Controlling Latin American Conflicts

Westview Replica Editions

The concept of Westview Replica Editions is a response to the continuing crisis in academic and informational publishing. Library budgets for books have been severely curtailed. Ever larger portions of general library budgets are being diverted from the purchase of books and used for data banks, computers, micromedia, and other methods of information retrieval. Interlibrary loan structures further reduce the edition sizes required to satisfy the needs of the scholarly community. Economic pressures on the university presses and the few private scholarly publishing companies have severely limited the capacity of the industry to properly serve the academic and research communities. As a result, many manuscripts dealing with important subjects, often representing the highest level of scholarship, are no longer economically viable publishing projects--or, if accepted for publication, are typically subject to lead times ranging from one to three years.

Westview Replica Editions are our practical solution to the problem. We accept a manuscript in camera-ready form, typed according to our specifications, and move it immediately into the production process. As always, the selection criteria include the importance of the subject, the work's contribution to scholarship, and its insight, originality of thought, and excellence of exposition. The responsibility for editing and proofreading lies with the author or sponsoring institution. We prepare chapter headings and display pages, file for copyright, and obtain Library of Congress Cataloging in Publication Data. A detailed manual contains simple instructions for preparing the final typescript, and our editorial staff is always available to answer questions.

The end result is a book printed on acid-free paper and bound in sturdy library-quality soft covers. We manufacture these books ourselves using equipment that does not require a lengthy make-ready process and that allows us to publish first editions of 300 to 600 copies and to reprint even smaller quantities as needed. Thus, we can produce Replica Editions quickly and can keep even very specialized books in print as long as there is a demand for them.

About the Book and Editors

Controlling Latin American Conflicts:
Ten Approaches
edited by Michael A. Morris and Victor Millán

Latin America remains a turbulent region, characterized by conflict and increased militarization,
despite the existence of regional juridical mechanisms
for controlling disputes. In this book, scholars from
both Latin and North America collaborate in presenting
ten original approaches to containing and resolving
conflict in the region. Stressing the need to closely
link contemporary approaches to conflict management
with the Latin American legalistic tradition, they
examine a broad scope of mechanisms ranging from
confidence-building measures to arms control agreements.
This book is the first systematic attempt to survey
arms control and to generate approaches for controlling
conflicts in Latin America.

Michael A. Morris, associate professor of political
science at Clemson University, South Carolina, is the
author of *International Politics and the Sea: The Case of
Brazil* (Westview, 1979). Victor Millán is a researcher
with the Stockholm International Peace Research
Institute (SIPRI) in Sweden.

Controlling Latin American Conflicts

Ten Approaches

edited by Michael A. Morris
and Victor Millán

Westview Press / Boulder, Colorado

A Westview Replica Edition

Published in 1983 in the United States of America by
Westview Press, Inc.
5500 Central Avenue
Boulder, Colorado 80301
Frederick A. Praeger, President and Publisher

Library of Congress Cataloging in Publication Data
Main entry under title:

Controlling Latin American conflicts.

(Replica series)
1. Latin America--Foreign relations--Addresses, essays, lectures. 2. Pacific settlement of international disputes--Addresses, essays, lectures. 3. Arms control--Addresses, essays, lectures. 4. Latin America --Politics and government--1948-   --Addresses, essays, lectures. 5. Latin America--Strategic aspects-- Addresses, essays, lectures. I. Morris, Michael A. II. Millan, Victor. III. Series.
JX1393.13C66 1983   327'.098   82-20039
ISBN   0-86531-938-3
Printed and bound in the United States of America.

10 9 8 7 6 5 4 3 2 1

Contents

Tables and Figures

Figures

The Contributors

Rubén de Hoyos is with the Department of Political
Science of the University of Wisconsin at Oshkosh,
where he heads the program of Latin American studies.

Susan Eckstein, Associate Professor of Sociology at
Boston University, is author of The Poverty of
Revolution: The State and Urban Poor in Mexico
and other works. She is currently writing a book
on Latin American revolutions.

Max G. Manwaring is on leave from his position as
Associate Professor of Political Science at Memphis
State University and was president of the Midwest
Association of Latin American Studies.

Victor Millán is a researcher with the Stockholm
International Peace Research Institute (SIPRI) in
Sweden, and has published articles and studies on
Latin American conflicts and arms control.

Carlos Moneta, formerly a Special Fellow at the
United Nations Institute for Training and Research
(UNITAR) and consultant to the Latin American Economic
System (SELA), has authored many articles on Latin
American affairs.

Michael A. Morris is Associate Professor of Political
Science at Clemson University, South Carolina. He
is the author of International Politics and the Sea:
The Case of Brazil (Westview Press, 1979), as well as
numerous articles in professional journals.

Juan Carlos Puig is a professor at the Simón Bolívar
University (Venezuela) and was the Minister of
Foreign Relations of Argentina. He has authored
many works on Latin American law and politics.

Martin Slann is Professor of Political Science at
Clemson University and is also the editor of Journal
of Political Science.

Augusto Varas is Professor and Researcher with the
Latin American Faculty of Social Sciences (FLACSO) in
Santiago, Chile and is Secretary General of the Chilean
Association for Peace Research (ACHIP).

1
Introduction

Michael A. Morris and Victor Millán

A CONFLICT-PRONE REGION

An upsurge in conflicts has occurred during the last decade in the entire Third World and in Latin America in particular. Since the beginning of the 1980s between 60 and 80 armed conflicts have taken place in the Third World, of a total of about 350 since 1945. Latin America, too, has become increasingly conflict-prone. Recent examples include the 1982 Argentine-British war over the Falklands/Malvinas, the armed clashes between Peru and Ecuador in 1981 and the beginning of 1983, and on-going armed conflict between Honduras and Nicaragua.

One of the major challenges in Latin America, as well as in other Third World regions, has been to control the escalation of conflicts with the existing procedural institutions and political organization. Purely political and legalistic measures for conflict control have often failed to be effective.

For example, the Organization of American States (OAS), under the tutelage of the United States, has aspired to provide a forum and mechanism for the peaceful settlement of disputes between Latin American countries. However, the organization generally has failed to constrain the expansion of conflicts or to limit them in recent years. The reasons are manifold, but two prominent factors may be mentioned. First, the OAS was set up to deal with localized intra-regional disputes, and even then only when all parties to a dispute chose to have a regional forum for settlement. Second, the OAS was intended by the United States to secure its pre-emptory authority against possible United Nations involvement in inter-American affairs. Thus, the use of the OAS by Washington to serve its national interests and the increasing reluctance of Latin American countries to use the OAS as a conflict settlement forum have prevented the organization from functioning in any but a paternalistic and partisan fashion. While this situation may change in the future, at present the

1

US "pre-emptory" authority has become difficult for many Latin American states to accept and its paternalism is openly rejected almost everywhere in the region. For example, the US proposal in the spring of 1979 that the OAS should consider sending a peace force to Nicaragua to expedite a transition to a post-Somoza regime was strongly rejected by most OAS members. Moreover, since the 1982 Falklands/Malvinas war, the proposal has again been raised to move the organization's headquarters away from Washington into the Latin American region, in order to facilitate the use of the organization as a forum for the resolution of Latin American issues, rather than as a tool of US foreign policy.

As traditional conflict resolution procedures have declined, Latin American conflicts themselves have become more difficult to control. Conflicts have proliferated, and have tended to become more complex and intractable. At present, in any attempt to discover common denominators for the profusion of conflicts in Latin America, one is faced with the fundamental problem of bewildering variety. These conflicts have often developed gradually from a mixture of several elements, for example, border disputes, historical animosities, economic and political system conflicts, the arms race, and the influence of great power rivalry.

Clarification of the kinds and number of Latin American conflicts is therefore a pressing need. Moreover, enhanced understanding of regional conflicts is crucial for generating more appropriate regional approaches to conflict control.

More than 30 conflict situations, varying in dimension and intensity, have been identified in Latin America (see Figure 1.1).[1] Conflicts between Latin American countries and with extra-regional powers also have been classified according to their main causes into the following five types:[2]

1) System conflicts involve ideological differences in regard to political and social values which lead to a struggle to impose (or resist the imposition of) these values. Included here are controversies between dictatorships and democracies, civilian and military regimes, and capitalistic and socialist models of development. While this type of conflict is not new to Latin America, it has become more prominent than before. The relative decline over the past several decades of the United States in the hemisphere and of inter-American institutions, together with the recent proliferation of Marxist-oriented regimes and armed movements in the region, especially in the Caribbean basin, have contributed significantly to heightened tension regarding system conflicts. The reassertion of the US presence in the Caribbean basin in the past several years has further contributed to polarization of regional politics. In many Central American and Caribbean cases, the weakness

Figure 1.1 Spectrum of current and potential conflicts in Latin America (by protagonists and types for 1980s)

SUBJECT \ OBJECT	Argentina	Bolivia	Brazil	Chile	Colombia	Costa Rica	Cuba	Dominican Rep.	Ecuador	El Salvador	Guatemala	Guyana	Haiti	Honduras	Jamaica	Mexico	Nicaragua	Panama	Paraguay	Peru	Surinam	Trinidad & Tobago	Uruguay	Venezuela	France	Netherlands	USA	United Kingdom	Soviet Union
Argentina	■	BD	BD	BC/DE															BD/E				BC/E					BC/D	
Bolivia		■	DE	CD															AC	DE									
Brazil	BD	BD	■									BC							BD				BD						
Chile	CD	CD		■			A													CD								CD	
Colombia					■												AC							CD					
Costa Rica						■	A										AC/E												
Cuba			A				■							A													AB/C		
Dominican Rep.								■					CD/E																
Ecuador									■											CD									
El Salvador							A			■				CD			AC												
Guatemala							A				■																	AC/D	
Guyana			CD									■												AC/D					
Haiti								AC					■														C		
Honduras							A			CE				■			AC/E												
Jamaica							A								■														
Mexico																■											BC/D		
Nicaragua			CD	AC/D			A							AC			■										AB		
Panama																		■									AB/CD		
Paraguay	CD	C	DE				A												■										
Peru			CD						CD											■									
Surinam												CD/E									■				CD				
Trinidad & Tobago																						■		CD					
Uruguay	CD		DE				A																■						
Venezuela				DE								BC/D										BC/D		■		CD			
France																									■				
Netherlands																										■			
USA							AE						BE				AE	A									■		AB
United Kingdom	AB/C		BC/D																									■	
Soviet Union																											AB		■

A : system/ideological conflicts

B : hegemonic/influence conflicts

C : territorial/border conflicts

D : resource conflicts

E : migration/refugee conflicts

of local states has exaggerated dependency on one or the other of the superpowers, thereby reinforcing system conflicts.

2) Hegemonic/influence conflicts involve claims of the great powers and of regional powers which result in attempts to increase and project their national power on the states in the region militarily, politically, economically, and socially. Rising regional powers in particular have benefited from greater diplomatic fluidity to extend their influence as the traditional US hegemonic position in the hemisphere has declined. Shifting power relationships have fuelled competition, especially in the context of proliferating conflicts and widespread militarization. Numerous, unresolved conflicts have motivated states, both large and small, to build up military capabilities, which for the first time have included the development of significant national military industries in several leading states. The renewal of great power competition in the region has paralleled rising competition among local powers, all of which complicates conflict control. The temptation on all sides to intervene has also increased as internal crises have spilled over into the international conflicts involving various states.

3) Claims involving the possession of, and sovereignty over, portions of land or water, as well as tensions arising between two or more sovereign states at their mutual frontier, lead to territorial/border conflicts. The concept of a "living frontier," expressed in Southern Cone geopolitical thinking, contributes to tensions constituting a potential for this type of conflict.

4) Resource conflicts involve disputes over verified or assumed resources in a given area, in which the conflict is due more to the value of the resource involved than the territory which contains the resource. Of particular importance at present in Latin America are tensions over energy resources and 200-mile offshore control, including jurisdiction for resource and related purposes over the 188-mile exclusive economic zone beyond the 12-mile territorial sea.

5) Migration/refugee conflicts result from differences in regional economic and political factors. Refugee problems have not only been motivated by political reasons, but also by economic reasons or a combination of both.[3]

There are only a few conflicts in Latin America whose etiology consists of a single-cause explanation. Most Latin American conflicts exhibit several elements of this typology, and the mix changes for each one of the individual parties over a period of time (see Figure 1.1). While in the past the dominant form of conflict was territorial/border, a mix of system/ influence and resource/migration causes dominates at

present and will continue to do so in the foreseeable
future. In the Central American region, system conflicts
predominate, while in the Southern Cone there is a
preponderance of territorial/border and influence/
resource conflicts.

To the extent that territorial/border conflicts
persist, their context has been altered. In many cases,
enhanced economic, military, and political capacities
of states have enabled them to pursue national self-
interest more assiduously. Enhanced capabilities have
also tended to shift the nature of territorial/border
concerns from sovereignty, status, and prestige toward
more ambitious protection or acquisition of resources
and pursuit of system/hegemonic aims. In other cases,
especially in Central America, the crisis in national
economic and social structures has transformed and
aggravated longstanding territorial/border conflicts.

It follows that conflicts with multiple causes
increasingly tend to overlap and link with one another,
most prominently in Central America. Frequent asymmetry
of causes between different actors in the same conflicts
further complicates the conflicts and their resolution.
A variety of motivations may encourage either party to
stimulate a dispute, while both sides need to collaborate
in conflict resolution.

Multi-causal, overlapping conflicts also tend to
aggravate military competition. Since the way in
which actors perceive and emphasize different causes
of conflict varies, the very definition and priorities of the causes tend to become an integral part
of the conflicts. Figure 1.1 expresses this dynamic,
dialectical character of contemporary conflicts through
the distinction between the "subject" and "object" of
multi-causal disputes. While the perspective of the
particular actor determines in part whether it is the
subject or object of a dispute, this relationship is
also influenced by relative power positions, which, as
noted, are currently in flux. A recurring temptation is
to benefit from or create a relative power advantage in
order to influence the nature and evolution of a conflict,
thereby playing an active role as a subject in shaping
the conflict outcome rather than being a helpless,
passive object of events. While this temptation to
influence the evolution of a conflict in ways favorable
to one's own interests characterizes all conflicts, the
fluidity and complexity of multi-causal, overlapping
conflicts accentuates this competitive tendency.

Changes in the nature of Latin American conflicts
therefore augur ill for peaceful resolution. Legal
solutions appear more appropriate for traditional
territorial/border conflicts than for contemporary multi-
causal, overlapping conflicts. And, as noted, traditional
legal institutions and measures have been weakened, and
in any event, only registered limited successes.

Because of the complexity of conflicts in the region, the traditional bilateral and multilateral conflict-dampening procedures that have been employed in the past are not likely to be sufficient to induce peace in the hemisphere. The identification and classification of contemporary conflicts is therefore important for the task of finding adequate measures to influence peaceful behavior of parties to a conflict, preventing the outbreak of hostilities, or if this cannot be accomplished, eventually re-establishing peaceful relations. Weakening the motivations for conflict, reducing the means for pursuing a conflict, and improving the mediatory and judicial mechanisms are new approaches that need to be applied. It is the pressing need to generate new approaches for regional conflict control which motivated this book.

GENERATING APPROACHES FOR REGIONAL CONFLICT CONTROL

Ten original approaches to containing and resolving conflict in Latin America are developed in the successive chapters of this volume. Chapter 2 surveys traditional diplomatic approaches to the control of Latin American conflicts, including their shortcomings, and indicates revisions and innovations that must be made to create a more effective system of regional conflict control. The focus then shifts in Chapters 3 and 4 from a regional perspective to national approaches for conflict control. Characteristics of national approaches are surveyed, respectively, of Caribbean basin and South American states, and again constructive alternatives are suggested. Yet another approach is to control conflicts through confidence-building measures, which has attracted considerable attention in the European context. Chapter 5 indicates how, with less fanfare but more results, Latin American states have already practiced de facto confidence building in the military field. Here, as well, recommendations for additional steps are made.
Inter-American organizations, that is, those involving both the United States and Latin American states, have played an important, if declining, role in regional conflict management (Chapter 2). Chapter 6 examines how cooperation between Latin American states, particularly in the context of the Latin American Economic System (SELA), constitutes an alternative approach to conflict management through international organizations.
Regional militarization has been occurring through the proliferation of nuclear technology and conventional weaponry, so Chapter 7 examines problems and opportunities for controlling the sources of armaments in Latin America. Chapter 8 complements this approach by analyzing how regional militarization and prospects

for control are expressed differently by military
sector or armed service, in this case naval conflict
and arms control.

The final chapters emphasize still other aspects
of the control of multi-faceted regional conflicts.
Chapter 9, in setting forth a quantitative approach for
monitoring Latin American arms control agreements,
complements earlier qualitative analyses of traditional
conflict control approaches (Chapter 2) and national
approaches (Chapters 3 and 4). Chapter 10 relies on a
case study approach to the control of Latin American
conflicts, which integrates national, inter-American,
regional, and global perspectives used elsewhere.
While this case study addresses the protracted, yet
abortive, negotiating process to resolve the Falklands/
Malvinas dispute, a number of other chapters, from
varying perspectives, deal in part with the impact of
the recent Falkland Islands war on Latin American
politics and regional order. Domestic conflict containment in Latin America, the approach adopted in
Chapter 11, adds yet another perspective to the survey
of regional conflicts and conflict management.
Chapter 12 concludes the survey by illustrating
consensus-building as an approach to conflict control
through comparison of two issues.

Several factors are responsible for the complementarity of the various contributions. As will become
evident through perusal of the following pages, the
authors share certain basic assumptions about Latin
American conflicts and conflict control. All the
contributors recognize that Latin America has become a
more conflict-prone region and that innovations in
conflict control are consequently all the more urgent.
The authors, in generating ten original approaches to
regional conflict containment and resolution, are also
reasonably optimistic about prospects for conflict
control. At the same time, there is acute awareness
of pitfalls. For example, Chapter 10 emphasizes that
protracted, yet abortive, negotiations to resolve
disputes can be counterproductive, and Chapter 11
focuses on the frequent linkage between domestic
conflict containment and oppression.

A shared assessment of major features of contemporary Latin American reality also helps unify this volume.
Many regional states, it is recognized, are undergoing
a period of domestic crisis, which tends to undermine
traditional domestic and regional institutions responsible for order and conflict control. US-Latin American
relations are likewise undergoing a crisis. At the
same time, the enhanced economic, military, and political
capacities of many regional states over the past few
decades have supported the widely shared desire for
greater domestic self-sufficiency and foreign policy
independence. These goals relating to domestic and

international self-determination do remain elusive for
weaker Latin American states, particularly as domestic
and international challenges have proliferated. Nonetheless, opposition to the increasing tendency to
intervene, both of the great powers and of rising
regional powers, remains intense. More positively,
even though the region is suffering a period of interlocking domestic and international crises, the Latin
American authors in particular retain faith in the
ability of the states in the region to overcome
current problems and eventually implement widely
shared democratic values.

By and large, this shared assessment of contemporary Latin American reality was reached independently
by the various authors, and the co-editors made no
effort to impose a conceptual framework on the authors.
At the same time, the authors were able to interact
and exchange views over a fairly extended period of
time, which helped refine and strengthen the consensus
about regional conflicts and conflict control. Initial
drafts of many of the papers were prepared for a panel
chaired by Michael Morris and Victor Millán (the
co-editors of this volume) at the Latin American Studies
Association meeting on March 5, 1982 at Washington, D.C.
Nearly all of the eventual contributors to the volume
were present at that occasion, and participated in
criticism of the existing drafts and planning for an
eventual published study. Subsequent correspondence
and discussions between the peripatetic authors likewise promoted complementarity of approaches.

This forging of mutually acceptable, complementary
approaches to conflict control transcends a mere
academic exercise. The academic contributors, including
the co-editors, are evenly balanced between Latin
America and the United States, and reflect many characteristic -- and diverging -- values of their respective
regions. In this instance, North and South American
scholars nevertheless have had much more success in
inter-American collaboration and consensus-building than
counterpart diplomats. On the one hand, the book documents the marked decline in inter-American consensus
regarding both the nature of regional conflicts and
appropriate approaches to conflict control. On the
other hand, the various approaches which follow here
are the fruit of a shared recognition of authors from
both parts of this hemisphere that they must be more
active and imaginative than their own governments in
generating mutually acceptable approaches for regional
conflict control.

The variety of perspectives embodied in the ten
approaches to regional conflict control should be
emphasized, since in this instance complex problems
require complex, multi-faceted solutions. In particular,

multi-causal, overlapping conflicts demand a variety of
methods and approaches to help stem the onrush towards
violence and disorder.

International conflict control ultimately depends
on stable, domestic order. Important instances of postrevolutionary order have unfortunately involved suppression of domestic class conflicts, so that long-term
stability remains uncertain (Chapter 11). Other states
which have not experienced revolutions have frequently
suppressed class conflicts as well, and would be more
stable and inclined towards conflict control were the
governments more democratic (Chapters 2 and 4). The
private sector can make important contributions to
peace, for example, in monitoring Latin American arms
control agreements (Chapter 9) or in human rights issues
(Chapter 12), although private sector groups have often
blocked consensus as well, as in the case of the exclusive economic zone (Chapter 12).

Ultimately, governments are responsible for conflict control, although their record has important
defects (Chapters 3, 4, and 10). Moreover, shifting,
hierarchical power relationships between states must
be a point of reference in deriving implications for
conflict control (Chapters 7, 8, 9, and 12).

Further complicating conflict control is the nexus
between internal and external politics (passim). Various
functional issues cut across domestic and international
affairs, with discrete implications for conflict
control -- law (Chapter 2); politics (Chapters 3, 4, and
10); economics (Chapters 6, 11, and 12); and military
affairs (Chapters 5, 7, and 8).

Different perspectives on international conflict
control likewise are sub-regional (Chapters 3, 4, and
8), regional (Chapters 5 and 6), inter-American (Chapters
2 and 12), and global (Chapter 7). Peculiarities of
specific conflicts may require appropriate conflict
resolution measures on a number of these levels simultaneously (Chapter 10). Specific issues (Chapter 12) and
sectors (Chapter 8) also have distinctive properties,
both with respect to conflict and its control.

The volume closes with a selected bibliography on
Latin American conflicts and conflict control. The
close relationship between regional conflicts and control
of these conflicts is reflected in the literature, so
that bibliographical materials related to both themes
are included.

NOTES

1. Here conflict situations refer to potential inter-state
armed conflicts where all the ingredients of a dispute exist,
whether or not the dispute has been formulated or crystallized.

2. See W. Grabendorff, "Tipología de los conflictos en
América Latina," Nueva Sociedad, 59 (Caracas, Marzo-Abril 1982):
39-46; and also Jack Child, Conflicts in Latin America: present
and potential (The American University, Washington, D.C. 1980)
unpublished.

3. Conflict types #4 and #5 both include a key economic
component, although this typology does not include mainstream
economic disputes since they generally do not pose the threat of
armed conflict. For example, issues involving trade, foreign
investment, and indebtedness have been causing increasing friction
between Latin American and developed states, although the
occasional specter in a former era of foreign intervention to
settle a debt or to counter an expropriation appears farfetched
today. Similarly, Brazil's emergence as South America's leading
economic power has had a variety of unsettling effects on its
neighbors, but cannot itself be considered as a key cause of
any eventual armed conflict.

2
Controlling Latin American Conflicts: Current Juridical Trends and Perspectives for the Future

Juan Carlos Puig

From the point of view of the peaceful solution of international conflicts, the countries of Latin America offer a paradoxical image. It is probable that in few regions of the world have so many praises been sung to peace, to understanding among brother countries, and to the need of avoiding war in every possible way. No other regional group has produced so many treaties, conventions and resolutions with the objective of promoting conciliation and understanding among States, and no other group possesses such a diversified and, at times, sophisticated panoply of juridical resources. However, frequently these nations have been inclined to adopt prejurisdictional forms of settlement, that is, forms which do not envisage compulsory jurisdiction or enforcement of the award. On the other hand, when some procedure of this kind was agreed upon, generally it only entered into force for a few states or it was displaced by diplomatic negotiations.[1]

It must be admitted that these contradictions and paradoxes have been evident ever since the days of Independence. At all the Latin American political congresses of the 19th century, beginning with that of Panama, the issue of the maintenance of peace has been ever present. Some of them contemplated a hermetical, pre-jurisdictional procedure as in the case of the Treaty of Perpetual Union, League and Confederation, Articles 13, paragraph 3, 16, and 17 (Panama 1826) and of the Continental Treaty, Article 21 (Santiago, Chile, 1856). More ambitiously, both the Treaty of Confederation, Article 10 (Lima 1848) and the Treaty on the Maintenance of Peace, Articles 1, 2 and 3 (Lima 1865) established, as a last resort, a compulsory procedure for the solution of conflicts.[2] However, none of these Treaties were ratified, which dramatically shows the gap that already existed in those days between noble ideals and cynical reality.

In this chapter I will analyze in depth this paradoxical situation, especially in regard to present times and with a view toward the possibility of outlin-

11

ing some solutions which, bringing normal practice into line with social reality, may encourage the peaceful solution of conflicts among Latin American states and forestall the crises that unavoidably lead to the use of force. With this in mind, we will deal first with the existing law in Latin America on this subject. Then, I will endeavor to give an idea of practice, that is, the way in which the norms detailed and explained in the previous section have been applied in concrete cases. Since the majority of these norms have not been applied, or at least not in the manner originally intended, we will look into the possible causes for this non-compliance. Later, I will outline feasible solutions and discuss practical means of implementing them.

EXISTING LAW

For the purpose of this study, juridical norms related to the peaceful settlement of conflicts among Latin American states can be classified as general and special norms, depending on whether they focus on any conflict or on one specific conflict category. In both cases, we can also distinguish between procedures which have been introduced by multilateral treaties and resolutions or by bilateral treaties. We will not consider existing conflict resolution possibilities for Latin American countries at the United Nations, since specific Inter-American procedures are more relevant to this book. The basic legal principle of impermeability between organizations has been observed, and has worked in practice as a <u>Grundnorm</u> to which specific principles for the solution of conflicts to be found in the United Nations Charter have been subordinated.[3]

General Procedures

Probably with the sole exception of the Saavedra Lamas Pact, multilateral procedures have arisen out of Panamericanism. Bilateral procedures, as a rule, consecrate arbitration, and were mainly agreed upon during the 19th century, many of them with the object of diminishing tensions stemming from important conflicts, almost always of a territorial nature.

<u>Multilateral procedures</u>. The Bogota Pact (American Treaty for Pacific Settlement) is the most important multilateral procedure, since it is a kind of codification of all possible solution procedures, both jurisdictional and pre-jurisdictional. It was intended to replace other Inter-American conventions which had specifically regulated certain peaceful settlement measures, but it only entered into force for a few states. As a result, the old treaties are still operative for the states which are not parties to the Bogota Pact.

More positively, the Charter of the OAS, in its 1967
Reform, gave the Permanent Council pre-jurisdictional
powers and established a subsidiary body, the Inter-
American Committee on Peaceful Settlement, which replaced the Inter-American Peace Commission. The latter
had been created by a simple Resolution of the Second
Consultative Meeting in 1940, and had had some measure
of success in the exercise of its functions, also of a
pre-jurisdictional nature.

     1. The Bogota Pact. This was adopted by the IX In-
ternational American Conference, in great measure due to
Latin American initiatives. It proposed to put in order the mass of treaties for peaceful solution that had
been adopted via Panamericanism and to culminate this
coordination with a hermetical jurisdictional mechanism,
something not achieved until then. The result is an
integral system of peaceful settlement which carefully
regulates all pre-jurisdictional procedures: good offices, mediation, investigation and conciliation.
     If a satisfactory arrangement is not achieved by
the application of these methods, any of the parties to
the conflict may have recourse to the International
Court of Justice, whose jurisdiction regarding any American State is recognized "ipso facto without the need
for any special Agreement while the Treaty is in force"
(Article 31). At that time, arbitration proceedings
are always open to the parties should they prefer them
to appearing before the International Court of Justice
(Article 38).
     From a strictly normative point of view, the Bogo-
ta Pact is, therefore, perfect, as it has no gaps or
fissures that would leave its functioning subject to
the will of the parties. That is why Latin American
jurists belonging to the ideologist-rationalist current
have applauded it without objection. J.M. Yepes, for
example, referred to it, as soon as it was adopted, as
"a true organic statute of what we could call the "pax
americana"."[4] However, the number of reservations that
were made at the time of its signature should not have
allowed for too many expectations right from the start.
Argentina, Bolivia, Ecuador, the United States, Paraguay, Peru and Nicaragua made reservations which, to a
greater or lesser extent, weakened its hermetical nature.

     2. Other Inter-American Treaties. Essentially,
these treaties concern the international instruments
superseded by the Bogota Pact. In fact, they are mentioned in the Pact, in its Article 58: the Treaty to
Avoid or Prevent Conflicts between the American States
of May 3, 1923; the General Convention of International Conciliation, the General Treaty of Inter-American
Arbitration, and the Protocol of Progressive Arbitra-

tion of January 5, 1929; the Additional Protocol to the General Convention for Inter-American Conciliation of December 26, 1933; the Anti-War Treaty of non-Aggression and Conciliation of October 10, 1933; and the Convention to Coordinate, Extend and Assure the Fulfilment of Existing Treaties between the American States, the Treaty on the Prevention of Controversies and the Inter-American Treaty of Good Offices and Mediation of December 23, 1936. To these there should be added the Treaty on Compulsory Arbitration adopted by the Second International American Conference (Mexico, 1902), but this was very preliminary and to all intents and purposes was replaced by the General Inter-American Arbitration Treaty of 1929.

These treaties only involve pre-jurisdictional procedures, that is, they do not lead to a solution that must be considered compulsory for the parties involved. Since these treaties continue in force for those states that have not ratified the Bogota Pact, the Pact has been added to the existing legal panoply, complicating even more the normative panorama.

3. Inter-American Peace Commission. The case of this pre-jurisdictional organ is very interesting because, although arising out of a simple Resolution within a framework of war (World War II), it was able to achieve considerable significance in the solution of Inter-american conflicts. In effect, it was during the Second Consultative Meeting (Havana, 1940) that Resolution XIV was adopted, entrusting the Council of the Panamerican Union with the creation of a Committee whose mission would be to "permanently see that those States among which there is, or may arise, conflict of any nature whatsoever, reach a solution as soon as possible, and to suggest to this end, without detriment to the formulae chosen by the parties or to the procedures to which they may agree, methods and initiatives conducive to this solution".

On this basis, the Council set up the Commission and established its headquarters in Washington. Later, at the Fifth Consultative Meeting (Santiago, Chile, 1959), concern for observance of non-intervention, respect for human rights, and exercise of representative democracy and promotion of economic development, led to a widening of the functions of the Inter-American Peace Commission in these fields and to its being granted the prerogative of initiative. Thus, by virtue of this Resolution (No. IV), the Commission was able to focus on the examination of: (a) methods and procedures to avoid activities generated abroad with the intention of toppling legally constituted governments or to provoke cases of intervention or aggression; (b) the relationship between violations of human rights or the lack of the exercise of representative democracy and political

tensions which affect continental peace, and (c) the relationship between economic underdevelopment and political instability. Although the Commission did not have
essentially jurisdictional functions, it exercised interesting competences of a pre-jurisdictional nature
(good offices) and produced recommendations to enable the
parties to make use of determined methods of settlement.

4. Charter of the OAS. General references to the
obligation of resolving controversies through peaceful
means were already to be found in the Charter of the OAS,
as approved in Bogota in 1948. Moreover, the present
Charter, reformed by the Protocol of Buenos Aires, in
its Chapter XIV, Articles 82 to 90, entrusts the Permanent Council of the Organization with specific competence
on this subject. The Council may exercise good offices
on its own or through the Inter-American Committee on
Peaceful Settlement, a subsidiary organ that replaced the
Inter-American Peace Committee. It also has investigative
powers, but in order to visit the territory of Parties
to the dispute, it must have the consent of the state
involved. Furthermore, "if one of the Parties continues
to refuse the good offices of the Inter-American Committee on Peaceful Settlement or of the Council, the Council
shall limit itself to submitting a report to the General
Assembly" (Article 88). This is therefore a strictly
facultative procedure, both as regards its functioning and
as concerns its content since, even when the intervention
of the Permanent Council is accepted, its faculties only
consist of assisting the parties and recommending those
procedures it considers adequate for the peaceful settlement of the controversy (Article 83).

Bilateral procedures. Latin American countries
mutually agreed to numerous treaties for peaceful settlement of disputes, especially arbitration, above all
during the 19th century and the beginning of the 20th
century. However, with some exceptions, they were not
hermetical. They included qualifying clauses that, due
to their diffuse nature, could prevent any initiative
in concrete cases. Such exemptions included vital interests, national honor, interests of third countries,
and constitutional matters. Moreover, they required,
to be given effect, a specific arbitration agreement
which contained the express consent of the parties.
Therefore, reticence of one of the Parties was enough
for so-called "general and compulsory" arbitration to
be non-functional in practice.
Of course, there were exceptions. Perhaps the most
typical of these were the Treaty of Arbitration between
Colombia and Chile in 1880 and the General Treaty of
Arbitration between Argentina and Chile in 1902. Of the
former, Paul Fauchille said: "This pact is the first
general, permanent, compulsory and unlimited arbitration

treaty known in the history of International Law. It
is often cited as the one which inaugurated the movement toward widespread and permanent arbitration in the
contemporary world".[5] With regard to the Argentine-
Chilean treaty, its hermetical nature and its adoption
at a time in which an arbitration procedure was under
way between the two countries in the hands of the same
judge as envisaged by the treaty, and which was successful, invested it with special relevance.[6]

Special Procedures

In the field of multilateral instruments, we will
consider the Inter-American Treaty on Reciprocal Assistance, a treaty on regional collective security which
also relates to the peaceful solution of conflicts; the
various treaties for Latin American integration, including the recent treaty setting up the Court of Justice of the Cartagena Agreement; and the system for the
protection of human rights in the Inter-American field,
which includes two organs of a jurisdictional nature:
the Inter-American Commission on Human Rights and the
Inter-American Court of Human Rights. In the field of
bilateral instruments, we will refer to various specific treaties of great relevance which have included methods for the solution of conflicts which may arise among
the parties in regard to the respective treaties.

Multilateral procedures. Curiously, in these treaties, especially those that refer to processes of integration and which espouse the Bolivarian ideal of American unity, one observes a characteristic reluctance to
incorporate juridically compulsory solution procedures.
Only now, through the two Courts of recent creation,
that of Human Rights (already installed) and
the Andean Court (still only on paper), is it possible
to perceive interest in a permanent institutional jurisdiction.

1. Inter-American Treaty on Reciprocal Assistance.
The essential objective of this Treaty is to organize
regional collective security, so that its task is not
that of resolving conflicts but rather that of checking
aggression and, at most, imposing sanctions on the aggressor. Although during the deliberations of the CEESI
(Special Committee to Study the Inter-American System
and Propose Measures for Restructuring It), the matter
of clearly establishing the difference between collective security and solution of conflicts was brought up,[7]
the fact is that the 1975 reform maintained the competence of the Meeting of Consultation on the subject of
"pacifying action". In effect, the former Article 7
has remained as it was, and bears the same number. According to this Article, in the event of a conflict

between two or more American states, the Consultative
body is empowered to adopt all the measures necessary
for the restoration or the maintenance of peace and security among American states, as well as for the solution of the conflict by peaceful means. Furthermore,
the rejection of pacifying action by a Party will be
taken into consideration in determining the aggressor
and in applying measures agreed to at the Meeting of
Consultation. The procedure is then special rather
than general in nature, since the conflict in question
must have the characteristics envisaged in the same
Treaty, i.e., it must at least be a question of an act
of aggression affecting the inviolability or the integrity of the territory or the sovereignty or the political independence of any state that is party to the same,
or of a conflict or a serious act that can endanger the
peace of America.

   2. Treaties regarding Latin American Integration
and Cooperation. In general, those treaties that regulate processes of Latin American integration and cooperation on a permanent basis have not really contemplated
operative procedures for the peaceful solution of conflicts. This was the case of the Treaty of Montevideo
of February 18, 1960, which established the Latin American Free Trade Association (LAFTA), and this omission
still holds in the new Treaty of August 12, 1980, which
created the Latin American Integration Association.
   LAFTA did adopt an additional protocol for the solution of controversies on September 2, 1967, which established an arbitral jurisdiction. The Court was to
be constituted on the basis of the decision of the parties, who would choose three members from a pre-established list of jurists, and there was also provision for
automatic constitution in lieu of agreement. The Parties recognized as compulsory, with no need for special
agreements, the jurisdiction of the Court to take cogni-
zance of and solve all controversies that might arise
in relation to a list of subjects that the Council of
Foreign Ministers of the Treaty of Montevideo would make
up and review yearly (Article 16).[8] Hermetical arbitration procedures also were contemplated in both the General Treaty of Central American Integration (Article 26)
of December 13, 1960, and the Treaty that established
the Caribbean Community (CARICOM), of July 4, 1973 (Articles 11 and 12 of the Annex).[9]
   More ambitiously, the Andean Pact members recently
drew up a treaty which creates the Court of Justice of
the Cartagena Agreement (May 28, 1979). This is a Court
of compulsory jurisdiction with competence to declare
void the decisions of the different bodies of the Pact
and to determine non-compliance of obligations con-
tracted by the member states. However, this Treaty has
not yet entered into force.

Finally, extremely important treaties of integration and permanent Latin American cooperation, such as those of the Plata Basin, Amazonic Cooperation, SELA, and OLADE, do not have any clauses relative to the solution of controversies.

3. American Convention on Human Rights (Pact of San José de Costa Rica). Two possible methods of obligatory solution of conflicts among member states have been established stemming from supposed violations of those human rights proclaimed by the Convention: firstly, the right of appeal to the Inter-American Commission on Human Rights, for which it is necessary to obtain the consent of the plaintiff "for an indefinite time, for a fixed period of time or on specific cases" (Article 45); then the right of appeal to the Inter-American Court of Human Rights, which also requires prior consent stated in a special declaration or by means of a special convention (Article 62).[10]

Bilateral Treaties. During recent years a series of treaties that are bilateral, but whose real aim is to permanently regulate matters of vital importance, have been drawn up between Latin American countries. The most significant examples concern hydroelectric systems in international basins. These include the Argentine-Uruguayan Agreement referring to the exploitation of the River Parana rapids in the area of Salto Grande (signed in Montevideo on December 30, 1946, but which only entered into force on October 27, 1958); the Yacyreta Treaty between Argentina and Paraguay of December 3, 1973; the Argentine-Paraguayan Agreement to study the possibilities of the River Parana resources on December 29, 1971; and the Brazilian-Paraguayan Treaty of April 15, 1973, on the exploitation of the River Parana hydraulic resources.

Even though these treaties regulate complex operations including preliminary surveys, construction, and operation of very costly works and establish international bodies to take over these tasks, they have not taken into account more or less hermetical procedures of obligatory solution of controversies. In general, they refer back to "the usual diplomatic channels". One exception is the Treaty of the River Plate and its maritime coast of November 19, 1973. In its Article 87 it recognizes the compulsory jurisdiction of the International Court of Justice at the request of either of the conflicting parties, when the conflict has to do with the interpretation or implementation of the Treaty. This procedure is to be used when the controversy has not been solved through direct negotiations, although a previous conciliatory procedure before the Administrative Commission can also be attempted (also at the request of one of the conflicting parties, Articles 68 and 69).

PRACTICE

Basic Trends

Having briefly analyzed current norms in Latin America relating to the peaceful solution of conflicts, now we must see how they are really applied. A norm, even though it is in force, does not guarantee in itself that the conduct demanded will, in fact, occur. Moreover, a large number of these norms are only in force for a limited amount of signatories of the particular treaty. And, in some cases, also, this "being in force" is theoretical because the treaty was either signed or ratified with certain reservations which completely undermined its procedural content.

What is, then, the real and concrete behavior of Latin American countries in this delicate matter of the solution of international conflicts? We believe that the main tendencies fall into the following conceptual headings: (a) Inapplicability of general procedures; (b) Relative success of the "pacifying action"; (c) Inoperative special procedures; (d) Preference for discretionary ad hoc procedures; and (e) Preference for the conflictive status quo.

Inapplicability of General Procedures. General procedures have not normally been applied due to the dearth of ratifications and the reservations that in many cases totally set aside compulsory jurisdiction. The lack of a substantial number of operative ratifications (that is to say, without reservations incompatible with the objectives of the treaty) hampers application among the few states that have fully ratified the treaties. Only the case of the conflict between Haiti and the Dominican Republic was able to be solved by applying both the Gondra Pact and the General Convention of Interamerican Conciliation.[11] Similarly, the Bogota Pact has not had autonomous application, since the few times it has been put into practice was on the recommendation of a Consultative Meeting or of the Interamerican Peace Committee.[12]

Relative Success of the "Pacifying Action". Probably due to the inefficiency of the Inter-American peace system, in some conflicts and concrete situations the Meetings of Consultation have played a part in the peaceful solution of conflicts by means of a "pacifying action".[13] The Interamerican Peace Committee played a similar pragmatic, pacifying role. The prejurisdictional competence of this body, and, at the beginning, its self-appointed pacifying role, brought about the understanding of the Parties in various conflictive

situations. Nevertheless, this limited success was
achieved in conflicts among small Latin American states
and especially in those cases in which the interest of
the United States was secondary from the point of view
of the content of the conflict itself, but significant
inasmuch as the maintenance of peace was concerned.
With the disappearance of the Interamerican Peace Committee, the functions it carried out were, to some extent, absorbed by the Permanent Council and its subsidiary body, the Interamerican Committee on Peaceful Settlement, but have not been exercised to date.

Inoperative Special Procedures. To date, the two
hermetical jurisdictional systems envisaged, that of
the protection of human rights and that of the Court of
Justice of the Cartagena Agreement, are inoperative.
The Pact of San Jose de Costa Rica has come into effect,
but the anticipated acceptance of the automatic submission to the Commission or the Court is very discouraging. Moreover,

> the procedure for the jurisdictional solution of
> differences, restricted today to the fifteen coun-
> tries that have ratified the Pact, is limited to
> three states as regards the competence of the Com-
> mission for Human Rights in regard to denunciations
> by one State party against another for violation of
> these rights and is reduced to the case of one
> State alone in regard to the competence of the In-
> teramerican Court.[14]

Although the treaty creating the Court of Justice
of the Cartagena Agreement has not yet entered into
force and, therefore, for the moment must be considered
inoperative, the fact that it has been ratified by all
the Andean countries save Venezuela is a good sign. In
the case of Venezuela, its approval by Congress is in
progress and it has already obtained approval by the
Senate. On the other hand, in the other processes of
Latin American integration, the outlook has been and
still is most unfavorable concerning jurisdictional or
hermetical solutions.[15] The procedures adopted have
never been applied and there has been a general preference for direct negotiation or a political solution.

Preference for Discretionary Ad Hoc Procedures.
In most cases where the parties to a conflict have applied a procedure for peaceful solution, this has generally been ad hoc and of a discretionary nature (direct
negotiation, good offices, mediation, investigation,
conciliation, recourse to international bodies). Such
discretionary ad hoc procedures reflect a marked preference for non-compulsory measures which allow for more
direct handling on the part of the Parties and a greater

margin for political compromise.

In the Latin American integration and cooperation movements, this preference has been the rule from the beginning. Similarly, with regard to conflicts of a different nature, there is a progressive tendency towards abandoning pre-established legal frameworks. For example, the conflict between El Salvador and Honduras was settled by the mediation of former Peruvian President José Luis Bustamante y Rivero, which led to the signing of a General Treaty of Peace on October 31, 1980. Similarly, Colombia and Venezuela directly negotiated their dispute regarding the frontiers of the marine areas on the Gulf of Venezuela, and will apparently follow the path of diplomatic negotiations in the future. The same may be said of the Venezuela-Guyana conflict.

Long-standing disputes such as those of Chile-Bolivia (Lauca River and access to the sea) and Ecuador-Peru (Rio de Janeiro Protocol of 1942) are likewise resisting the application of legalistic procedures, while direct negotiation has resolved the controversy between Brazil and Argentina regarding competitive exploitation of the hydraulic resources of the Upper Parana. New conflicts looming on the horizon (such as the recent one between Colombia and Nicaragua and, in general, those of the Caribbean) do not augur reliance on institutionalized solutions either.

The Argentine-Chilean dispute over the Beagle Channel also illustrates obstacles to pre-established legal procedures. Once previously-agreed-upon arbitration procedures were initiated by a unilateral request of the Chilean government, Argentina's first reaction was to propose new negotiations. A compromise was finally reached whereby the two parties submitted by mutual agreement to arbitral jurisdiction, formally retaining the arbitrator designated by the Treaty of 1902 (the Queen of England), but in practice referring the controversy to examination by an arbitration court made up of five judges from the International Court of Justice (Preamble to the Agreement). However, the award made on this basis, which was released on January 31, 1977, was rejected by Argentina. Both governments subsequently renewed negotiations on the dispute and later entrusted the matter to the consideration of His Holiness the Pope as a mediator, with a view to obtaining a proposal for a possible solution to the controversy. More recently, the Argentine government denounced the General Treaty on the solution of controversies between the two countries that had been signed on April 5, 1972, whereby pacific settlement was entrusted to the International Court of Justice, although subsequently (September 1982) Argentina reconsidered the matter and pledged to keep the Treaty alive for the Beagle Channel case.

<u>Preference for the Conflictive Status Quo</u>. Not
only is it possible to detect a preference for non-compulsory, <u>ad hoc</u> recourses for the solution of conflicts;
many conflicts remain without solution and nothing
seems to compel the parties (or at least one of them)
to agree even to a non-compulsory procedure. As a result, tensions continue to build up and will unavoidably break out into ever more serious crises, above all
because the new characteristics of the international
system and the new realities under which Latin American
states are living increase considerably the possibilities of conflict. It therefore becomes imperative and
urgent to determine the causes responsible for limited
juridical success in controlling Latin American conflicts, and on this basis to suggest possible solutions.

EXPLANATIONS

<u>Diversity of Causes</u>

Why have matters reached this stage in Latin America? That is, why do conflicts endure and multiply?
Why do those that are resolved find settlement through
totally discretionary mechanisms that are very vulnerable from the juridical point of view? Why does one perceive generalized and growing mistrust towards the application of more reliable hermetical jurisdictional
procedures?
Those who have tried to find answers to these urgent questions have, generally, also started from the
juridical field, although without stopping to examine
specifically the normative deficiencies with respect to
social reality. For example, it is said that the poor
success of jurisdictional procedures in Latin America
is due to the fact that the states of the subcontinent
are very zealous of their "sovereignty", or to the fact
that, within the internal political system of our countries, the executive branch has always predominated and
tends to overshadow the importance of the other
branches, especially the judicial.[16]
An objective examination of these criticisms clearly shows their superficiality. In the 19th century
when the states of Latin America were more concerned
with the preservation of their sovereignty and were
much more "presidentialist", they did not hesitate in
settling their conflicts by arbitration. It therefore
seems logical to presume that there is no simplistic,
legal explanation for the problems that have arisen and
that, unavoidably, reference must be made to complex
causes. We believe accordingly that the explanations
are varied and that they can be classified into three
groups: international politics, domestic politics and
juridico-normative causes.

International political causes. These causes are
related to the structure and the functioning of the international system and can be narrowed down to two: (1)
the progressive autonomy of Latin American countries
and (2) the decline in the relative power of the United
States over the continent.

1. Progressive autonomy of Latin American countries. The reality of the past few years shows that,
for various reasons, Latin American countries and especially, but not exclusively, the more important ones in
the area, are handling their affairs in a more autonomous manner within the international system. As we have
explained in previous works, it is possible to perceive
a vocation towards autonomy in the Latin American ruling
classes of today that shows up in the transition from
paracolonial dependence to national dependence and from
this latter state to heterodoxical autonomy.[17] This is
one basic reason for the current reluctance regarding
jurisdictional solutions.

Judicial reality (in the broad sense) shows that
in crucial cases (and in international law the immense
majority are in this category) the judge, in accordance
with the factual characteristics of the case, conceives
a reasonable solution and then tries to justify it within "positive" law through an interpretation that is
discretional to the extent to which the applicable norm
is divorced from the will of the legislator. In this
sense, the solution of an international conflict via
jurisdictional channels (and especially via those of
arbitration) is always "political".

In view of this reality, the acceptance of compulsory jurisdiction has an adverse psychological implication for the ruling classes of small and medium-sized
countries, because of circumstances stemming from the
international system which reward those who accept it
and punish those who are recalcitrant. While arbitration and various forms of peaceful solution were frequent among our countries from the 19th century up to
very recently, this was not due to the fact that those
judgments and proposals for solutions were better or
more adjusted to existing law than at present. What
happened was that, one way or another, enforced or imposed solutions were protected by the international system. The small and medium-sized countries of the pe-
riphery were in no position to resist the pressure exercised on them by the great powers in order that,
first, they should consent to a peaceful form of solution, and, later, that they should accept the judge's
verdict.

The backstage machinations of certain past cases
of arbitration, which have now come to light, clearly
show great power pressure. The arbitration between Venezuela and Great Britain with regard to the frontier

conflict in Guyana during the last century is a case in point.[18] (The award was handed down on October 3, 1899.) Similarly, the manipulation suffered by the Drago doctrine at the Second Hague Conference, which conditioned its basic principle of non-compulsory collection of the public debt to the submission of the conflict between creditor and debtor to the decision of a court of arbitration, also clearly shows that the preference for jurisdictional solutions was conditioned by the structure of the international system and the action of the great powers.

In the same way, the recent arbitral award in the case of the Beagle Channel, to which we have already referred, is neither more or less "political" (in the sense in which we have used the word to describe the judge's method) than the previous decisions adopted by Her Britannic Majesty to settle conflicts between Argentina and Chile.[19] If Argentina's reactions now have been different, it is because times have changed. The rejection of the arbitral decision now finds support in the growing "permissiveness" of the international system and in the "psychological" appreciation of the real autonomy the country enjoys.

2. The decline in the relative power of the United States over the continent. The United States is a super power and its potential is colossal. However, for several reasons, which will not be analyzed here, its relative power (from the political point of view) has declined on the continent. This has undoubted repercussions on the problem of the settlement of conflicts on the sub-continent and on the emergence of conflicts. From this point of view, the new US low profile implies a decrease in the disciplinary strength of the dominant power within its bloc and, consequently, a reduction in its capacity to control conflicts. It should be well understood that this capacity has not disappeared, but simply that it is less influential than before. The sterile, last-minute telephone call from President Reagan to General Galtieri of Argentina on the occasion of the 1982 Argentine recovery of the Malvinas Islands vividly demonstrates this decline in US ability to deter or control conflict. Consequently, while conflict potential has increased in recent years in Latin America, recourse to definitive solution procedures has also diminished.

Domestic political causes. From this perspective, there are two preponderant explanations: (1) the possibility of obtaining political consensus by manipulating international conflicts in lieu of domestic legitimacy and (2) the fear that jurisdictional solutions may have destabilizing effects domestically.

1. Manipulation of international conflicts to obtain domestic consensus as a substitute for political legitimacy. This psychological action recipe is widely known. If a government has domestic difficulties due to problems that have no short-term solutions, the external conflict, ably promoted and exaggerated (when it has not been even created artificially), can deviate the attention of public opinion and generate, even if only temporarily, a consensus held together by national sentiment. As it can easily be understood, this danger is greater in those systems where popular participation in decision-making is limited or practically non-existent.

Accordingly, conflict potential has increased in the region due to the proliferation of authoritarian regimes or pro forma democracies which are continually facing acute problems of domestic legitimization. From this point of view, it is understandable that Latin American states are endeavoring not to find themselves constrained by pre-established conflict-resolving machinery with rigidly arranged procedures and deadlines that cannot be extended.

In this context, international conflicts that are artificially magnified can produce particularly dangerous domestic consequences because of a "boomerang" effect. On the one hand, the government involved may not want to be bound by peaceful solution measures, in order to exercise at will the challenge represented by the conflict. On the other hand, it may find itself trapped by the very euphoria it aroused, when it is later prevented from negotiating and reaching a compromise on issues which propaganda up to that moment had presented as vital.

This is the vicious circle into which, unfortunately, many governments fall, especially authoritarian ones. To achieve a consensus, they magnify the international controversy, but once they have achieved it, they must find a solution congruent with the objectives whose achievement was so firmly advocated, because otherwise the consensus will become diluted and the government will be left even more unprotected and lacking in support that at the beginning. This dramatic vicious circle is exceedingly dangerous because it pushes the government into an escalation of acts (and omissions), whose final outcome, due to the dialectic process set in motion, cannot be other than war. The case of the Malvinas provides a singularly vigorous illustration of this diabolical dialectic process.

2. Possible destabilizing effects of jurisdictional solutions. Governments are afraid of losing control of the solution of controversies due to destabilizing effects that may result from a settlement that does not

completely meet expectations which, rightly or wrongly,
public opinion has generated. This observation applies
to any peaceful solution procedure, even discretionary
ones. Once the settlement or the proposed solution has
been reached, governments face the need to convince
public opinion, and it is at this stage that the destabilizing potential appears. It is very easy for political sectors opposed to the government to clothe partisan ends with the national interest by criticizing a
decision that is not too favorable for the country
(something that is very frequent because seldom do solutions give full satisfaction to either of the Parties
involved).

Juridico-Normative causes. In the strictly judicial field, it is usually said that the inoperativeness
of the jurisdictional systems is due to the fact that
the states are not inclined to accept in advance permanent institutional jurisdictions and that, therefore,
ratification of treaties in existence should be achieved
or else other more acceptable ones should be drawn up.
Basically, the argument is a tautology: there is no
peaceful solution because there are no treaties in
force, and there are no treaties in force because states
do not like peaceful solutions.
The real question that should be analyzed within
this context is, to our understanding, whether there
are specific juridico-normative causes which might dis-
courage states, in this case the Latin American ones,
from adhering to the hermetical jurisdictional course.
This is primarily due to lack of credibility and trust
in international courts, which results from structural
shortcomings related to: (1) the recruiting of the
judge; (2) the inadequacy of applied law; and (3) the
"diplomatization" of the procedure.

1. Recruitment of the judge. As the presentation
of a candidate to undertake prejurisdictional or jurisdictional international functions is not usually a vital
matter for the state, the choice is normally left in
the hands of the corresponding bureaucratic apparatus,
i.e. the Foreign Ministry. Since, in order to be appointed, it is necessary to have the votes needed, which
are those of the states, the international election
campaign and vote-trading become the patrimony of the
same intimately related internal and international bu-
reaucracies. The result of all this has been that in
recent years the curricula of candidates and, therefore, that of the judges finally chosen, have been essentially of diplomatic extraction or proceeding from
international organizations. This explains why the
most renowned internationalists never reached, for example, the International Court of Justice. As Leo
Gross so aptly states:

Some of the jurists whose works are frequently cited in individual opinions and whose writings may well qualify as "the teachings of the most highly qualified publicists" and therefore as "subsidiary means for the determination of rules of law" have not been elected because the States of their nationality do not belong to any efficient vote-trading bloc in the United Nations.[20]

What the experience of international jurisdiction has shown in the last few decades is that this diplomatic predominance has been one of the factors which has contributed to the discredit, for example, of the International Court, for the simple reason that diplomatic skills are not appropriate for jurisdictional adjudication. When a decision has to be made, the perception of the diplomat is very different from that of the jurist. The diplomat is accustomed to adjust to his instructions, to eschew personal responsibilities, and to act on behalf of the state. As a judge, it is understandable that he should try to sidestep the issue in controversial cases, and to dispose of them at the preliminary hearings by trying not to decide in regard to the merits. If the decision is inevitable, he will endeavor to reach conclusions that are not too vulnerable from the point of view of the international situation by bearing in mind the constellation of power appreciated by a diplomatic mind. Such considerations would not affect the jurist, who will always try to give the case an operative solution, influenced or not by justice, according to whether he follows a positivist or a jus naturalist course.

It is a question of differences of approach, which in the diplomatic case is non-functional for the purpose of achieving a reliable and foreseeable jurisprudence, since the situational context is predominant. In order for the Court to once again awaken the confidence of jurists and of professional judicial circles, it must be "adequately composed of public international lawyers".[21] Similar conclusions apply to the selection of international judges for arbitration courts and even conciliators and mediators.

2. _Inadequacy of applied law_. The law of the international community is a juridical order that is applied to a human group that is going through a period of profound crisis and transformation. Every time that these situations arise, the judge who has to apply existing law to disputes which are each day more controversial, finds himself faced with a dramatic dilemma. If he considers the law just as it appeared at the time of its adoption, he finds obsolete norms which are inoperative vis-à-vis a reality that has advanced with giant steps. If, on the contrary, he finds inspiration

exclusively in justice, he may adopt solutions that are
not operative either, that is, that are so far removed
from the actual conditions of the international system
that they do not meet up to the expectations of the international community within which the court should reinforce its credibility. Consequently, the task of the
international magistrate is exceedingly complex and
calls for a profound knowledge of the law of the international community in its normative dimension and of
its underlying trends, as well as a very keen and up-
to-date perception of justice and of international social reality. C. Wilfred Jenks, who knew international
jurisprudence so well, had occasion to refer to this
problem in a well-known book:

> The law is in process of rapid growth and the pro-
> cess neither can nor should be arrested, but the
> uncertainty incidental to such a process of growth
> is a heavy liability when seeking the acceptance
> of a larger measure of compulsory jurisdiction by
> commitments of general application which are not
> limited to the interpretation of a particular in-
> strument or to matters within some well-defined
> field.[22]

Jurisprudence, being what it is, cannot be static
and, through the procedures we all know, it is constant-
ly being updated to reality. However, gradual and in-
terstitial adaptation that promotes confidence and
trust is undermined by the permanent contradiction among
successive International Court judgments. Such inade-
quacies of applied law do not attract the status quo
countries because they fear an erratic revolutionary
verdict, nor do they convince the newer arrivals, because they are always concerned about the possibility
of a decision tied to some ancient law that came to
light in the colonial era.

3. Diplomatization of the procedure. It is also
possible to detect a marked tendency toward "diplomatiz-
ing" the procedure before the International Court. It
is generally diplomats who supervise the preparation of
cases and who even act as agents and advisors. Not in-
frequently, international legal scholars of a country
that is Party to a dispute are not even consulted.
Even former judges of the International Court of Justice
have been left on the sidelines in jurisdictional proceedings! Although this can be explained above all by
professional jealousy and by the tradition of rivalry
between Latin American foreign ministries and national
internationalists, it is no less true that this attitude promotes consideration of the case within the diplomatic framework noted above, which in no way favors
consolidation of peaceful means for the solution of
conflicts.

SOLUTIONS

Complex proposals for complex causes

After the diagnosis and the etiology, we must now look for remedies. The usual temptation is to limit oneself to proposing juridico-normative solutions. Thus, for example, the prescriptions offered by Francisco Orrego Vicuña simplify the procedural framework, confirm the preference for discretionary proceedings, and draw up a solemn treaty for the renunciation of the use of force and threats of the use of force.[23] We do not deny that these proposals are worthy of consideration, but the above examination of causes instead focused attention on the deeper, structural nature of deficiencies stemming from the international political framework, from the internal political context, and from the basic law and the procedural system. To accept prevailing structural problems and draw up new undertakings to refrain from resorting to the threat or use of force, apart from being repetitious, does not constitute a sufficient guarantee for the preservation of peace. Recent history shows very clearly that the legal obligation not to use force, even when contained in an apparatus of collective security, is not sufficient if not accompanied by a reasonable mechanism of peaceful change. Otherwise, the tensions that accumulate due to the gap between applied law and real expectations are so deep that they finally justify an outbreak of violence.

In this part, we will deal instead with possibilities of attacking the structural causes of the progressive Latin American mistrust regarding methods for peaceful solution and its dramatic consequence, which is the multiplication of controversies, the increase of tensions, and potential crises of real magnitude looming in the foreseeable future. In order to help resolve the basic problem, the following measures could encourage a peaceful solution: (1) the creation of a Latin American system of peaceful settlement; (2) the participation of public opinion in the establishment and functioning of the system; (3) the adoption of measures to foster confidence for peaceful solution of conflicts; (4) non-government participation in the recruiting of international jurists; (5) removal of the secrecy surrounding prejurisdictional and jurisdictional bodies; (6) de-ideologization of applied law; and (7) adequate publicity about procedures for a peaceful solution.

1. Creation of a Latin American system of peaceful settlement. International political causes undermine an institutionalized peace system when its functioning is subjected to conditions stemming from the interna-

tional system such as direct or indirect influence of
the great powers. For example, within the OAS, the
creation of an Inter-American Court has often been
brought up, but the project never prospered due to the
considerations made previously regarding the preponderance of the USA. It is understandable that the United
States should prefer to be influential in the solution
of conflicts, rather than accept the establishment of a
jurisdictional structure that would reduce its concrete
possibilities in any way.

In fact, the United States has not ratified either
the Treaty of Compulsory Arbitration of 1902, nor the
Protocol for Progressive Arbitration, nor the Bogota
Pact, in short, those treaties which in some way represent a certain degree of compulsion in their jurisdictional procedures. Neither has it ratified the Pact
of San José de Costa Rica.

On the other hand, the greater autonomy currently
enjoyed by the countries of Latin America could very
well sustain a sub-continental system of peaceful solution for their own conflicts. For example, it has been
suggested at times that the OAS be replaced by an Organization of Latin American States. Similarly, it is
possible that the creation of a Latin American System
of Peaceful Settlement that does not adversely affect
the existing bodies, especially the inter-American ones,
could efficiently contribute to the preservation of
peace in Latin America, which would in turn benefit the
whole of America. The creation of the Court of Justice
of the Cartagena Agreement, which in two short years
has been ratified by practically all its members (Venezuela alone is missing, but negotiations are well under
way to this effect), is a very encouraging sign.

The Latin American System of Peaceful Settlement
could be very flexible and could offer the possibility,
should the parties involved so wish, of a preliminary
option for jurisdictional or pre-jurisdictional methods.
Furthermore, in order to avoid the lifelessness that
characterizes the International Court of Justice, it
should be conceived as a system concerned not only with
traditional diplomatic conflicts, but also with those
generated by the various processes of regional integration under way.[24] The system should undoubtedly also
adjust to the structural characteristics that are the
subject of our exposition in the following paragraphs.

2. Participation of public opinion in the establishment and functioning of the system. As we have seen
above, one of the principal obstacles to international
adjudication, from the point of view of the internal
policy of the state, is the destabilizing potential of
an adverse finding. An alternative is to introduce some
mechanism that will allow for the specific expression
of the will of the people who, after all, are the ulti-

mate beneficiaries or losers, be it directly or indirectly, of the international cases. Such insertions should be introduced in two crucial moments of the process of peaceful solution: (a) on the establishment of the system of peaceful settlement that includes compulsory jurisdiction and (b) on the acceptance or rejection of the solution proposed by pre-jurisdictional methods before a compulsory decision is reached.

In the first place, a Latin American state should not ratify the Treaty establishing the Latin American System of Peaceful Settlement without prior consultation with its inhabitants through a plebiscite that results in a favorable recommendation. In this way it would be definitely established that the responsibility for having accepted a system for the peaceful solution of conflicts is not exclusively that of the government in power at the time, but that it is shared and backed by the people who, therefore, also assume responsibility for the future consequences of such a decision.

A formula for peaceful settlement also should be envisaged making popular consultation possible. What we propose is that the conflict be submitted to a jurisdictional procedure only in the event that a previous pre-jurisdictional step has been fruitless. But this pre-jurisdictional step (mediation, for example) must have novel characteristics: the proposal of the mediator would be submitted to a plebiscite for approval, and the court would only intervene in the case of a negative result. Naturally, the consultation regarding the will of the people that we propose should be surrounded by all the guarantees of tolerance, impartiality and freedom that will render it really significant. If this were not the case, the proposed remedy would have a boomerang effect.

This procedure would have many advantages: it would force the mediator to scrupulously weigh all the arguments; it would oblige the interested parties to present their arguments carefully; it would compel those responsible for the negotiations to consult all the relevant groups of public opinion; in turn, it would oblige these groups to take an interest in the conflict and take stands during the pre-jurisdictional negotiations; and, above all, it would subject the stands of the interested parties to ample debate by public opinion through its natural organs of expression. Mediation undertaken subject to these conditions would, in the immense majority of cases, render it unnecessary to resort to jurisdictional recourse which, in any case and due to the mere fact of its existence, would also give impetus to consensus without any need to enter into the examination of the case. In this way, satisfaction would be given to the current Latin American tendency to prefer an agreement through the emergence of a reasonable and responsible consensus.

The intention is, above all, to avoid the government monopoly in the solution of international conflicts in Latin America and their resulting manipulation with the pernicious consequences we have analyzed above. With the system we propose, it could easily be seen that the fears of destabilization are groundless and that governments can act with greater efficiency and security when they realize that they have the backing of their peoples, obtained through fair consultation. In addition to this, the temptation to utilize international conflicts for purposes of offsetting internal dissent would be avoided, a temptation to which governments and political parties often succumb.

3. Adoption of confidence-building measures for peaceful solution of conflicts. On the occasion of the Conference on Security and Cooperation in Europe, also called the Helsinki Conference (1975), the possibility was debated of adopting confidence-building measures among the states participating in the Conference. The intention was to contribute towards reducing mistrust and tension stemming from the lack of information regarding military activities. The Helsinki Act regulated this question and prescribed certain "confidence-building measures", such as prior notification of military manoeuvres and troop movements and exchange of observers. Chapter 5 of this volume relates the confidence-building approach in detail to Latin America, so the discussion here is limited to the role confidence-building measures can play in preparing the atmosphere for the achievement of a peaceful solution between contending parties.

Generally, the examination and analysis of conflicts among Latin American countries are undertaken individually by the respective governmental, diplomatic, military and academic circles of the Parties to the conflict. Although, at times, there is no lack of balanced national opinions, the partiality of the forums in which the debate takes place often leads to a biased opinion. The exchange of opinions actually takes place at the diplomatic level or, what is even worse, in confidential pre-jurisdictional or jurisdictional contexts. The respective public opinions are usually informed only when the result of the negotiations is already in sight, when the solution already has been proposed, or when the award or sentence has been pronounced. But by that time the fait accompli precludes any meaningful public deliberation, since it imposes a feedback that completely alters the situation.

Would it not be possible--and this is our concrete proposal--that exponents of the arguments of the other country, that is, the other Party to the controversy, also be present in the national forums and that, thereby, the real arguments of the opponent be known, under-

stood and discussed before the conflict is submitted to
a peaceful procedure? The academic world seems to be
the most appropriate one for this type of constructive
discussion, but it would also be possible to hold it in
other settings: political, military, business, labor,
cultural, journalistic, etc. The majority of Latin
American countries now possesses institutions that seem
very appropriate for this type of dialogue: the national
war schools or national defense schools, where qualified
civilians and representatives of diverse sectors of national activity take part, in addition to senior officers of the armed forces, as professors and students.

Dialogues and debates such as those we propose
would tremendously facilitate a peaceful solution. It
would be possible to hear the real arguments of the adversary, to understand his true motives, to appreciate
the possible vulnerability of one's own, and, above all,
to duly weigh the negative repercussions of the prolon-
gation of the conflict on the overall spectrum of the
international relations of the states involved and, at
times, on the internal context itself. We therefore
feel that, in the same way the Helsinki Act regulates
the procedure to be followed for the implementation of
measures for fostering confidence in the matter of military deployment and related action, the Latin American
System for Peaceful Settlement should envisage and regulate the adoption of confidence-building measures,
such as those we propose, for the settlement of controversies.

4. Non-government participation in the recruiting
of international jurists. Governments have completely
monopolized the nomination and appointment of persons
to carry out pre-jurisdictional and jurisdictional functions in the international sphere and, unfortunately,
this has become common practice as well in the formation
of the courts lately created in America. Thus the
judges of the Inter-American Court of Human Rights are
elected by the states that are Parties to the Convention
from a list of candidates proposed by those same states
(Art. 7 § 1, of the Statute), and the judges of the Court
of Justice of the Cartagena Agreement are appointed on
the basis of lists presented by each member country and
by the unanimous vote of the plenipotentiaries accred-
ited for such a purpose (Art. 8). We have already seen
the negative consequences of this manner of choice from
the point of view of the integrity and foresight of the
court and of the stability and adequacy of applied law.

Even recognizing that, in view of the current
structure of the international regime (and as long as
it remains unchanged), governments should be basically
responsible for the designations, we still believe that
definite efforts should be made to achieve a widening
of the recruitment base. In the Latin American System

of Peaceful Settlement, the universities of each country should also be able to present a slate of candidates
that could include as little as one national--thus
bringing about the incorporation of jurists of other
states in which the universities are not really autonomous and, therefore, where they would not be nominated
unless officially sponsored. Self-nomination should
also be allowed.

Finally, adequate publicity should be given to the
names of the candidates presented and to their respective curricula, including such publications and research
work as may be considered most adequate in justification
of their candidacy. The scientific shortcomings of
many candidates would thus be manifest, and this would
serve as a brake on the presentation of unqualified
candidates. It was precisely the lack of adequate publicity of the merits of the candidates for judges of
the International Court of Justice that was stressed by
the panel appointed by the American Society of International Law to debate upon the future of the Court.
One of the recommendations was that the national groups
"should submit statements of the personal qualifications
of the candidates nominated by them to be included by
the Secretary General in the list of candidates."[25]

5. Removal of the secrecy surrounding pre-jurisdictional and jurisdictional bodies. Public opinion,
the universities, and influential groups of society
should all have a vivid perception of the functions of
international courts and of the tasks, purposes, and
expectations of the judges. To this end, the judges
themselves (in the wide sense) should promote public
contacts and rapprochement. There is a need to make
international judicial bodies known, to expose their
achievements, to recognize their failures, and to lis-
ten to criticism. In the Latin American System of
Peaceful Settlement, we propose, as a part of the functions of the judges, that they would give courses and
seminars at universities and teaching institutions in
the region during the judicial recess as well as take
part in panel discusions, round tables and other academic meetings in which special attention is focused on
the peaceful solution of conflicts in Latin America and
the structure and the workings of the system.

6. De-ideologization of applied law. An adequate
selection of justices will be one of the guarantees
that the solutions will be juridically appropriate. In
this aspect, however, the universities of the region--
and especially their law schools--will have to work
very hard to ensure that the teaching of and research
into the law governing the international community correspond to the real expectations of a region that possesses important possibilities for potential autonomy.

It is essential, above all, to understand and counter
the implicit ideologization of the doctrines and theo-
ries of International Law and of International Relations that we, Latin Americans, normally employ and
which, having been conceived in the developed centers
of the West, are biased in their favor.[26] We therefore
believe that the Latin American System of Peaceful Settlement will be successful to the extent that it coher-
ently and consistently applies law that is instead in-
spired in justice which does not forget the realities
of our region.

7. Adequate publicity about procedures of peaceful
solution. Finally, the Latin American system should
contemplate adequate publicity for all its procedural
steps. An international "case" is not only of interest
to the agents, advisors and lawyers of the interested
parties. It also involves entire peoples. Consequently, applications, arguments, memorials, rejoinders, and
hearings should be published and made known and even be
debated. Proposals for solutions should also be publi-
cized. We firmly believe that the de-mythification of
international procedures will contribute towards a preference for and acceptance of peaceful solutions.

FINAL CONCLUSION

Epilogue for crusaders

We are very much aware that a good part of the solutions put forth imply radical changes in the habits,
the attitudes, and, above all, in the psychology of the
actors on the international stage and that, for these
reasons, it is very problematical (although not impossible) that they will ever be adopted. However, this
is the field on which the destiny of our region is at
stake, and with it, that of humanity. We therefore
fervently believe that we, Latin Americans, must strive
untiringly to build a region at peace. We emphasize
"peace", because our great objective should not be mere
pacification, that is, the absence of war, but orderly
co-existence guided by justice and tempered by charity.
Then this region at peace could also, to some extent,
set the course for other states and especially those
which have senselessly embarked on an arms race for
mass destruction that is incomprehensible even from the
point of view of military science.

To achieve this end, it is essential that those of
us who uphold these ideas should unite and defend them
passionately in an endeavor to influence the sometimes
mistaken decisions taken by those who govern our countries. The well-trod paths are no longer of any use,
as they unavoidably lead us to destruction.

Senator José Franco Montoro, of Brazil, has put

forth a proposal that seems to us to be of great importance in bringing together those who are actively concerned: that of establishing a Latin American Front for
the Defense of Democracy and Basic Freedoms, comprising
social, political and economic forces which need not
necessarily belong to governmental or official circles.[27]
Obviously, the Front could also promote the peaceful
solution of conflicts in our countries. If at one time
it could be said that war was too important a matter to
be left exclusively in the hands of the military, has
not the time perhaps arrived for concluding that the
preservation of peace is now such a serious problem for
the future of humanity that its solution cannot be left
in the hands of diplomats alone?

NOTES

1. All through the nineteenth century, arbitration was exceedingly frequent among Latin American states, as also between them
and European states. Suffice it, for example, to thumb through A.
M. Stuyt's classical Survey of International Arbitrations, 1794-
1970 (A.W. Syjthoff, Leyden, 1972) to see that Latin American countries, in spite of being "Johnnies Come Lately" in the international community of those times, were well ahead of many other European
states in the number of arbitrations arranged and of arbitration
awards enforced. It should be borne in mind, however, that these
arbitrations, formally agreed to, were actually imposed in great
measure, due to the characteristics of the international system of
those days, either because one of the parties to the conflict was
an European power and the arbitration was an elegant way of achieving its own objectives, or because the crises which would arise
out of the conflicts could alter the regional status quo. Numerous examples could be cited but perhaps a very significant one of
the former case could be the Venezuelan-British arbitration case
of 1899, while a good example of the latter might be the Argentine-Chilean case of 1902. On the other hand, the Central American
states established the Central American Court of Justice through a
convention in 1907, which was active during ten years. Nevertheless, the predominant participation of the USA in the inception of
this Court is well-known, as is also the fact that the convention
was not renewed at the expiry of the first term of ten years as a
consequence of the verdict it handed down regarding the conflict
between El Salvador and Nicaragua in regard to the Bryan-Chamorro
Treaty which directly affected US interests.

2. Cf. Juan Carlos Puig and Delia Colombo Imaz, "El fracaso
de la iniciativa latinoamericana en el panamericanismo. Ensayo
de interpretación socio-política", in Política de poder en América
Latina, eds. J.F. Petras et al (Pleamar, Buenos Aires, 1974), pp.
49-84.

3. In actual practice, every time a Latin American state appeared before the UN indicating its preference for this forum as

an alternative procedure of conflict resolution, the procedure always led to a dead end, either because the Security Council declared itself incompetent (Guatemalan case, 1954) or because, even assuming competence, measures taken by the OAS prevailed in practice (Dominican case, 1965).

4. J.M. Yepes, 'La Conferencia Panamericana de Bogota y los progresos del panamericanismo', en Revista de Derecho Internacional (Havana), 54 (1948), p. 181.

5. Paul Fauchille, Traité de Droit International Public (Pedone, Paris, 1926), Vol. I, 3rd. Part, p. 604.

6. The arbitrator agreed upon was HRH of Great Britain. In case one of the Parties were to break off friendly relations with Great Britain, the arbitrator's role would be assumed by the Swiss Government. On the other hand, should a disagreement arise between the Parties as to the contents of the arbitral agreement, it was for the arbitrator "to fix the agreement, the date, place and formalities of the proceedings, as well as to solve all procedural difficulties which could appear in the course of the proceedings".

7. See Mary Jeanne Reid Martz, 'OAS Reforms and the Future of Pacific Settlement', Latin American Research Review, 12 (1977): 178-179.

8. An "Interim Mechanism for the Settlement of Disputes" had been previously adopted, but it did not lead to a hermetical procedure. Resolution 165 (CM-I/III-E).

9. CARIFTA (Caribbean Free Trade Association) had only foreseen a pre-jurisdictional procedure for the settlement of disputes (Article 26, Treaty of April 30, 1968).

10. With reference to the system of human rights protection before the entry into force of the Pact of San José (a system which is still applicable to the states which are not parties to the latter), see Héctor Gros Espiell, 'Le système intéramericain comme régime régional de protection des droits de l'homme', Recueil des Cours de l'Académie de Droit International, 1975. The transition period has been thoroughly analyzed by Thomas Buergenthal, 'La Comisión Americana sobre Derechos Humanos: problemas escogidos', and by Andrés Aguilar, 'La Comisión Interamericana de Derechos Humanos y la entrada en vigencia de la Comisión Americana de Derechos Humanos o Pacto de San José de Costa Rica', in articles published in Mundo Nuevo, Revista de Estudios Latinoamericanos, 2 (1979), Nos. 5-6. The problem, which is impossible to elucidate here to its full extent, is important, since the "old" Human Rights Commission had much more limited competence than the "new" one.

11. Maria Teresa Infante Caffi, 'La solución pacífica de las controversias', in Rodrigo Díaz Albónico (ed.), Antecedentes, balances y perspectivas del Sistema Interamericano (Editorial Universitaria, Santiago de Chile, 1977), p. 155.

12. Thus, in the conflict between Costa Rica and Nicaragua (1948-1949), at the suggestion of the Organ of Consultation, both governments agreed upon a Pact of Friendship whereby they acqui-

esced "in applying the American Treaty on Pacific Settlement, to which they give full force, to any controversy which may arise between them, even before the aforementioned Treaty be formally ratified and, therefore, before it comes into force among the American Republics". In another conflict between the same countries in 1955, a new agreement was entered into with the purpose of regulating the functioning of the Commission of Investigation and Conciliation established according to the Pact of Bogota. And, finally, in the conflict between Honduras and Nicaragua in 1957, also on the basis of the recommendation of the Organ of Consultation, the Parties applied the judicial procedure foreseen in the Pact of Bogota. See OAS, Tratado Interamericano de Asistencia Recíproca, Vol. I (1948-1959), pp. 59, 206 and 294.

13. César Sepúlveda, 'The Reform of the Charter of the OAS', Recueil des Cours de l'Académie de Droit International, 137 (1972), p. 97.

14. Héctor Gros Espiell, Perfeccionamiento del régimen jurisdiccional internacional, paper presented at the Conference "Segundas Jornadas Latinoamericanas de Derecho Internacional", Viña del Mar, Chile, December 1980 (sponsored by the Institute of International Studies of the University of Chile), pp. 11-12.

15. David J. Padilla, 'The Judicial Resolution of Legal Disputes in the Integration Movements of the Hemisphere', Lawyer of the Americas, 11:75-95.

16. Ibid., 91-93.

17. For a more detailed elaboration of this point, see Juan Carlos Puig, 'Integración y Autonomía. A propósito de la reunión del Foro Latinoamericano en Caracas', Revista Argentina de Relaciones Internacionales, 1 (1975), pp. 5-29.

18. Héctor Gros Espiell, Introduction to Frederick de Martens, Rusia e Inglaterra en Asia Central (Ediciones de la Presidencia de la República, Caracas, 1981), pp. 16 ff.

19. Juan Carlos Puig, 'El laudo arbitral británico en el caso del Río Encuentro', Estudios de Derecho y Política Internacional, Juan Carlos Puig (ed.) (Depalma, Buenos Aires, 1970), p. 186 ff.

20. Leo Gross, 'Conclusions' in The Future of the International Court of Justice (Oceana, New York, 1976) p. 744.

21. Gerald Fitzmaurice, Chapter XIII, in Leo Gross (ed.), The Future of the International Court of Justice, p. 484.

22. C. Wilfred Jenks, The Prospects of International Adjudication (Stevens, London, 1964), pp. 106-107.

23. Francisco Orrego Vicuña, 'Análisis de la práctica latinoamericana en materia de solución de controversias', Derecho de la Integración, 4 (1974), pp. 20 ff.

24. Following this line of reasoning, Felipe Salazar suggested the creation of a Permanent Latin-American Court in his article 'Solución de conflictos en organizaciones interestatales para la integración económica y otras formas de cooperación económica',

Derecho de la Integración, 11 (1978), p. 33.

25. Gross, op. cit., p. 730.

26. Juan Carlos Puig, Doctrinas Internacionales y Autonomía Latinoamericana (Ediciones del Instituto de Altos Estudios de A-mérica Latina, Caracas, 1980), pp. 15 ff.

27. José Franco Montoro, A luta pela democracia na América Latina (Brasilia, 1979).

3
Controlling Conflict in the Caribbean Basin: National Approaches

Victor Millán

INTRODUCTION

Despite their heterogeneity, the countries of Central America and the Caribbean region share certain basic peculiarities. Most of them belong to the Western Hemisphere alliance system, which also comprises the United States and the South American republics, and their geographical position is far from the main theatres of military conflicts in the world. This, together with the predominance of a common Iberian ancestry, especially on the Central American isthmus, has contributed to a strong regional consciousness. However, the presence of the United States in the area creates a situation in which a group of weak states is associated in an alliance system with a major power that is viewed by its weaker allies as both a protector and a threat.[1]

Within the Central American isthmus, and to a lesser extent in the Caribbean area, the armed forces have traditionally been active and determinant in politics and government, while in the latter decades their strictly military functions have steadily decreased. The militarization of the region, as illustrated by the growth of military expenditure accompanied by an increasing role for military institutions in national economic, social and political affairs, is primarily connected with domestic politico-social issues rather than with problems of international security.

The declaration in 1823 by US President Monroe--that interference by any European power in the affairs of the newly emerging Latin American republics would be considered an unfriendly act toward the United States itself--established the right for the USA to "protect" Latin America. It was based on the assumption that the two regions of North and Latin America shared common interests which the northern power had the right to interpret. Thereafter, aggressive expansionism was added to the defensive paternalism of the Monroe Doctrine. Since 1823, the United States has conducted more than 70 mil-

itary operations in Central America and the Caribbean
without a declaration of war.[2] In addition, political
instability within the countries of the region has weakened the capacity of the alliance system to deal effectively with either external or internal conflicts.[3]

Ghosts from the past are present today in the post-
Viet Nam era of declining US internationalism and détente, and a new Cold War era has reached the region.
Washington's grip on Central American and Caribbean affairs has become problematic both cognitively and oper-
ationally. Certain countries of the region, most noticeably Mexico, Nicaragua, Panama, Colombia and Venezuela, have begun to reject many of the traditional
forms of US influence in their domestic policies and,
more important, have adopted foreign policies based on
particularistic notions of national interest and sovereignty.

The objective of this paper is to review and analyze current developments in foreign and domestic policy
in the Central American and Caribbean states, in the
light of increasing levels of ongoing internal and inter-
state conflicts. International as well as regional or
national efforts to develop mechanisms for peaceful
change--crisis management, peace-making and peace-keep-
ing operations--will be examined in conjunction with on-
going or potential conflicts.

DEFINITIONS

The term 'Central America and the Caribbean', which
is a sub-region of Latin America, is commonly applied to
the group of nations of the Western hemisphere immediately south of the United States, including the present
possessions of France, the Netherlands, the United Kingdom and the United States.

In this chapter, the term 'Central America' refers
to Mexico and the Central American isthmus, i.e., Guatemala, El Salvador, Belize, Honduras, Nicaragua, Costa
Rica and Panama. 'The Caribbean' includes the islands
in the Caribbean Sea. The term 'Caribbean Basin', which
is geopolitical in the sense that countries and territories defined by it are the targets of common diplomatic
and strategic efforts, covers the areas of the Caribbean
archipelago plus Mexico, the Central American isthmus,
Colombia and Venezuela. A conflict between two or more
parties is defined here as a situation where the aims,
interests and values of two or more parties are considered by them to be incompatible. 'Inter-state conflicts' or 'international conflicts' include all those
claims to political leadership, territorial and boundary disputes or controversies over natural resources,
ideological and security interests and migration conflicts which have an impact on the political situation
in the region described here. These can be differenti-

ated from 'internal conflicts' or 'intra-state conflicts' which include internal war, coups d'état, guerrilla war, revolution, insurrection, rebellion, and civil
disorder, as well as all hostilities in which the organized armed forces of a state are used on at least one
side. Finally, 'controlling conflicts' is used to de-
note all measures intended to prevent, moderate, terminate, limit or freeze organized conflicts at the internal and international level, as well as measures meant
to build up confidence and understanding among parties
and thereby produce a national or international climate
conducive to a peaceful settlement of disputes.[4]

CONFLICTS: INTERNAL AND EXTERNAL DIMENSIONS

The current crisis in Central America consists of
three critical situations, namely, the position of Nicaragua, the civil war in El Salvador, and the conflict
between Cuba and the United States.

The present situation in Central America is much
the result of the slow disintegration of outdated social
and political systems and of strategic considerations on
the part of the United States. In the Caribbean, an
additional important reason for the high level of instability is the distortion of regional structures due to
the alignments of countries with former colonial powers.
Further, there are the common problems faced by all
small states: competing models for development and a
striving for secession and independence.[5] Almost all
internal conflicts are between groups seeking to change
the status quo and other groups fighting to maintain it.
This raises the question as to whether the Western concept of stability which involves a gradualistic approach
to change is, in fact, relevant in the Central American
and Caribbean context in view of the structural changes
which are taking place in the region.

Central America and the Caribbean

The countries of the Central American isthmus have
limited natural resources. Most of them depend on exports of a single, agricultural product--coffee or ba-
nanas--with the exception of oil and some minerals in
the case of Guatemala. The basic source of current conflict (that is, the political and/or economic struggles
in the region) is over control of the scarce natural resources of the region, and, most importantly, over control of the land, from which food to feed the masses of
people and export crops to generate foreign exchange is
produced. A lack of participation in decision-making by
the majority of the population, the fact that all do not
enjoy equal rights, and the absence of a fair distribution of income and wealth lead to discontent, provoking
'impatient' groups in society which attempt to seize

power. Existing socio-political and ideological concepts pave the way for a polarization of the masses, and
this leads in turn to the introduction of new revolutionary ideas.

The inherent and persistent instability of most
countries in the region has prompted the establishment
and constant increase of armed and paramilitary forces
(figure 3.1) to enable their regimes to hold on to power
and to defend themselves against the competing forces
within the country. Perceptions of actual civil wars at
home and greater threats from abroad lead to an ever-
increasing share of national budgets to be spent on armaments. This fact entails an increased economic burden,
and aggravates the political consequences of internal upheavals.

External threats have commonly been exploited to
distract attention from internal tensions and 'development problems' (e.g. the conflicts between Guatemala-
Belize, Honduras-Nicaragua, El Salvador-Honduras, and
Costa Rica-Nicaragua). This clearly has the effect of
further aggravating mutual threat perceptions. In addition, the armed forces represent a danger to fragile
political structures (e.g. in Guatemala, Honduras and
El Salvador).

In order to draw relevant conclusions about the
nature of the regional conflicts and the problems of
security, the internal and the external dimension of
those problems, as well as the links between them, must
be examined. These links become stronger with the deterioration in the resilience (their capability to adjust
themselves to new situations) of the individual countries in the region. Thus, the greater the threats to
security which originate domestically, the greater are
the external threats faced by that country. Sources of
domestic instability are political, economic, social and
even cultural and ideological in nature. Therefore, the
realm of security in the region involves a wide spectrum
of issues and is not solely a military matter in the
conventional sense. Moreover, the US administration's
deep involvement in internal affairs in the region has
led to an acute political sclerosis and uneven economic
development. Direct involvement such as the provision
of military assistance and advisers to Guatemala, El
Salvador, Honduras, and indirect involvement such as the
US policy of aggressive destabilization in Nicaragua and
Jamaica (until 1980), the constant threat of US invasion
against Cuba or economic sanctions against Grenada, Cuba and Nicaragua, and their exclusion from the Caribbean
Basin Initiative of the Reagan administration announced
on February 24, 1982 have contributed to the fact that
the region is now convulsed by revolution, civil war,
border skirmishes or even clashes, economic disruption,
refugee camps and clandestine arms networks.[6] In short,

the internal conflics have become increasingly inter-
nationalized in the past year, where no external actor
has been more prominent than the United States itself.
Thus the projection of the East-West conflict pattern
on the region by the US administration--particularly the
presentation of El Salvador as a "textbook case of indirect armed aggression by the communist powers"--has
created few options in the search for peaceful ways out
of a potential quagmire in El Salvador, Guatemala and
elsewhere in the Caribbean basin, in the meantime jeop-
ardizing the common Western hemisphere interests protecting basic human rights and preventing conflicts that
might compromise regional security.

Mexico and the region

Until the past decade, Mexico was indifferent to
the political existence of Central America. In spite
of its economic development, natural wealth and large
population, Mexico did not entertain schemes for regional leadership. After the oil boom which brought about
rapid economic, social and political development, the
concern of Mexican governments with the evolution of
Central America has grown.
Three specific fears have prompted Mexico's new
interest in the region. (a) Prolonged political instability amongst the countries of Central America would,
at the very least, create a refugee problem in Mexico.
(b) Regional conflicts might tend to increase the power
of the military within the Mexican political system.
For example, the Mexican military worries about its
ability to defend oilfields which lie to the north of
the convulsive Guatemala and responds by pressing for
more numerous, better trained and better equipped
troops to keep the guerrillas out of southern Mexico.
(c) Last, but by no means least, successful revolutions
in El Salvador and Guatemala would place Mexico's political system under a great strain. Opposition groups in
Mexico, feeling that history was on their side, would
be tempted to pursue more aggressively their demands
for an equitable distribution of Mexico's wealth. Radical leaders might try to rally dissatisfied peasants
and workers to their cause; conservatives, on the other
hand, would feel threatened by events in Central America
and urge that steps be taken to control leftist groups
within Mexico. Whilst the Mexican political establishment is confident of its ability to co-opt or repress
any leftist pressure, it is concerned that domestic unrest could justify the strengthening of the Mexican military forces and, thereby, diminish the civilian influence in the ruling of the country. The political
institutions and ideology that have made Mexico stable
could then begin to erode.
Mexico is playing an important role in convincing

the US administration of the need for changing policies
toward the region. It has rejected direct or indirect
plans for military assistance to right-wing dictatorships.

Mexican foreign policy has concentrated mainly on
maintaining its important relations with the United
States. However, it has also adopted a sophisticated,
comprehensive, pragmatic and consistent foreign policy
toward Latin America, based on the legacy of the Carranza Doctrine of 1918,[7] which remains valid even after
more than sixty years. Mexico is convinced that military force is not the way to settle conflicts. Since
1931 when it became a member of the League of Nations,
it has promoted several regional initiatives to remove
fears of armed conflicts and nuclear war. The 1967
Treaty of Tlatelolco--which prohibits the testing, use,
manufacture, production or acquisition by any means, as
well as the receipt, storage, installation, deployment
and any form of possession of nuclear weapons in Latin
America--is one proof of such efforts. The 1978 Conference, convened by Mexico to deal exclusively with the
problem of conventional arms control in the region,[8] the
first of its kind in the history of Latin America, is
another such effort.

Mexico differs with the USA on many matters in this
geographical area, ranging from its interpretation of
the nature of the current government in El Salvador and
its dealings with the current government of Nicaragua,
to holding virtually diametrically opposed views on the
nature and significance of the Cuban revolution.

The decision to break relations with the Somoza regime in May 1979 marked a new Mexican activism in the
region. Mexico has subsequently taken action to influence events in Central America. Firm support has been
given to the Sandinist regime in Nicaragua. Former President López Portillo travelled extensively, including a
visit to Cuba. While keeping diplomatic relations with
the Salvadorean junta, Mexico, together with France, has
granted official opposition status to the Farabundo Mar-
ti Liberation Front (FMLN) and the Democratic Revolutionary Front (FDR) as one representative political
force, with the legal right to enter into negotiations
with the government to find a political solution to the
crisis. Mexico has given generous economic assistance
to the region through a joint petroleum-financing agreement with Venezuela and joined Panama and Venezuela in
offering jointly their "good offices" to mediate in El
Salvador. The Mexican-Venezuelan San José Agreement of
1980 guarantees supplies of oil to nine countries in the
Caribbean Basin (Barbados, Costa Rica, Dominican Republic, El Salvador, Guatemala, Honduras, Jamaica, Nicaragua and Panama), at prices that are, in effect, a dis-
count on prevailing world prices. Part of the purchase
price of petroleum is converted into low-cost loans for

development, providing a crucial stabilizing element in
the region, and foreshadowing a new future for international economic relations in the region. Mexico has
traditionally shown good will toward movements for social change in Latin America. For example, it was the
only country in Latin America that opposed sanctions and
a diplomatic break with Cuba in the early 1960s. Mexico
has in fact maintained both economic and political relations with Cuba. Mexico refused to back the OAS (Organization of American States) on sanctions against Cuba,
and voted against ousting Cuba from the inter-American
system. Nor did it vote in favor of the inter-American
peacekeeping force for the Dominican Republic in 1965.
Mexico justified its positions on the basis of the two
principles that have their roots in the Carranza Doctrine, which has determined its approach to foreign af-
fairs--non-intervention and self-determination. Mexico's
emphasis on these principles is clearly related to its
feelings of vulnerability vis-à-vis the United States.
When the Reagan administration, in the beginning of
1981, moved towards a harder line against Cuba, Mexico
showed its determination to maintain links with Havana
by signing a sugar agreement and a broad energy agreement for propane gas, and helping Cuba to expand its refining capacity and to search for its own oil and to as-
it in buying whatever related equipment was needed on
the world market.[9] Mexico has also served as a bridge
and communicator between the USA and Cuba, encouraging
meetings in Mexico City (1981) and Havana (1982), convinced, as the Mexican Foreign Secretary put it, that
these talks could be successfully pursued towards the
goal of removing obstacles in the way of Cuban-American relations and paving the way for peaceful settlements in Central American conflicts.[10]
    Three aspects of current US-Mexican relations can
be distinguished: (a) the conflict situation in Central
America and their differing proposals for its solution;
(b) the array of normal bilateral relations which include trade, energy, illegal immigration, air routes/
tourism and water sharing; and (c) the political climate
of the relationship which reflects the views of the establishment and influential sectors within both nations.
The Reagan and López Portillo administrations made
progress in the latter two issues by competent diplomacy
and increased efforts toward open dialogue. The first
issue, however, is the most important, least well understood and has the most immediate political consequences.
    Thus, the prospects for a special relationship be-
tween Mexico and the United States, based on reciprocal
concessions and mutual respect, will be affected by the
foreign policies of both countries in regard to Central
America and the Caribbean. If both countries continue
to diverge significantly on issues of foreign policy in
this region, their differences may affect the normal

bilateral relationship and make it difficult, if not impossible, for them to be forthcoming and cooperative
with each other Like the United States, Mexico believes
that there are other alternatives available to help
solve Central American conflicts than the "Cuban solution" to right-wing military dictatorships. Contrary to
the United States, however, Mexico doubts the viability
of a moderate or centre-democratic solution and instead
foresees centre-leftist regimes, that are pluralistic
but not necessarily democratic, as the most likely outcome in the region. Thus, Mexico's hypothesis assumes
that since US administrations failed to halt the Sandinist victory in Nicaragua in 1979, and since the revolutionary forces in El Salvador and Guatemala have continued to grow during the past years, the only strategy
that can possibly succeed in ending the political violence is to exert a moderating influence on the extreme-
left by supporting centre-left forces. The August 1981
Mexican-French Declaration recognizing the Salvadorean
opposition as a representative political force to take
part in negotiations aimed at ending the conflict in El
Salvador, is a good example of this discreet but offi-
cially-sanctioned approach. There is no doubt that the
USA and Mexico are important actors in the region, both
having common security interests in avoiding inter-state
war between their supporters and reducing tension in the
internal affairs of the countries in the region.

Cuba and the Region

     Although militarization has often been justified by
national security considerations, it is in most cases a
response to the social and political conditions prevailing in individual Latin American countries. This was
particularly the case after the 1959 Cuban Revolution,
which engendered fears of similar upheavals elsewhere.
Both US and Cuban policies have had an important impact
on the overall situation in Central America and have, to
a great extent, influenced political and social developments in the states of the region. The traditional view
of US interests in the Western hemisphere emphasizes a
litany of security, economic and political interests.
Historically, primacy has always been given to US security interests, inhibiting direct military threats to
the United States or to its military assets in the region, safeguarding vital maritime routes, including the
Panama Canal, and ensuring US access to strategic raw
materials. The Caribbean is a part of the southern border of the United States, whose involvement in the Basin
is perceived not as a matter of choice but of necessity.
The United States has an important security interest in
ensuring that Cuba does not pose a security threat in
the region. A substantial portion of world seaborne
commerce passes through the Caribbean, some of it

through the Panama Canal. Almost 40 per cent of the total amount of petroleum imported by the USA, compared to
19 per cent in 1960, comes from that region (from Venezuela, Mexico, the Bahamas, which is a petroleum tran-
shipment and refining center, the Netherlands Antilles,
and Trinidad and Tobago). Half of the US import of
bauxite and aluminium comes from the Caribbean, especially from Jamaica and Surinam--the USA imports about 90
per cent of its industrial requirements of these materials. In addition, the Dominican Republic alone supplies
about a twelfth of all US requirements of primary nick-
el.[11]
US policies toward the Caribbean Basin in the late
1970s responded to increased perceptions of change within the region and beyond. During the late 1970s, Cuban
fears were heightened by indications that the United
States had stepped up the military, political and psychological struggle. During the crisis of the discovery
of a Soviet combat brigade in Cuba in August-October
1979, President Carter issued Presidential Directive 52,
ordering the State Department to consult with the CIA,
DoD, and AID to devise new strategies to curb what he
perceived as Cuban interventionism and to undermine Havana's influence in the Third World. The Directive
called for increased economic aid and the sale of military equipment to Central American and Caribbean governments. In the meantime, the US administration autho-
rized the creation of a Caribbean joint task force, the
increased surveillance of Cuba by SR-71 spy aircraft and
other devices, and the holding of military manoeuvres
at Guantanamo naval base as well as in the Caribbean
Sea. Between 30 October and 7 December 1981, forty-one
US Navy ships, including two aircraft carriers, took
part in manoeuvres in the Caribbean code named 'Redix-81',
with participation of some NATO members. In 1982,
'Redix' manoeuvres, with 39 ships and more than 200 aircraft, were repeated. At the beginning of March 1982,
six NATO nations, including the USA, participated in a
marine exercise, 'Safe Pass 82', held in the Gulf of Mexico. During the 10-day manoeuvres, nearly 30 ships,
about 80 aircraft and nearly 10,000 men carried out operations concerned with maintaining control of the sea
lanes of communications and ensuring safe passage of
alliance shipping through the mid-Atlantic. Moreover,
in a move to reinforce US military power near Cuba and
the rest of the Caribbean, the US Navy announced its
intention to reopen the former naval station in Key
West, Florida, since, as the Navy Secretary John F.
Lehman Jr. said, "a forward operating base at Key West
would support naval operations and exercises in the
Florida Straits between the United States and Cuba and
improve the Navy's response to possible contingencies
in the Caribbean area".[12] The United States is also
seeking agreements for air and ground base facilities

in Colombia, Honduras and Haiti, as a part of an effort
to bolster their defenses, and as a political and psychological symbol--a means of showing support and backing to friendly regimes.[13] Thus, the USA and Honduras
concluded an agreement on May 7, 1982, that give US aircraft access to Honduran air bases at Puerto Lempira,
Comayagua and La Ceiba.[14] The Reagan administration requested $21 million for the fiscal year 1983 to improve
airfields in Honduras.[15] The USA already had an agreement with the Honduran government to use its Pacific
Ocean naval base in the Gulf of Fonseca, which borders
on Honduras, El Salvador and Nicaragua. In addition,
the Honduran government leased the Cisnes Island (Swan
Island) in the Caribbean Sea for 90 years to the USA,
enabling the US Navy to monitor all shipping coming from
the Caribbean Sea to the Gulf of Mexico. The United
States also has air, ground or naval facilities in An-
tigua, the Bahamas, Cuba (Guantanamo Bay), Panama, Trinidad and Tobago, Puerto Rico, Turks and Caicos Islands,
and the Virgin Islands.

On the other hand, Cuba has allowed the Soviet
Union naval facilities at Cienfuegos, for Soviet submarines and surface warships, an air base at San Antonio
de los Baños for reconnaissance aircraft, and an elec-
tronic-surveillance installation south of Havana near
Lourdes. On the northern coast of Cuba, the Soviet
Union operates a string of early-warning radars that can
detect aircraft as far away as 300 miles. Moreover, the
Soviet Union set up a satellite tracking station in Ja-
ruco, Havana province in 1973, for reception and trans-
mission of signals in the Intersputnik system.[16] Cuba
has justified the Soviet presence as well as its armament program by what it perceives to be the constant
threat of US invasion. Thus Cuban Vice-President Carlos
Rafael Rodríguez declared at the Second Special Session
of the United Nations devoted to Disarmament, that his
country nearly doubled its military capability in 1981
because the Reagan administration refused to rule out
the possibility of a military attack on Cuba. Cuba
complained that from 1959 to 1979 the USA, using the
Guantanamo base, has been responsible for 12,668 provo-
cations and incidents, including the murder of Cuban
border guards, as well as violations of Cuban airspace
and territorial waters.[17] Furthermore, the Cuban government feels that it has an internationalist duty to
help liberation movements all over the world, as well as
to defend the security of certain states. Cuba is present in Angola and Ethiopia at the request of those governments (in Ethiopia, the Cuban build-up took place
after Castro's efforts to mediate the Ethiopian-Somali
dispute had failed).[18] In Central America and the Caribbean, Cuba's influence remains limited to close collaboration with Nicaragua's revolutionary government,
and with Grenada, Guyana, Surinam and Jamaica (until

1980). Cuba has assisted these countries with medical
personnel, teachers, construction workers, managers,
agronomists and other technicians, as well as provided
training for the police and military forces of these
countries. Cuba states that it is providing assistance
to guerrillas in El 'Salvador and Guatemala at a modest
level, whilst the USA claims that this has been more
substantial. Cuba has at times been a moderating actor,
urging political moderation on the Sandinist government,
the retention of a mixed economy and a non-aligned foreign policy, and has advised them to continue accepting
US aid and foreign investment. The prospects for the
spread of Cuban influence in the region and elsewhere
are generally perceived by the USA as significant. The
USA-Cuban relations have been characterized not only by
mutual hostility, but also by mutual paranoia.

USA and the Region

     The US Republican Platform for the 1980s, adopted
on July 15 at the party's national convention in Detroit,
underlines the premises of the "new" policy of the Reagan
administration: "we will return to the fundamental principle of treating a friend as a friend and self-pro-
claimed enemies as enemies, without apology. We will
make it clear to the Soviet Union and Cuba that their
subversion and their build-up of offensive military
forces is unacceptable".[19]
     The US administration has responded to its percep-
tions of Cuban and Soviet activities in the Caribbean
basin, and to the events in Nicaragua, Grenada, El Salvador and Guatemala, by sharply increasing both its interests and its commitments in the region. Under Carter,
the United States' reaction had led to a dramatic change
in US foreign assistance policies toward the region, including a decision to give $75 million in economic aid
to revolutionary Nicaragua in 1980. In February 1982
the Reagan administration suspended payment of the final
$15 million, and remilitarized some of its policy re-
sponses. This policy of remilitarization includes a reassertion of US military activities, and reinforcement
of US military command procedures in the region (US-Hon-
duran joint military manoeuvres in July 1982 near the
Nicaraguan border, as well as the US military bases and
facilities in Honduras) and an increase in US security
assistance[20] (see figure 3.2).
     During the past two decades the US-Cuban percep-
tions of their relationship as well as their view of
Central American internal conflicts have gone through
a process of stereotyping--the devil-image syndrome--
where both sides attribute all problems to the behavior
of the opposite party with support of revolutionary language or great rhetorical extravaganza.
     The Reagan administration's policy toward regional

conflicts has been determined by fear of the Cuban example rather than the realities of the conflicts themselves, which have their genesis in decades of economy
inequality and political oppression. Thus Washington
has lost sight of the regional dynamics, focusing only
on the East-West dimension of the local conflicts.

The inefficacy of the US policy towards Cuba and in
the region as a whole, as well as the failure of Central
American and Caribbean governments at the end of the
1970s, introduced a new variable into the conflict situation in the area: namely, internal and external conflicts are now inextricably bound up with each other.
Outside support for the parties involved in internal
conflicts thus introduced a new, conflict-intensifying
dimension. Not only neighboring states and the USA but
also the leading regional powers (Mexico, Cuba, Colombia
and Venezuela) tended to intervene, more or less openly,
on behalf of one or the other of the political systems.
Thus, with the intensification of popular insurrections
and class struggles, a trend developed during the 1970s
by which other actors used the intervention of neighboring states as an excuse for their own direct or indirect
interference in internal conflicts.[21] Central America
and some states of the Caribbean remain affected by a
number of serious border and territorial disputes, a
fact that heightens the level of these conflicts, and
reduces the possibilities for a 'political solution' to
internal conflicts, which generally are less susceptible
to prevention, moderation and settlement, than inter-
state conflicts.

INTERNATIONAL DIMENSIONS OF THE CONFLICTS

The types of conflict which have broadened geogra-
phically in the past decade range from disagreements
over the demarcation of a boundary and disputed sovereignty over a much larger territory (Guatemala-Belize;
Honduras-El Salvador; Honduras-Nicaragua; and Nicaragua-
Colombia), to ideological differences between two states
which lead to system conflicts, including here controversies between democracies and dictatorships, civilian and
military regimes, and capitalistic and socialist models
for development, as well as varying attitudes to the at-
tainment of human rights and disagreements over national-
ization of foreign property (Cuba-USA; Dominican Repub-
lic-Haiti; Honduras-Nicaragua; USA-Grenada; USA-Guate-
mala; USA-Nicaragua; and Costa-Rica-Nicaragua). Other
forms of conflict include those over verified or assumed
resources of raw materials in a given area, including,
to a growing extent, economic considerations stemming
from the trend towards general acceptance of a 200-nau-
tical mile exclusive maritime economic zone (Guatemala-
Belize, Nicaragua-Colombia, Costa Rica-Nicaragua, El
Salvador-Honduras, Nicaragua-Honduras, Venezuela-Trini-

dad and Tobago, Venezuela-South Antilles, Venezuela-Colombia) and migration and refugee conflicts due to different levels of economic and political development and stabilization, which lead to labor migration and refugee problems motivated by political, economic or humanitarian reasons (Mexico-USA, Guatemala-Mexico, Haiti-USA, Cuba-USA, Haiti-Dominican Republic, El Salvador-Honduras, Honduras-Nicaragua, Nicaragua-Costa Rica, Colombia-Venezuela, Guatemala-Belize).

An analysis of the types of conflict involved discloses their wide-ranging nature and complexity, partly because of the considerable shift within conflict type and the increasing overlap of conflict causes. Thus a given conflict may have components of several elements of this typology, and the mix may shift for each one of the individual participants over time. In many cases, a nation's publicly-stated objectives in a conflict also may be quite different from its real ones, even if propaganda and political argumentation try to claim the opposite (thus the example of the boundary disputes between El Salvador and Honduras, the conflict situation between Honduras and Nicaragua, Guatemala-Belize, etc.). It is often and naturally quite possible for a government to use a conflict situation as a pretext for starting a conflict as a tactical measure when the primary issues lie elsewhere.

During the past two decades, the predominant forms of conflict in the region have been border and territorial, while in the present situation the dominant scenarios lie in ideological, resource and influence forms of conflicts. Ideological confrontation (system conflicts) between widely differing political value systems are the type of conflict which are particularly evident in Central America and the Caribbean. It seems that the forms of conflict more prone to peaceful settlement and conflict resolution are border and territorial, while the least amenable to settlement are ideological influence, resources and migration (to the extent that the resources and migration involved are considered substantial). Thus, Central American and Caribbean conflicts in the short and mid-term will be more severe and long-lasting, and less susceptible to traditional methods of mediation and conciliation.[22]

However, one can question this assumption (most often accepted by political scientists dealing with conflicts in Latin America). In effect, the main dividing-line in the conflict situation in Central America and the Caribbean is not between ideology/resources and borders/territories, but between, on the one hand, issues and goals that can be identified because they deal with a quantity such as land-borders, territories and resources, and, on the other hand, issues and goals which deal with a quality, like freedom, human rights or general ideology (i.e. changes of status quo in a

particular country). While this slightly changes the
classification of conflicts, the effects on a scenario
could be great. Assuming that the quantity-based conflicts are more easily subject to control measures than
the quality-based ones, in the future, quality-based
conflicts, i.e. the ideologically influenced conflicts,
will probably increase and be less susceptible to the
conflict-dampening processes used in the past (in border
and territorial claims).

Peace efforts

Another aspect is the active participation of Central American and Caribbean states in attempts to manage
international conflicts within their own regions. Conflict management has traditionally been characterized by
massive foreign influence, particularly that of the
United States, but national approaches by both states
and non-state actors have been gaining greater prominence. Prominent national approaches have been mostly
confined to larger regional powers (e.g. Cuba, Venezuela and Mexico), while smaller states in the region have
in the past generally pursued passive foreign policies.
Nevertheless, recent unrest in Central America and the
Caribbean has tended to involve smaller states more directly in conflict, which has led them to become more
concerned with conflict management. It was generally
acknowledged that minor states were not usually expected
to pursue an independent foreign policy, but simply to
accommodate on the best terms available the regional
designs of their most powerful neighbors. However, in
addition to Cuba, Mexico, Venezuela and USA, Panama,
Costa Rica, Nicaragua, Honduras and Guyana have begun to
assume roles in forming regional policy towards the internationalization of peace.
A series of proposals has been promoted by these
minor republics aimed at relaxing tension and increasing
stability and development in Central America and the
Caribbean area. They have requested a systematic dialogue between the interested parties and a genuine
readiness to grant mutual concessions without abandoning
essential principles and legitimate interests. These
proposals and initiatives range from appeals to Cuba and
the United States to improve their relations, to schemes
favoring a negotiated political solution to the Salvadorean conflict. Other resolutions deal with the most
acute conflict, that between the United States and Nicaragua and Nicaragua and its neighbors, by demanding
that the government of the United States rule out any
threat or use of force against Nicaragua.
The feasibility and desirability of the creation of
a system of mutual non-aggression pacts between Nicaragua and the United States, on the one hand, and between
Nicaragua and its neighbors, on the other, has also
been considered.

Panama. Facing the situation in Central America at the end of the Carter Administration and following the election of Reagan, Panama has attempted to resolve the armed conflict in El Salvador by negotiations. The US Bowdler Plan was originated and backed by Panama, when representatives of the US State Department and the Frente Democrático Revolutionario (FDR) of El Salvador held talks on peace initiatives in Tegucigalpa in January 1981. The plan contained five main points: (a) an immediate ceasefire; (b) reorganization of the Salvadorean National Guard and a shake-up in the security forces; (c) reorganization of the Salvadorean government, to bring in FDR representatives; (d) elections to be held at a later date; and (e) a program of economic reforms, with US help. The FDR later rejected the ceasefire proposal as a precondition for further negotiations, and elections were held in April 1982 without the participation of the opposition to the El Salvador government.[23]

Panama has not ceased in its efforts to pursue a politically negotiated agreement for El Salvador. Indeed, in July 1982, Panama managed to bring the Salvadorean armed forces, the opposition and a personal representative of Fidel Castro to the same table, for an informal meeting where they sought to work out the basis for a negotiated political settlement of the El Salvador war. The General Secretary of the Democratic Revolutionary Front stated at the end of August 1982 that they would be prepared to work for a political settlement if access to the press and other freedoms were guaranteed. Moreover, he said that the opposition leaders were not asking for positions in the government nor making their political demands preconditions for a negotiated settlement of the war. However, the government of El Salvador has shown little willingness to meet these requirements, which would include actions to create a political forum for the opposition, lifting the state of siege that has been in effect in El Salvador for more than two years, general amnesty for political prisoners, and the repeal of laws restricting labor union activity.

In April 1982, the UN Security Council considered a complaint by Nicaragua against the government of the United States, where the Nicaraguan representative referred to an imminent invasion of his country and warned of the danger that this constituted for peace in the region and in the world.[24] In light of this, Panama presented a draft resolution to the Security Council cosponsored by Guyana[25] regarding the deterioration of the situation in Central America and the Caribbean. Panama's proposal recalled resolution 2131 (XX) on the inadmissibility of intervention in domestic affairs of the UN member states and the protection of their independence and sovereignty, and resolution 2160 (XXI) on strict observance of the prohibition of the threat or use of force in international relations. The Panama resolution enjoins, by means of various specific measures, respect for the territorial borders between the countries and their respective sovereignties, and avoidance in any way of the destabilization of the region or tne internal system of any of its components. Permission should not be given for the use of territory for launching destabilizing actions against other countries, for arms trafficking nor the training or transit of combatants. The draft resolution appeals to all member states to refrain from direct, indirect, overt or covert use of force against any country of Central America and the Caribbean, and to the parties concerned to have recourse to dialogue and negotiation which would lead to the search for a peaceful solution to the problem of Central America and the Caribbean. The Panama resolution co-sponsored by Guyana was not adopted because of the negative vote of the United States, a permanent member of the Security Council. Nicaragua called the veto a serious threat to Central America, implicitly confirming its apprehension about US intentions regarding military aggression.

Another Panamanian proposal has been an attempt to synthesize into the basis for a negotiated consensus the declared policy aims of the principal regional powers: the United States, Mexico, Cuba, Venezuela, and the Central American countries directly involved.

Panama also seeks to secure a system of non-aggression pacts between the Nicaraguan government and the United States, and between Nicaragua and its neighbors in the US-backed Central American Democratic Community (Guatemala, Honduras, El Salvador and Costa Rica), and to open a process of détente between the United States and Cuba.

Mexico. Panama's proposal differs little from proposals put forward by Mexico's President. In a speech in Managua on February 21, 1982, the Mexican President identified three areas of tension in the region: (a) the United States' relations with Cuba, (b) the United States' relations with Nicaragua, and (c) the United States' attitude towards the Salvadorean civil war. He suggested that parallel negotiations should take place, on the theory than interrelated solutions should be found to interrelated problems. The Mexicans believe that if US-Cuban relations could be restored after 23 years of almost total absence of communication, the remaining Central American and Caribbean conflicts could be solved. Thus, Mexico has encouraged meetings between the two countries in order to remove one of the main obstacles in Cuban-American relations--the Cuban military presence in Africa--by getting them to agree to an internationally-guaranteed arrangement regarding

Angola and Namibia. In the case of Nicaragua, the Mexican President presented a three-point strategy: (a) the
USA should renounce any threat or use of force against
Nicaragua, (b) the anti-Sandinista forces training in
Honduras and Florida with tacit or direct US support
should be disbanded, and the government of Nicaragua
should simultaneously renounce the purchase of weapons
and aircraft and reduce the size of its armed forces.
Finally, (c) Nicaragua should conclude a series of non-
aggression pacts with its immediate neighbcrs and the
USA.   The proposals made by Mexico's President were
well received internationally, especially by Nicaragua,
Cuba and the opposition in El Salvador.   Such was not
the case in the United States.   The Mexican proposals
were incorporated into the Declaration of Managua, and
were subsequently approved by the Permanent Conference
of Latin American Political Parties (COPPPAL),[26] which
demanded as its first condition a lessening of tension,
and the starting of dialogue and negotiations based on
strict respect for the principles of non-intervention,
free self-determination, and a peaceful solution to conflicts in the region.   The Mexican aim in the short
term has been achieved, because it has provided some
members of the US Congress and international public
opinion with a new banner under which it could unite to
press the Reagan administration to proceed with caution
in the region.   However, it has not brought about real
negotiations.   Nevertheless, the López Portillo proposal
must be seen as a longer-term policy. It is an attempt
to find peaceful mechanisms for dealing with problems
in conflict areas.   The fact that this area is in an
irreversible process of change where the emergence of
opposition movements is regarded by the USA as part
and parcel of Soviet expansionism leads the Mexicans to
believe that the only way to eliminate the danger of a
globalization of the conflict is to propose a form of
international politics based on dialogue, rapprochement
and negotiations.   Mexico is, in fact, seeking an agreement on certain rules about what is permitted and what
is not.   Since the US government views the events in
Central America and the Caribbean as a Soviet Union in-
trigue through their Cuban proxies, the Mexicans feel
that only by altering this analysis can peace be guaranteed.   The USA would gain in confidence and understanding by talking to the Cubans, thus leading to an
improvement in the overall situation.

   USA.   The United States responded to the López
Portillo peace proposal with the eight-point plan presented to the Nicaraguan government on April 8, 1982,
which calls for the following: (a) an end to Nicaraguan
support for insurgencies in neighboring countries;
(b) a political declaration by the United States whereby it would enforce the Neutrality Act, which makes it a

crime to plan or launch invasions of other countries
from US territory; (c) a joint US-Nicaraguan statement
pledging not to interfere in each other's affairs, nor
in the affairs of others in the region; (d) a limit to
the size of military forces in the region, a ban on the
import of heavy offensive weapons into the region, and
a reduction in the number of foreign military advisers;
(e) an international verification process to monitor
compliance with these provisions, conducted by outside
observers from the Organization of American States
(OAS) or the United Nations; (f) a resumption of US aid
to Nicaragua, including Nicaragua in the Administration's Caribbean Basin development plan (CBI); (g) a
series of confidence-building measures including cultural and other exchanges; and (h) reaffirmation of Nicaragua's prior commitment to a system of political
pluralism, a diversified economy and non-alliance.

Nicaragua. Nicaragua answered the US plan for improving relations on 14 April 1982, expressing a willingness to discuss the US eight-point plan proposal but
insisting on the participation of Mexico as a mediator.
The United States has expressed a preference for bilateral talks, but it has not publicly ruled out some
kind of role for Mexico in setting up the negotiations.
The Nicaraguan counterproposal to the US plan contains
several restatements of points made public at the United Nations' Security Council in March 1982 by the Nicaraguan Head of State, Daniel Ortega, including the following principles: (a) Nicaragua is ready to improve
the climate of relations with the United States through
negotiations; (b) Nicaragua cannot accept that it
or any other country in the region should be considered
the geopolitical preserve of the United States or as a
part of its so-called strategic frontier, a concept
that restricts the exercise of sovereignty and independence of the states in the region; (c) Nicaragua can,
therefore, in no way represent a threat to the security
of the United States; (d) Nicaragua is ready to sub-
cribe to non-aggression pacts with all neighboring
countries of the Central American area in order to ensure peace and the internal stability of the zone; (e)
the USA should put a halt to measures and covert plans
which have been denounced but which have
never been officially denied, such as secret destabilization plans and the organization or financing of paramilitary forces, advised and trained by US military personnel in Honduras and by active and retired military
personnel from Argentina and other South American countries. In addition, the USA should refrain from using
Honduran territory as a base for armed aggression and
terrorist operations against Nicaragua; (f) the presence of US warships in the waters of Central America
and off the coast of Nicaragua should be stopped, as

should the US over-flights by spy-aircraft violating
the air space of Nicaragua; and (g) the United States
must explicitly promise not to attack Nicaragua, and
must renounce any plans for an economic, financial or
commercial boycott.[27]
  The two sets of proposals amalgamate the concerns
of both sides, which are in many respects the same, addressing such issues as the integrity of Nicaragua's
borders, perceived threats of US aggression against Nicaragua, and the militarization of Central America in
general and Nicaragua in particular. There is scepti-
cism about the real intentions of the USA in opening up
talks with Nicaragua (the same could be said about US-
Cuban talks), and both parties question the willingness
of the other to negotiate seriously. Since the two
packages of proposals were put forth, Nicaragua has
pushed the United States to set a date for talks, without receiving a response. The Nicaraguan government
holds that the eight-point US plan was merely a political device aimed at internal public opinion in the USA
and at improving its international image. Moreover,
the Nicaraguan government has indications that the US
administration has moved further, with the reported acceptance by President Reagan of the National Security
Council budget of $19.9 million, to promote destabiliz-
ing and covert actions against Nicaragua that entail
economic sabotage, attacks, training and arms shipments
to anti-Nicaraguan forces, and stepped-up presence of
US warships in surrounding waters and US reconnaissance
airplanes overhead.[28] In a turn-about, the USA demanded
that Nicaragua halt alleged arms deliveries to the Salvadorean opposition and the use of Nicaraguan territory
as a base for subversive operations. As a result of
these allegations, Nicaragua declared a state of emergency for 30 days, extended since March 1982, because
of concern about US "aggression". The nation has been
on a war-footing since then, with constitutional guarantees suspended and full censorship enforced.
  The US administration's failure to deny these alle-
gations--that it is financing, if not coordinating,
military and paramilitary actions against Nicaragua
from Honduran territory and seeking to destabilize the
Nicaraguan government by covert actions--constitutes a
potential violation of several treaties binding the
United States, including articles 2 (paragraphs 3 and 4)
and 33 (paragraph 1) of the Charter of the United
Nations, articles 3 (paragraph g), 14, 18, 19 and 21 of
the amended Charter of the Organization of American
States, and articles 1 and 2 of the Protocol of Amendment to the Inter-American Treaty of Reciprocal Assistance.

  Honduras. Honduras, the second-poorest nation in
Latin America after Haiti, with its first freely-elected
civilian government in 10 years (November 1981), is be-

coming more involved in the conflicts in Central America. After having signed a peace treaty with El Salvador in 1980, which formally ended the 11 years of hostility between them, Honduras has had a close partnership with the El Salvador military institution. The fact that Honduras shares borders with Guatemala, El Salvador and Nicaragua is the main cause of Honduras' growing militarization and provides an almost unmitigated panorama of uncertainty. As the military is strengthened by massive US aid in hardware, the temptation to continue its tradition of meddling in civilian affairs will probably prove irresistible. The civilian government of Honduras, in the wake of armed involvement in the region, and deeply concerned that external forces are threatening the country's stability, has therefore called for a reduction of weapons and troops in Central America to levels strictly necessary for defense, territorial integrity and public order. On March 23, 1982, the Minister of Foreign Affairs of Honduras presented before the Permanent Council of the Organization of American States a detailed proposal for the internationalization of peace in Central America.[29]

The Honduras proposal contains six points, calling for: (a) general disarmament in the region, including not only a halt to the arms race but also a genuine reduction in armaments and in military strength, including agreements on the type of weapons to be limited and prohibited as part of this general disarmament plan; (b) a reduction in foreign military personnel on an objective and reasonable basis, as well as any other elements likely to create suspicion and unease or to distort the identity of the respective nations; and (c) the setting-up of a process of international supervision and monitoring which would cover countries where there are conflicts and sensitive features which may affect peace in the region, such as ports, airports, border areas, and strategic sectors. Honduras is prepared to submit its territory, without reservations, to any type of international supervision or monitoring for the basic purpose of securing and strengthening peace; and favors (d) discussion of, and agreement on, the most appropriate procedures and mechanisms for halting the traffic of arms in the region; (e) absolute respect for delimited and demarcated borders and the jurisdictional frontier-lines of states in the region; and (f) the establishing of a permanent, multilateral dialogue between countries in the region, as well as at the internal level, in order to strengthen democratic and pluralistic systems.

In connection with this peace initiative, Honduras has started a series of meetings with the Foreign Ministers of Costa Rica, El Salvador and Guatemala, resulting in the newly-created organization called the Central American Democratic Community (mentioned above) and calling for a meeting of army commanders to discuss

the Honduran proposal for regional peace. Honduras has
also initiated talks with Nicaragua concerning border
incidents between these two countries. The conflict
between Honduras and Nicaragua has become potentially
significant, as Honduras is the alleged conduit for
weapon shipments originating in Nicaragua and destined
for insurgent forces in El Salvador. Honduras and Nicaragua have two of the largest and best-equipped armed
forces in the Central American isthmus, and both have
been moving towards closer identification with states
hostile to each other: Honduras with the USA and Nicaragua with Cuba. Honduran armed forces have become involved in fighting the opposition movement in El Salvador, and have conducted joint military manoeuvres with
the Salvadorean armed forces and with the USA.[30] These
actions have raised tensions with Nicaragua. The Sandinist government has accused the Honduran armed forces
of involvement in armed clashes along the border between the two Central American countries as well as of
supporting and encouraging the former Somozan guardsmen
settled in Honduras. The proposed peace initiative has
been jeopardized by Honduras allowing its territory to
be used for US military bases and facilities, receiving
an increasing number of US military advisers, and becoming the second largest receiver of US military aid
in the Western Hemisphere after El Salvador (see figure
3.2). Unless Honduras unilaterally starts to reduce its
weaponry, following Costa Rica's post-war example, to
dismantle foreign military bases, and to uphold the
strict neutrality of its territory, the Honduran good-
will and perhaps sincere desire to reduce tension in
Central America would be nothing more than a repetition
of the Latin American diplomatic rhetorical extravaganza, which so far has failed to achieve adequate mechanisms for peaceful settlements of disputes.

  Costa Rica. In 1948 Costa Rica disolved its armed
forces, freeing the country from the threat of coups.
Since then, the country has had the resilient characteristics of an established democracy and an equitable
distribution of economic benefits among the population.
However, in the past years, the economy of Costa Rica
has suffered from continuous deterioration, which has
been translated into falling economic growth rates, accompanied by a burgeoning oil-import bill and an ever-
growing public sector, combined with a sharp rise in inflation and severe balance-of-payment problems. Thus
the country is now being tested in its ability to deal
forcefully with economic and social problems. The
scope of the nation's problems makes it clear that Costa Rica's democracy is at a crossroads.
  Costa Rica is no longer immune to the problems of
Central America, but unlike its northern neighbors,
there are no death squads, political "missing" persons

or human rights abuses, and the police forces are under
the direct control of the Supreme Court. However, the
economic crisis and the unprecedented increase of political protest in the country could severely shake its
organizations and long tradition of stable democracy
and could strongly challenge Costa Rica's status in the
near future, with the ever-present risk that the internal unrest could be manipulated by outside forces.
Should Costa Rica be drawn into the civil strife affecting its neighbors, an increase in domestic political
violence and a deterioration in the human rights situations will be inevitable. Therefore, Costa Rica is
concerned with the Central American conflicts, fearing
the risk of their spilling over into a larger-scale
conflict that would affect the entire region and therefore dragging the country into the whirlwind of polarization and violence.

Costa Rica has endorsed the Honduras proposal to
the Nicaraguan government, seeking a verifiable agreement on ending border incursion and freezing the import
of major weapons. Costa Rica has also made efforts to
mediate in the internal conflict of El Salvador by conducting discussions with both parties to the conflict,
in order to reach a political solution through dialogue
without any prior conditions between the Salvadorean
opposition and the government. A settlement in El Salvador, as Costa Rica foresees, would remove a central
irritant factor in US-Nicaraguan relations, while
opening a dialogue with Nicaragua would facilitate a
peaceful solution in El Salvador, by increasing the
pressure on the opposition and the ruling establishment
in El Salvador to negotiate a political solution.

In 1982, Costa Rica and Nicaragua agreed to establish a border commission, in order to solve the problem
of anti-Sandinist forces operating against Nicaragua
from Costa Rica. It has been suggested that both countries should jointly patrol the northern border, in order to combat illegal flows of weapons and insurgent
forces. Moreover, in August 1982, Costa Rica, Belize,
Nicaragua, Dominican Republic and Venezuela, signed a
joint declaration in Santo Domingo pledging their commitment to ideological pluralism, self-determination,
and avoidance of force as a means of resolving international conflicts.[31]

CONCLUDING REMARKS

The spectra of conflicts and actors is widening in
Central America and the Caribbean and can be contained
only with difficulty in the face of revitalized militarization.

The prospects for evolving a more stable order in
the Western Hemisphere do not appear particularly promising in the aftermath of political-military upheaval

in the Caribbean Basin. However, the idea of controlling conflicts and establishing a code of conduct of behavior for nations in their inter-state relations have a strong appeal in a world troubled by tension, insecurity and the threat of annihilation. The
Central American and the Caribbean dilemma has been
aggravated by the increasing lack of correspondence between economic development, social mobilization, and political participation. Economic development has occurred in these regions without any extension of political participation. Meanwhile, social mobilization has
steadily continued as a result of social-economic
changes, so that, without an answer to demands for
popular participation, the likelihood of a political
crisis remains only a matter of time.
     The US foreign policy in dealing with Central Amer-
ica and the Caribbean nations has presented a historic
pendulum pattern from neglect and inaction to that of
direct intervention. Both courses of policy have been
counterproductive and have failed, basically because of
a faulty analysis of the realities of the area, i.e.
high levels of poverty and social misery, corrupt power
structures, enormous class differences, high rates of
illiteracy, terror, torture and other forms of repression.
     There can be no solutions imposed on Central Amer-
ica and the Caribbean from the outside. The only viable
solutions to the problems of the region are those which
emerge from within the area itself and which correspond
to the interests and needs of the inhabitants as determined by them. Those solutions must respect the people's right of self-determination and the political independence, sovereignty and territorial integrity of
the states of the region. Thus, the problems of Central America are not susceptible to military solutions,
especially where such solutions are promoted by outside
interests. The providing of military material, the encouragement of violent confrontation, and the rhetoric of
intervention and threats of destabilization do nothing
but lead to great tension and instability in the region
and the widening of the arena of conflict.
     Steps that could favor a relaxation of tension
and promote stability and development in Central America
and the Caribbean must include: (a) a substantial improvement in relations between Cuba and the United
States; (b) the creation of a system of mutual non-aggression pacts between Nicaragua and the United States,
as well as between Nicaragua and its neighbours; (c) a
negotiated political solution to the Salvadorean conflict between all the parties to the conflict; (d) the
abolition of arms-trafficking; (e) a ban on the impor-
tation of heavy weapons and limitation on all armaments
and armed forces to those required for defense; (f) the
control of frontiers under reciprocal and verifiable

conditions, including international supervision; (g) a
withdrawal, under effective conditions of reciprocity,
of foreign troops and military and security advisers;
and (h) the promotion and adoption of measures of confidence-building aimed at reducing inter-state tensions
and creating the prerequisites for better understanding
between the peoples and countries of the region.

NOTES

1. John C. Dreier, 'The Western Hemisphere', in The role of
alliances and other interstate alignments in a disarming and disarmed world (Washington Center of Foreign Policy Research, School
of Advanced International Studies, Johns Hopkins University, Washington, D.C., July 1965), No. 2, p. 37.

2. War powers legislation, 1973. Hearing before the Committee
on Foreign Relations, United States Senate, Ninety-third Congress,
First Session, April 11 and 12, 1973 (US Government Printing Office, Washington, D.C., 1973), pp. 126-156. Also Ramiro Guerra,
La Expansión Territorial de los Estados Unidos (Ediciones de Ciencias Sociales, La Habana, 1975, 4a. edición).

3. Between 1945 and 1980, only two of the Central American
republics--Mexico and Costa Rica--escaped military intervention in
politics.

4. The literature on this topic is extensive. See: Barbara
Anne Wilson, Typology of Internal Conflict: An Essay (Center for
Research in Social Systems, The American University, Washington,
D.C., May 1968); Lincoln P. Bloomfield, Amelia C. Leiss et al, The
Control of Local Conflict: A Design Study on Arms Control and Lim-
ited War in the Developing Areas, prepared for the US Arms Control
and Disarmament Agency (Washington, D.C., US Government Printing
Office, 1967), Vol. I; World Armaments and Disarmament, SIPRI Year-
book 1968/69 (Almqvist & Wiksell, Stockholm, 1969), p. 363; Jozef
Goldblat & Victor Millán, 'Militarization and Arms Control in Latin
America', in World Armaments and Disarmament, SIPRI Yearbook 1982
(Taylor & Francis Ltd., London, 1982); R.P. Richardson, Jr. & S.
Waldron, An Analysis of Recent Conflicts (Center for Naval Analysis,
Department of the Navy, Washington, D.C.), Report CRC144,1966; Volker
Matthies, Der Greenzkonflikt Somalia mit Äthiopien und Kenia: Ana-
lyse eines Zwischenstaatlichen Konflikts in der Dritten Welt (Ham-
burg, 1978), p. 16; Arturo A. Fernández, 'Tipología y Análisis de
los Conflictos Internacionales Actuales', Estudios Sociales Centro-
americanos (San José, Costa Rica, Septiembre-Diciembre 1981), No.
30, Año X, pp. 85-124; Wolf Grabendorff, 'Tipología y Potencial de
los Conflictos en América Latina', Nueva Sociedad, No. 59, Marzo-
Abril 1982, pp. 39-46.

5. Wolf Grabendorff & Helga Strasser, Interstate Conflict Behavior and Regional Potential for Conflict in Latin America (Stif-
tung Wissenschaft und Politik, Research Institute for International
Affairs, Ebenhausen, West Germany, September 1980), pp. 26-27; Nor-
bert Lechner, La Crisis del Estado en América Latina (El Cid, Edi-

tor, Caracas, 1977); Guillermo Molina Chocano, 'Crisis Capitalista, Inflación y Papel Económico del Estado', Estudios Sociales Centro-americanos (San José, Costa Rica, Enero/Abril 1981), No. 28, Año X, pp. 9-41; 'Estados Unidos: Perspectivas Latinoamericanas', Cuadernos Semestrales (Mexico, D.F.), Nos. 5 and 6, 1st and 2nd semesters 1978; and Antonio Cavalla y Luis Maira, 'Proposiciones Metodológicas para el Estudio de la Política Norteamericana hacia América Latina', Estudios Sociales Centroamericanos (San José, Costa Rica, Septiembre-Diciembre 1980), No. 27, Año IX.

6. For evaluation of US policy toward Central America, see Richard E. Feinberg, 'Central America: No Easy Answer', Foreign Affairs, Summer 1981, Vol. 59, No. 5, pp. 1121-1146; Paul E. Sigmund, 'Latin America: Change or Continuity?', Foreign Affairs: America and the World 1981, Vol. 60, No. 3, pp. 629-657; 'Struggle in Central America', Foreign Policy, Summer 1981, No. 43, pp. 70-103; William M. Leogrande and Carla Anne Robbins, 'Oligarchs and Officers: The Crisis in El Salvador', Foreign Affairs, Summer 1980, pp. 1084-1103; NACLA Report on the Americas, Vol. XIV, No. 1, Jan-Feb 1980, Vol. XIV, No. 2, Mar-Apr 1980, and Vol. XVI, No. 2, Mar-Apr 1982; and William M. Leogrande, 'A Splendid Little War: Drawing the Line in El Salvador', International Security, Summer 1981, pp. 27-52.

7. César Sepúlveda, 'Transformación y Desarrollo del Derecho Internacional en México y en la América Latina (1900-1975)', Anuario Jurídico, 5 (1978), pp. 117ff; César Sepúlveda, 'Vigencia actual de los principios de la política exterior del Estado Mexicano', Relaciones Internacionales, Vol. VII, Julio-Diciembre 1979, No. 26-27 (Mexico), pp. 5-18.

8. J. Goldblat & V. Millán, ibid., pp. 414-422.

9. New York Times, 21 February 1981; International Herald Tribune, 10 February 1981; Financial Times, 5 August 1982.

10. New York Times, 10 March 1982; Newsweek, 24 May 1982; Susan Kaufman Purcell, 'Mexico-US Relations: Big initiatives can cause big problems', Foreign Affairs, Winter 1981/82, Vol. 60, No. 2, pp. 379-392.

11. The Caribbean Basin Policy. Hearings before the Subcommittee on Inter-American Affairs of the Committee on Foreign Affairs, House of Representatives, Ninety-seventh Congress, First Session, July 14, 21 and 28, 1981 (US Government Printing Office, Washington, D.C., 1981), p. 21.

12. Washington Post, 10 June 1982; Latin America Weekly Report, 23 April 1982, p. 12.

13. International Herald Tribune, 5 March 1982.

14. Aerospace Daily, 21 May 1982; Newsweek, 22 March 1981; and International Herald Tribune, 6 August 1982, p. 3.

15. The DoD overall military construction budget requested for the fiscal year 1983 totals $7.8 billion. The House and Senate Armed Services Committee approved the $21 million to improve airfields in Honduras to which US forces would have access in case of

trouble in the Caribbean. Among the specific projects under consideration are the lengthening of the runways and expansion of the aircraft parking ramps to accommodate larger aircraft, and construction of underground fuel storage tanks. The Honduran request was included in an administration request for $45 million for unspecified contingency facilities in other countries, Congressional Quarterly, Weekly Report, Vol. 40, No. 25, 19 June 1982, p. 1485.

16. Gramma, Havana, 24 August 1980, p. 12.

17. Historia de una Usurpación: la Base Naval de Estados Unidos en la Bahía de Guantánamo (Editora Política, La Habana, 1982), pp. 66-67.

18. Donald E. Schulz, 'The strategy of conflict and the politics of counterproductivity', Orbis, Vol. 25, No. 3, Fall 1981, p. 700.

19. 1980s Republican Platform Text. Congressional Quarterly, Weekly Report, 19 July 1980, p. 2054.

20. Latin America Weekly Report, 30 July 1982, pp. 1-2.

21. Grabendorff & Strasser, ibid, p. 14.

22. Jack Child, 'Conflicts in Latin America: present and potential' (American University, Washington, D.C., September 1980); pp. 6-10, and Grabendorff & Strasser, ibid., pp. 23-27.

23. The Bowdler Plan is named after the outgoing Assistant Secretary of State for Inter-American Affairs, William Bowdler, and the proposal was thought to have the backing of President Reagan's transition team. Latin America Weekly Report, 23 January 1981, p. 1.

24. UN Document S/14913.

25. UN Document S/14941.

26. COPPPAL (The Permanent Conference of Latin American Political Parties) was set up in October 1979 in Oaxaca, Mexico, during a meeting of Latin American political parties representing 22 political organizations from 14 nations, convened by Mexico's PRI (Institutional Revolutionary Party). The participating organizations signed the Constitutive Declaration of Oaxaca, a document in which the principles and constitution of COPPPAL were formalized with the purpose of contributing to a greater understanding of the serious problems of the region. Signatories pledged to join in the search for such solutions as will lead to peace and development and expressed their desire to unite actions of international solidarity with democratic processes in favor of social justice and genuine liberty in Latin America. For more details on COPPPAL and its activities, see Comercio Exterior de México (English edition), Vol. 28, No. 5, May 1982, pp. 173-79; United Nations Document S/PV. 2335, pp. 28-31; and Washington Post, 24 February 1982.

27. Mesoamerica, Vol. 1, No. 4, April 1982; Comercio Exterior de México, Vol. 28, No. 4, April 1982; and ALAI-Servicio Informativo, Vol. 6, No. 18, 27 May 1982. Also, UN Document S/PV.2335,

pp. 3-32.

28. UN Document S/14913.

29. UN Document S/14919; New York Times, 24 March 1982, p. 13; Le Monde, 26 March 1982, p. 3; and ALAI-Servicio Informativo, Vol. 6, No. 18, 27 Mayo 1982.

30. Latin America Weekly Report, 30 July 1982; New York Times, 4 July 1982.

31. Latin America Weekly Report, 20 August 1982.

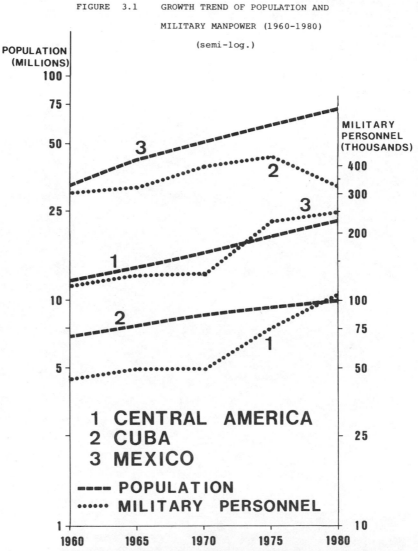

FIGURE 3.1 GROWTH TREND OF POPULATION AND
MILITARY MANPOWER (1960-1980)
(semi-log.)

1 CENTRAL AMERICA
2 CUBA
3 MEXICO

---- POPULATION
•••••• MILITARY PERSONNEL

Source: The Military Balance, The International Institute
for Strategic Studies, London 1960-1981-1982; United Nations
Statistical Yearbooks; Press-cuttings.

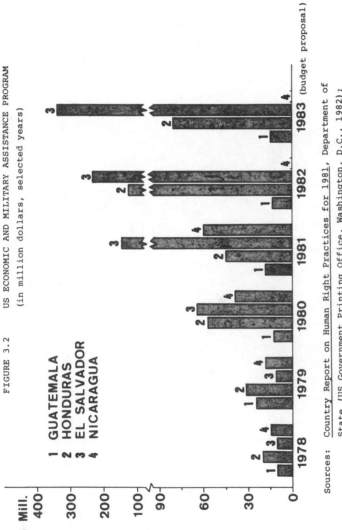

FIGURE 3.2   US ECONOMIC AND MILITARY ASSISTANCE PROGRAM

(in million dollars, selected years)

1 GUATEMALA
2 HONDURAS
3 EL SALVADOR
4 NICARAGUA

Sources: Country Report on Human Right Practices for 1981, Department of
State (US Government Printing Office, Washington, D.C., 1982);
Washington Report on the Hemisphere, vol. 2, N°. 11 & 16,
February 23 and May 4, 1982) COHA, Washington, D.C., 1982)
International Report, August & December 1982 (Center for Inter-
national Policy, Washington, D.C.); Foreign Assistance and Re-
lated Programs Appropriation for 1978, 1979,.1980, 1981, 1982 and
1983 (US Government Printing Office, Washington, D.C.)

4
Controlling Conflict in South America: National Approaches

Augusto Varas

INTRODUCTION

The 1981 armed conflict between Ecuador and Peru, as well as the 1982 Anglo-Argentine confrontation over the Malvinas, have dramatized the ineffectiveness of the mechanisms for resolution of tensions and conflicts among South American countries. Because of the presence of significant regional military powers on this continent, there has been renewed concern about the causes of this type of confrontation.

In order to achieve a stable system of conflict resolution in South America, it is necessary to reduce American interventionism in the region, to assure mobilization of internal forces for democracy in all South American countries, and to promote measures for greater participation of the citizenry in the control of the armed forces and decision-making in the resolution of conflicts.

DISARMAMENT AND ARMS CONTROL PROPOSALS AND AGREEMENTS

Before World War II, Latin American governments set forth different arms limitation proposals and agreements. For example, in 1902 Argentina, Brazil and Chile signed a disarmament agreement, the so-called "Pactos de Mayo", which compelled re-sale of some ships previously ordered by Argentina to Japan and by Chile to the UK. In 1923, Latin American Ministries of Foreign Affairs agreed on a declaration to prevent armed conflict between Latin American nations. A similar declaration was signed by all Latin American countries in 1933, and in 1936 the Conference on Peace Consolidation adopted a recommendation which urged the limitation of the arms race in the region. After World War II, through the Inter-American Reciprocal Assistance Treaty (1947) and the Bogota Pact (1948), Latin American governments pledged not to use force in inter-american relations, whenever a peaceful solution to conflict was available, and set up a continental assistance plan to aid indi-

vidual countries in the case of an armed attack. More
recently, Latin American governments[1] have participated
in different global and regional arms limitation proposals and agreements, both nuclear and conventional
(see Table 4.1).

The relatively limited participation of Latin American countries in arms limitation proposals contrasts
starkly with the damaging effects of the arms race in
the region. According to the available data, only three
Latin American countries can be considered active parties in the field of arms limitation proposals. Brazil
and Mexico have participated in the presentation of most
of the main proposals at the United Nations, and Argentina has supported some of them. The other Latin American countries have remained rather distant from disarmament and arms control initiatives and have been, at
the most, passive elements. Even the active countries
have a record of contradictory policies toward disarmament and arms limitation proposals. Such is the case
with Argentina, Brazil, Colombia, Peru and Venezuela,
which have supported general and complete disarmament,
although they are the main forces within the regional
arms race. Most Latin American governments act similarly when they are faced with immediate and realistic
disarmament proposals as, for example, in the case of
the ten per cent military budget cut proposal, which
was endorsed solely by the region's main military power,
Brazil. A year later, at the 1974 Ayacucho Meeting,
representatives of various South American countries
agreed on a general declaration about disarmament, but
they have not subsequently implemented its arms limitation recommendations. Finally, Mexico has followed a
consistent disarmament policy in making proposals of
her own, supporting almost all the initiatives of this
kind in the United Nations and playing an active role
in the implementation of disarmament policies. Despite
this positive record, Mexico has not supported the ten
per cent military budget cut nor arms transfer limitation proposals.

The governmental record of ratification of major
arms limitation agreements varies from country to country (see Table 4.2), although general regional practice
is not encouraging. For example, Argentina's active
participation in disarmament and arms limitation proposals is in strong contradiction with its policy toward actual agreements. Argentina has ratified only
two of seven major postwar agreements: the Antarctic
Treaty, due to its need to freeze the conflict with
Chile and Brazil over this area, and the Outer Space
Treaty. Similarly, Brazil, a very active party in making disarmament proposals, has not ratified any nuclear
disarmament agreement. Only Mexico has maintained a
consistent policy throughout the last decades. Three
small Latin American countries--Panama, Nicaragua, and

the Dominican Republic--have signed and ratified the
Sea Bed Treaty. Disagreements about resulting problems
of maritime jurisdiction have undermined support for
this treaty. Argentina, Brazil and Chile have consistently refused to ratify fully nuclear disarmament
agreements. This is due to their desire to keep the
nuclear weaponry option open. Chile has, in fact, developed a nuclear research and development program in
recent years.

Similarly, recent nuclear policies in Peru may be
explained in the light of nuclear developments in Argentina, Brazil and Chile. Peru has ratified the main
regional denuclearization agreement, but, impelled by
nuclear development in the other Southern Cone countries, it has accepted Argentine technological and
scientific support to develop a nuclear research and
development program of its own. Concern with maintaining a nuclear balance in the area threatens to set off
a small-scale nuclear race.

A related pattern characterized the Meeting of Experts after the Ayacucho Summit. In the 1974 Declaration of Ayacucho, Bolivia, Venezuela, Panama, Argentina,
Colombia, Chile and Ecuador agreed to limit armaments
and promote peace and order. There were two subsequent
meetings of experts to carry out these purposes, the
first, in Lima, Peru in February 1975, and the second,
in Santiago, Chile in September of that same year. At
the second meeting, a task force was appointed to develop a proposal for disarmament and arms limitation in
the Andean area. A list of forbidden weapons was established, but it has been impossible to reach an agreement so far.[2]

Even though the 1974 Declaration of Ayacucho did
not have any real effects, its fundamental principles
were reiterated in the joint communique of the foreign
relations ministers of the same countries in 1978. In
it the signatory countries expressed their willingness
to explore jointly with other countries in the area the
conventional arms in the region. A similar initiative
occurred in August 1978, when representatives of twenty
Latin American and Caribbean countries agreed upon a
declaration relating to conventional disarmament in general and called upon the rest of the countries in the
region to collaborate in this direction. This meeting
also considered the possibility of more specific consultations regarding the limitation of arms considered excessively harmful or having indiscriminate effects.
Likewise, the possibilities of recommending measures
tending to restrict the commerce of such armaments to the
region were posed. Finally, in September 1980, Colombia, Costa Rica, Ecuador, Panama and Venezuela agreed
upon a Charter of Conduct, which called for the peaceful
resolution of controversies and reiterated the princi-

ples of the Declaration of Ayacucho. In that same year,
some measures of mutual confidence were put into practice, especially joint naval manoeuvres, as well as
land and air manoeuvres among diverse armies and air
forces of bordering countries. This was complemented
by the invitation of foreign dignataries to witness the
military manoeuvres of those countries.

In sum, government policies reflect a widening gap
between disarmament and arms limitation proposals and
agreements, both global or regional, and actual disarmament measures. The different government policies on
this matter are mostly defined by the military, in relation to national strategies and specific inter-american political contingencies. Because of these priorities in national policies, the relative failure to implement disarmament and arms limitation measures contrasts with the "success" of the regional arms race,
which has pushed military expenditures to more than six
billions dollars in 1981.

Control of conflicts and foreign policy

The group of initiatives intended to control agreements in South America has had meager results. A general explanation valid for every one of the South American countries refers to the autonomy which the respective armed forces have acquired through the definition
of defense policy, as well as the acquisition of adequate means and mechanisms to carry it out. This relative autonomy of the armed institutions, in essence,
arises from a profound crisis of the State in each
country of the area, which has led the armed forces to
determine the overall direction of national policy.
Because of this, there is a tendency to scorn diplomatic mechanisms and international political alliances,
while the potential of military force to achieve adequate external security is overestimated. Once the
theoretical underpinnings of the policy become infused
with this view, the context of security in each South
American country begins to depend more and more strictly on the way that its own armed forces perceive and
define security.

A recurring characteristic of the military way of
defining the security context is the linking of foreign
policy to the internal socio-political situation in each
country. To that extent, South American foreign policy
is linked indissolubly to the strategy of internal submission of the civil to the military, with foreign policy initiatives as dependent variables of such an internal strategy. Thus, in the field of military relations, the perception that the armed forces of a South
American country have of the others is strongly determined by the nature and ideological orientation of the
respective governments. Of greatest significance is

the increased autonomy of the armed institutions which
has led to a situation in which these very institutions
are the ones to define the type of relationship possible among regional armed forces. International political-military initiatives will then be strongly affected
by the way in which domestic military elements are constituted historically in each particular case. In a
context of generalized military autonomy, each military
organization defines its own security context starting
from indigenous factors and from the perception of how
they are linked to the intra-regional international situation.

Colombia is one of the Latin American countries
that confronts the greatest difficulties in the internal
political arena because of the active presence of some
important national guerrilla groups. The extent of
armed action of M-19 and the FARC (Revolutionary Armed
Forces of Colombia), the armed branch of the Colombian
Communist Party, is unique on the continent. Unlike
restricted guerrilla outbreaks in Venezuela, the Colombian guerrilla movement is a destabilizing force for
local politics. The armed forces have undertaken an
expensive program of military purchases to confront
this internal threat, including the purchase of armored
vehicles, automatic rifles, submachine guns, and TOW
launchers.

Along with this renewal of materiel for purposes
of internal order, the Colombian Navy has incorporated
ships and submarines purchased from Germany. This
strengthening of naval power is oriented particularly
toward the defense of Colombian claims in litigation
with Nicaragua in the Caribbean. Although Colombia politically supported the Sandinist revolution, the Nicaraguan claim over the San Andres Islands placed a note
of tension in the relations between both countries.
Likewise, the expansion of the Central American conflict,
as well as the eventual crisis that could arise in the
Canal Zone, led Colombia to define its internal and external security context as a unit. That is, Colombian
security planners associated the internal guerrilla
threat with the ideological-political support given to
the guerrillas by Nicaragua, which also wished to reopen talks on the territorial dispute.

Because of these interlocking internal and external
conflicts, Colombia has looked to the USA for support
and has itself supported the so-called Central American
Democratic Community, while it launches an intense offensive against the M-19 guerrilla movement. In this
way, the management of internal and external conflicts
of Colombia at this time tends to put more emphasis on
military force than negotiation and diplomacy, in contrast to Venezuela, which is moving toward a model more
propitious to the negotiation of international issues.

A similar pattern is witnessed in Ecuador, where
the process of military autonomy has reached levels

greater than those historically observed. After a long
period of military governments of diverse types, the
Ecuadorian armed forces, taking advantage of the oil
bonanza, initiated a process of growing arms purchases
and increases in military spending. At the same time,
the democratization that was initiated in Ecuador did
not undermine the autonomy of the armed institutions,
thereby leaving them free to rely on their own definitions of the goals and appropriate means for national
defense. For these reasons, in spite of a recently
elected democratic government, the Ecuadorian armed
forces carried out a new military campaign in 1981
against Peru, repeating the war which they lost in 1942
over the Amazon area. Whoever the initiator of the conflict may have been, recently installed democratic governments in both Ecuador and Peru were not able to prevent war.

The Peruvian response to the Ecuadorian military
presence on its northern border was the massive deployment of armament and national mobilization. Given the
disproportion in size of military forces between the
countries, the potential Ecuadorian threat to Peruvian territory was insubstantial. Of particular significance is the fact that in both countries the initial
confrontation and massive response were fundamentally
military affairs directed by the high institutional com-
mands. In both cases, the recently elected civilian
governments only performed a support function for mobilization and could not act through diplomatic channels
nor multilateral mechanisms such as the Organization of
American States or the Andean Pact. This same situation
was repeated in 1982 during the Malvinas conflict, when
the Peruvian government tried to encourage political and
diplomatic negotiations. Again, the armed forces emphasized military means and gave military aid to Argentina. Here the contradiction between the perceptions
of regional reality of a civilian government and the
armed forces was shown in all its magnitude.

Furthermore, the contradictions between the civilian government and the armed forces involved the kind
of diplomacy that had been practiced during the two
former military governments. Under Velasco Alvarado
and Morales Bermúdez, the Peruvian foreign ministry
played a fundamental role in the direction of foreign
policy and reflected the will of the military. But the
election of President Belaúnde resulted in a gap between the foreign ministry and the Presidency, and, to
that extent, a gap between the latter and the armed
forces. For such reasons, Belaúnde's intention of being
an active President promoting international negotiation
did not receive the support of the foreign ministry and
was blocked by the complete autonomy of the armed forces.

Both Ecuador and Peru therefore show that the autonomy of military institutions is unimpeded by the ex-

istence of a civilian democratic government that has
not achieved complete control of internal politics. In
the context of weak government direction, the armed
forces can take the initiative independently of presidential orders.

The most noteworthy case of military autonomy is
that of the Argentine armed forces in relation to the
1982 Malvinas conflict. When the military government
of Galtieri became increasingly isolated from a social
and political base of support, historical tendencies
toward a "heterodox autonomy"[3] became associated with a
counterfeit nationalism with strong chauvinist connota-
tions. The weak military government hoped that reliance on old nationalist theses offered a possibility of
recuperating its position in the internal order.

Related lessons may be derived from the way in
which Chile and Peru have attempted to resolve the problems regarding the outlet to the sea requested by Bolivia. In spite of the existence of military governments in Chile and Peru in 1977, discussions on a sea
outlet for Bolivia were initiated, a subject which had
not been touched upon in Chile since the signing of the
Lima Treaty in 1929. The rhetoric of both military
governments, which appeared to be willing to resolve
the problem of Bolivia's land-locked position, nonetheless hid a political calculation that contained self-
serving geopolitical and military considerations. Thus,
the Chilean proposal of a passage for Bolivia to the
sea, although it did not contradict the terms of the
Treaty of 1929, was made without conducting previous
diplomatic consultations with Peru, for which reason
the latter reacted with deep reservations. On its side,
Peru reacted by formulating a counterproposal that was
unacceptable to Chile, since the internationalization
of the sea outlet for Bolivia only delayed the question
and did not resolve the problem thoroughly. In this
way, both military governments ostensibly catered to
Bolivia in the hope of neutralizing the other. As a
result, Bolivia found the solution once again delayed,
with an eventual Chilean-Peruvian conflict still pend-
ing.

A potential solution to the Bolivian land-locked
situation was therefore squandered due to consider-
tions peculiar to the governing armed forces, which subordinated viable political goals to purely tactical military considerations. A similar pattern characterized
Argentine behavior in relation to the border conflict
involving the Beagle Channel. There, Argentina's rejection of the 1977 British arbitration ruling positioned it to attempt to impose its view through the
force of arms. Subsequently, Papal mediation was likewise questioned by the Argentine military government,
which tried to take advantage of a favorable conjunction
of military forces and diplomatic circumstances in order

to isolate Chile and force it to cede its juridical positions.

In sum, the intrusion of military considerations
in the affairs of Latin American countries tends to limit and distort possible solutions to conflicts that are
initiated through diplomatic routes or negotiation.
These solutions tend to be replaced by those relying on
force or are otherwise obstructed by considerations of
a military nature

In contrast to the type of cases previosly analyzed, some recent evidence indicates that internal political factors can bring about revision of retrograde
foreign policy positions and encourage mechanisms of
negotiation over confrontations entailing the use of
force. For example, Venezuela has had an historical
posture favorable to disarmament initiatives and armament control, and has enhanced its international standing in recent years because of oil and imaginative diplomacy.

Nevertheless, some recent Venezuelan developments
do not augur well for moderation. There have been increases in military spending and rising arms imports.
This military modernization effort has put special emphasis on a supposed Cuban threat in Central America
and the Caribbean by favoring armed opposition to revolutionary activity in the area in association with
the United States. This policy was reinforced by the
presence of the Christian Democrat Duarte in El Salvador, who retained power until 1982 and who received
full support of the counterpart governing party, COPEI,
of Venezuela. Together with Venezuelan demands for the
Essequibo region of Guyana, an image of Venezuela more
concerned with military solutions than political or
diplomatic negotiations is projected. However, in the recent past, two important factors show how the relationship between the internal situation and foreign policy
can produce different results according to how they are
combined. A first element is the electoral defeat of
Duarte in El Salvador and the domestic political erosion
that this meant for the Venezuelan governing party, CO-
PEI, which faces a presidential election in 1983. Since
the political formula attempted by Herrera Campins
failed and Duarte was replaced by an ultra-right winger,
internal support of the COPEI foreign policy suffered
and threatened to weaken electoral support for 1983.
In the second place, together with the failure of the
Central American policy of Venezuela, the hard-line reaction of the government of Guyana in response to Venezuelan demands for the Essequibo led the Christian
Democrat government to seek Venezuelan incorporation
into the Non-Aligned Movement. The effect of this application was the neutralization of the Non-Aligned
Movement as an international support force for Guyana.
These recent events have coincided with a Venezuelan

economic-financial crisis, which is likely to make management of future internal discontent increasingly difficult.
   As a consequence, even though Venezuela chose to
build up its military power in a former period, given
the confluence of current internal and external factors,
its rulers have now opted for a moderate policy of diplomatic initiative, rather than emphasizing the use of
force. A more moderate policy includes greater reluctance to associate with US efforts to isolate Nicaragua
in Central America, a less aggressive attitude toward
Cuba, and a more stable political relationship with Mexico for cooperation in the area.
   However, the reaction of the Venezuelan armed
forces regarding this change of policy is yet to be
known. Other imponderables include the extent to which
the armed forces have become oriented toward reliance
on the use of force, and the degree to which they will
insist that their modernization program be carried
through, even though the Venezuelan budget already suffers from a deficit. Such a course of action, in tandem
with increasing military autonomy, would reverse the
present policy tilt toward moderation. The recent initiative of Guyana to purchase armaments from Brazil similarly does not favor entrenchment of negotiating tendencies in Venezuela over the militarist options.
   Finally, the Brazilian case illustrates a pragmatic, international policy that favors negotiation over
the imposition of force. This is most notable, since
Brazil is the top military power in South America.
Faced with various disputes and pressured by armed
forces that perform a political function of primary importance, Brazil has still been able to act in the region in a non-conflictive, though determined, way. Numerous disputes with neighbors have been resolved
through negotiation with each one of the countries in
question. Especially in the case of Argentina, the
Brazilian Foreign Ministry has tried to achieve joint
cooperation agreements in the hydroelectric and nuclear
areas, as well as a considerable number of other negotiations and agreements.
   The explanation of this apparent anomaly is found
in the development of the professionalism of Itamaraty,
the Brazilian Foreign Ministry, which has been able to
make its perspectives prevail over those of the military.[4] This civilian control of Brazilian foreign policy is particularly striking in trade and financial relations with socialist countries. The civilian economic
leadership in Brazil has neutralized the Brazilian military in that respect, in order to pursue broad agreements, such as those established by the governmental
and entrepreneurial mission headed by the Minister of
Planning, Delfim Neto, in 1981.[5]
   Nevertheless, one of the consequences of the 1982

Malvinas conflict could be the increase of harsher
forces in relation to the resolution of controversies.
For example, the Brazilian Navy has observed with concern the presence of extra-continental powers in the
South Atlantic, and, in the aftermath of the Malvinas
conflict, its high command has increased pressure for
greater budgets and accelerated naval modernization.
As a result of such an international situation, civil-
military tensions in Brazil could increase. Another
factor that could present a greater margin for internal
conflict in this field is the on-going process of political liberalization ("abertura"). To the extent that
the opposition continues to register important successes, the armed forces may feel that their position
is threatened, which together with the post-Malvinas
external situation, could make a moderate negotiating
position on the part of Itamaraty more difficult.

In synthesis, the capability of controlling inter-
state conflicts in South America through appropriate
foreign policies depends on several factors. It increasingly depends on internal political conditions,
especially on the capacity for civilian control that
the respective governments have in relation to their
armed forces, as well as on the security context of
each South American country. In a security situation
perceived as favorable and in a situation of weak civilian control, the armed forces will impose their
perspective of confrontation. On the contrary, if there
is civilian control and/or if the security context of
that country is seen by the particular armed forces as
unstable, negotiating tendencies will be imposed even
when pressures for high military budgets are maintained.

US policy toward the region

The strategic importance of South America has often
been exaggerated, particularly by the Latin American
armed forces themselves. From the mid-1950s until the
beginning of the 1970s, the continent did have political-ideological importance for the USA, but it did not
perform any strategic military function.[6] The military
relations of the region with the USA thus acquired a
more ideological-political than strategic connotation.
For the same reason, as soon as the political orientation of South American governments changed--Velasco in
Peru, Allende in Chile, Torres in Bolivia, and Perón in
Argentina--or when the orientation of the American administration toward the region was modified--Carter and
human rights, for example--military relations with the
USA showed their fragility and confronted a serious
crisis. The crisis of the so-called "panamerican military system" at the beginning of the 70s was a result,
therefore, of the politicization and ideologization of
the relations between South American and US armed
forces.

The crisis of panamerican military relations during
the Carter administration had led countries with military governments such as Argentina, Brazil and Chile to
terminate military aid ties because of US criticism of
their human rights practices. Nevertheless, it was
precisely during this period, between 1976 and 1980, that
Argentina and Chile received the greatest financial support from the USA.

With the Reagan administration, a new stage was
initiated in military links between South America and
the USA. The United States has tried to harmonize its
permanent interests in the region through support for
de facto governments, all of which are clearly oriented
to the right and strongly repressive in internal matters. This has led to normalization of diplomatic and
military links between the USA and right-wing dictatorships in South America.

Following the 1982 Malvinas conflict, renewed emphasis was placed on links with South American armed
forces. It was considered necessary to reestablish and
improve panamerican military relations in order to dis-
courage extracontinental influence and, at the same
time, assure the "governability" of those countries.
In the Argentine case both factors overlapped. On the
one hand, the armed forces were involved in an offensive military action that was intolerable for the USA.
On the other hand, the failure of the Argentine armed
forces meant a move toward eventual civilian rule,
which, from the US view, increased its ungovernability.

As a consequence, the role that the USA is likely
to play in the region for the remainder of the Reagan
administration will be greater involvement in political-
military matters, greater indifference to questions related to human rights, and greater attention toward
matters of a financial order or of foreign debt service.
These characteristics point towards greater control of
intra-regional conflicts. This new US policy orientation contrasts with previous US policy, which was less
interventionist and which therefore possessed a lesser
capacity to manage conflicts in the region, such as was
demonstrated in the Chilean-Argentine crisis in 1978
and the Peruvian-Ecuadorian confrontation in 1981. This
perspective of mounting involvement for what remains of
the Reagan administration can only be put in practice
in smaller South American countries or in others with
similar characteristics. It will not be possible in the
case of Brazil, which has already ceased to be a pref-
erential ally of the United States in order to acquire
an autonomous role in the region. An important source
of conflict that may emerge throughout the coming years
involves contradictions between the policies of these
two countries, to the extent that Brazilian pragmatism
might clash at any moment with the new US interventionism.

Toward a South American Policy on Control of Conflicts

Since we foresee greater US involvement in the South American region and since we associate this with greater US capacity to control conflicts that may arise there, we cannot do more than lament this conclusion. Besides being threatening to the respective sovereignties of the Latin American states involved, such a US-directed system of control is not adapted to South American realities and hence creates a high level of volatility and instability. A system thus conceived can only rest on frustrated and dissatisfied military sentiments, which in any event would revive intra-regional competition and sharpen conflicts.

A viable, stable system of conflict resolution implies some type of non-interventionist hemispheric link, insofar as inter-American relations are concerned. Insofar as internal South American politics are concerned, democratically-expressed civilian forces must have the real ability to maintain control over armed institutions. Development of an effective system of conflict control in South America supposes that both conditions be observed.

Assuming that these necessary, but not sufficient, conditions could be met, some additional general ideas flowing from them may be expressed, in order to elaborate a national policy of effective control of conflicts in the region. The development of means of mutual trust, which is a first step in decreasing intra-regional tensions, should be complemented by a group of typically local measures that are oriented in the same direction but vary with the specific circumstances of each South American case. Following the same order of the above exposition, the principal criteria for the group of countries made up by Argentina, Colombia and Ecuador will be described first.

For different internal political reasons, these three countries seem to be incapable of submitting their armed institutions to effective civilian control. In the Argentine case, the lack of institutionalization of its own state structure has led to autonomy of the armed forces, which was expressed acutely through interservice differences that had important effects on the 1982 defeat in the Malvinas. Similarly, in the Ecuadorian case, the armed forces exhibit very high levels of autonomy, even in the framework of a democracy such as exists in the country, although this has not led to such fragmentation of the military command as in Argentina.

For such reasons, a first measure in this respect is to submit all armed institutions to civilian control by an Executive that is selected on representative and legitimate bases. The unity of civil command over the entirety of the armed services is a fundamental condition for obtaining satisfactory results.

A second measure is to tighten the relationship between the civil sectors and the structures for conflict resolution at the regional level. For example, the conflict resolution mechanisms in the Organization of American States, as well as potential mechanisms of the Andean Pact and the Latin American Economic System (SELA), should be broadened to include existing nongovernmental organizations that have played a role of importance in the reduction of inter-state tensions. Reference can be made to the Catholic Church, youth movements such as the Peace and Justice Service, labor organizations of all kinds, women's organizations and other intellectual and cultural groups. All such groups have been historically isolated from decisions affecting conflict resolution, although their opinions are particularly relevant since their membership is composed of those principally affected by the increase in tensions. To the extent that conflict resolution mechanisms are reformed to include non-governmental organizations and more such mechanisms are created, popular participation in the search for peaceful and stable solutions would be reinforced. In this respect, it is fitting to call attention to the important effort that intellectual, artistic and Catholic groups made in Argentina and Chile in successfully containing the danger of war in 1978 over the Beagle Channel.

In the case of Peru and Chile, as well as in all those nations where there are historical problems of unresolved boundary disputes, it is necessary, along with mobilizing the above-mentioned conflict resolution mechanisms, to initiate a progressive search for consensus on subjects as acute and sensitive as the outlet to the sea for Bolivia. Such consensus-building would involve overcoming Peruvian reticence toward a solution that would imply terminating the border dispute with Chile, as well as promoting a more reasonable Peruvian diplomatic style of greater collaboration. More generally, consensus-building would involve initiating negotiations at an academic-intellectual level, which do not oblige the parties, so that agreements potentially acceptable to governments could be determined. Nevertheless, as long as the autonomy of the armed forces is not limited in the Peruvian case and Chile does not restore a fully democratic system, it will be very difficult to advance decisively in these matters. To the degree that a civilian presence is stabilized in Bolivia, it may facilitate initiation of successive tripartite meetings at the academic level for conflict resolution.

Finally, in the cases of Venezuela and Brazil, it is a question of strengthening those positive tendencies that exist in both countries through the enforcement of the aforementioned recommendations. Along with deepening civilian control and opening multilateral organisms to the participation of non-governmental institutions, it is necessary to emphasize consensus-building. The new participation of Venezuela in organizations such as the Non-Aligned Movement and the greater proximity of Brazil to intra-regional organizations such as SELA and the Andean Pact could accelerate the positive trends evident in both countries.

In summary, an effective system of conflict resolution depends on the ability of South American countries to reduce US interventionism in the area, and requires a system of stronger intraregional alliances. Likewise, it depends on the complete rule of democracy in these countries as a necessary condition for the full participation of the citizenry in the control of the armed forces. Along with these guidelines, it is necessary to reform those bilateral and multilateral intergovernmental organizations charged with conflict resolution in such a way as to give greater participation to non-governmental entities. Finally, it is necessary to seek agreements, whether bilateral or multilateral, settling specific disputes, beginning with the meeting of those who are directly involved in the disputes and interested in peace. To the extent that this group of conflict resolution recommendations promotes popular participation in decision making, democracy will be strengthened at the regional level and inter-state conflicts, which in the great majority of cases are due to narrow interests, will be contained.

NOTES

1. It should be emphasized that this analysis focuses on South America, disregarding the situation in Central America.

2. Different positions regarding the list of weapons to be limited or eliminated from Latin American arsenals vary in accordance with the strategic position of these countries and their different warfare hypotheses. As a result of these differences, a third meeting of experts never took place.

There was a consensus over the prohibition of biological, chemical, toxic and nuclear weapons, ballistic missiles, carriers, cruisers and nuclear submarines. There were, however, definite differences between Colombia, Chile and Ecuador, on the one hand, and Bolivia, Peru and Venezuela, on the other, regarding missile ranges. The former supported prohibition of strategic missiles and the latter wanted to maintain this option free and prohibit 50-kilometer range missiles. Peru was against prohibiting artillery above 105 mm. and Colombia and Chile supported the prohibition of all type of bombers. Col. Gerardo Cortés Rencoret, 'Los tratados de armamentos en América', Seguridad Nacional (January-

March 1978).

3. Juan Carlos Puig, 'Política Internacional Argentina', un-published paper presented at the Seminario sobre Políticas Exteriores Comparadas de América Latina, Caracas, 4-6 October 1982.

4. In this respect, see Alexandre S.C. Barros, 'The Formulation and Orientation of Brazilian Diplomacy', unpublished paper presented at the Seminar on Comparative Latin American Foreign Policies, Viña del Mar, Chile, 20-23 September 1982.

5. See Augusto Varas, 'Las Relaciones de América Latina con los Países Socialistas: Los Casos de Argentina, Brasil, Chile y Perú', unpublished paper presented at the Seminar on Comparative Latin American Foreign Policies, Viña del Mar, Chile, 20-23 September 1982.

6. See James C. Haar, 'Ayuda Militar para la América Latina', Military Review, May 1969.

TABLE 4.1

Types and number of Latin American Proposals and/or Declarations related to Arms Limitation and Disarmament (does not include signed treaties)

	General and complete disarmament	Cessation of nuclear weapons tests	Non-proliferation of nuclear weapons	Nuclear weapon-free zones	Preventing arms race on the sea bed	Preventing arms race in outer space	Chemical and biological weapons	Environmental warfare	Military budgets	Arms transfers	Declaration of Ayacucho
Argentina	2			1	1		2				x
Bolivia				2						1	x
Brazil	3	4	4	3	1	1	3		1		
Chile	2			2							x
Colombia	2									1	x
Costa Rica			1								
Dominican Republic											
Ecuador				2						1	x
El Salvador										1	
Guatemala											
Haiti											
Honduras											
Jamaica			1								
Mexico	8	4	4	3	3	2	4	1			
Nicaragua											
Panama											x
Paraguay										1	
Peru	1										x
Trinidad & Tobago	1										
Uruguay											
Venezuela	1									1	x

Source: Data derived from United Nations, Report of the Preparatory Committee for the Special Session of the General Assembly devoted to disarmament, Volume V, New York, 1978.

TABLE 4.2
Date of ratification of major post-World War II Agreements

	Antarctic Treaty	Partial Test Ban Treaty	Outer Space Treaty	Treaty of Tlatelolco	Non-Proliferation Treaty	Sea Bed Treaty	Biological Warfare Treaty
Argentina	1961	–	1969	–	–	–	–
Bolivia	–	1966	–	1969	1970	–	1975
Brazil	1975	1965	1969	1968*	–	–	1973
Chile	1961	1965	–	1974*	–	–	–
Colombia	–	–	–	1972	–	–	–
Costa Rica	–	1967	–	1969	1970	–	1973
Dominican Republic	–	1964	1968	1968	1971	1972	1973
Ecuador	–	1964	1969	1969	1969	–	1975
El Salvador	–	1965	1969	1968	1972	–	–
Guatemala	–	1964	–	1970	1970	–	1973
Haiti	–	–	–	1969	1970	–	–
Honduras	–	1964	–	1968	1973	–	–
Jamaica	–	–	1970	1969	1970	–	1975
Mexico	–	1963	1968	1967	1969	–	1974
Nicaragua	–	1965	–	1968	1973	1973	1975
Panama	–	1966	–	1971	1977	1974	1974
Paraguay	–	–	–	1969	1970	–	1976
Peru	–	1964	–	1969	1970	–	–
Trinidad and Tobago	–	1964	–	1970	–	–	–
Uruguay	–	1969	1970	1968	1970	–	–
Venezuela	–	1965	1970	1970	1975	–	–

Source: Derived from SIPRI, Arms Control, Taylor & Francis, London, 1978.

* While Brazil and Chile have ratified the Treaty of Tlatelolco, the Treaty is not yet in force for either state, since both have refused to waive the requirements laid down in Article 28.

5
Regional Confidence-Building in the Military Field: The Case of Latin America

Victor Millán

INTRODUCTION

One of the main tasks for the 1980s will be the search for practical ways and means to increase trust in the field of political-military relations in the Western hemisphere.

Increased rivalry or open conflicts, as exemplified by the recent armed clashes between Peru and Ecuador (1981), Argentina and Great Britain (1982), delicate border situations such as those between Nicaragua and Honduras, Nicaragua and El Salvador, Chile and Argentina, Venezuela and Guyana, and the Reagan Administration's hardline strategy in Central American and Caribbean countries, threatening military interventions and economic blockade, have been major issues of concern in the region. The intensification of Central American conflicts in particular has led to a fear of renewed polarization of inter-state relations in Latin America.

There is consequently a growing concern that the relative stability which exists at present will break down, leading to increased regional militarization and an explosion of the arms race. Due to the precarious situation in the humanitarian field and the socio-economic crisis, security and trust have become more elusive. Great imagination and courage are needed to discover new instruments and mechanisms by which conflicts between Latin American states and vis-à-vis the USA might be resolved.

REGIONAL SECURITY

Most of the Latin American states belong to the inter-American collective security system. The three main juridical instruments which regulate the relationships of the states in the region in the field of peace and security are: (a) the Charter of the Organization of the American States (OAS) of 1948, amended by the Protocol of Buenos Aires in 1967, (b) the Inter-American Treaty of Reciprocal Assistance (the Rio Pact) of 1947 with a <u>Protocol</u> of amendment approved in San José (Costa Rica) in 1975, but still not in force (only seven members have ratified it), and (<u>c</u>) the <u>American Treaty on Pacific Settlement</u> (the <u>Pact of Bogotá</u>) of 1948.[1]

The situation in Latin America is different from that which prevails in Europe, where two major military alliances confront each other and threaten each other's security. Confidence-building measures (CBMs) evolved in Europe from a need to agree on some concrete forms of cooperation which could contribute to dispelling mistrust of foreign military establishments, particularly mistrust between West and East, and thereby reassuring potential adversaries and reducing the likelihood of conflict.

The concept of confidence-building measures whether in Latin America or Europe is aimed at reducing interstate tensions and focuses on a step-by-step reduction of mistrust and fear thereby helping to develop confidence, better understanding and more stable relations between nations.[2] The concept derives from the realization that states need to be reassured that certain activities of other states do not threaten their own security. Such a degree of confidence can only be achieved if the amount of information available to governments enables them to make satisfactory forecasts and to predict the actions and reactions of other governments within their political environment. CBMs would contribute to the establishment of a favourable climate for the conduct of negotiations and the conclusion of agreements on arms-control and disarmament.

Nevertheless, despite the absence of hostile military blocs and the existence of the juridical instruments mentioned above, relations between Latin American states are frequently characterized by rivalry or open conflict. Also, the factors determining the prevailing security situation differ in many cases from those existing in Europe, which is characterized by the two-bloc confrontation. Confidence-building measures, adapted to the Latin American milieu, could help to create the climate and conditions conducive to the removal of inequalities in the political, social, and economic fields, as underlying causes of tension and conflict, thereby creating a prerequisite for arms-control and disarmament negotiations in the region.

Certain appropriate mechanisms for this purpose already exist within the region. The above-mentioned treaties, which are themselves designed to guarantee peace and stability throughout the Western hemisphere and contain a number of clauses aimed at building confidence among American states, constitute one such mechanism. However, the <u>term 'confidence-building'</u> has not been used in the same context as in the <u>Document on Confidence-Building Measures</u> in the Final Act of the Conference on Security and Co-operation in Europe of 1975.

MECHANISMS FOR CONFIDENCE-BUILDING MEASURES

Measures aimed at building confidence between American states are specified in chapter II, article 3, item c of the Charter of the Organization of American States (OAS) amended by the Protocol of Buenos Aires, where it is declared that good faith shall govern the relations between states. According to article 17, respect for and the faithful observance of treaties [should] constitute standards for the development of peaceful relations among states, and treaties and agreements should be public. Article 19 seems to be important in the light of pressure from the USA and other states on Central American affairs. This article declares that no state may use or encourage the use of coercive measures of an economic or political character in order to coerce the sovereign-will of another state and thus obtain from it advantages of any kind. Chapter V of the OAS Charter --Pacific Settlement of Disputes--contains a number of articles on the settlement of international disputes which may arise between American states and which should be submitted to peaceful procedures. Moreover, in case of conflict, article 59 requires a Meeting of Consultation of Ministers of Foreign Affairs in order to consider problems of an urgent nature and of common interest to the American states. Thus article 60 considers that any member state may request such a Meeting of Consultation; and in case of an armed attack within the territory of an American state or within the region of security delimited by treaties in force, a Meeting of Consultation shall be called immediately by the Chairman of the Permament Council of the Organization (article 63). Also the OAS Charter established an advisory defense committee, composed of the highest military authorities, to deal with matters relating to defence against aggression (articles 64, 65 and 66).[3]
The parties to the Inter-American Treaty of Reciprocal Assistance (1947) are under obligation to submit the controversies among them to the procedures in force in the Inter-American System. According to articles 3 and 11, the Meeting of Foreign Ministers should serve as the Organ of Consultation in order to agree upon measures that should be taken in case of an armed attack by any state against an American state. Moreover, the provisions contained in the American Treaty on Pacific Settlement, particularly those referring to Commissions of Investigation and Consultation (article XV), also aim at building confidence between the American states. Another example of a multilateral instrument capable of building international confidence is the Treaty of Tlatelolco, which prohibits the testing, use, manufacture, production or acquisition by any means, as well as the

receipt, storage, installation, deployment and any form
of possession of nuclear weapons in Latin America.[4]
Treaty obligations are administered through the Agency
for the Prohibition of Nuclear Weapons in Latin America
(OPANAL) and the peaceful use of nuclear energy is permitted under the control of the International Atomic Energy Agency (IAEA).

REGIONAL APPROACH

Other confidence-building measures have been developed at the regional level. In the 1967 Declaration
of Punta del Este, the Presidents of Latin America expressed their intention to avoid those expenditures that
are not indispensable for the performance of the specific duties of the armed forces. A more elaborate effort
to strengthen regional confidence may be found in the
1974 Declaration of Ayacucho, commemorating the 150th
anniversary of the battle which ended Spanish domination
in South America. The six states then members of the
Andean Group--Bolivia, Chile, Colombia, Ecuador, Peru
and Venezuela--plus two non-members--Argentina and Pana-
ma--undertook to promote and support the building of a
lasting order of international peace and co-operation
and to create the conditions for effective limitation
of arms and an end to their acquisition for offensive
purposes, so that all possible resources might be devoted to the economic development of every country in
Latin America.[5] In addition, the Parties to the Ayacucho Declaration agreed to act through the Foreign Ministers in the event of any situation that could affect
peaceful coexistence between their countries.
Several consultative meetings of the Andean countries took place after the signing of the Declaration
of Ayacucho with a view to translating its provisions
into an internationally binding instrument. In 1978 a
conference was convened in Mexico City, to deal exclusively with the problem of conventional arms-control in
the region. The participants (Argentina, Bolivia, Colombia, Costa Rica, Cuba, the Dominican Republic, Ecuador, El Salvador, Guatemala, Haiti, Honduras, Jamaica,
Mexico, Nicaragua, Panama, Peru, Surinam, Trinidad and
Tobago, Uruguay, and Venezuela) recommended inter alia
initiation of studies and talks concerning possible limitations on transfers of certain types of conventional
armaments to Latin America and between countries in the
area, as well as limitations on conventional weapons
considered to be excessively injurious or indiscriminate
in their effects. In September 1980 representatives of
Colombia, Costa Rica, Ecuador, Panama, Peru, Venezuela
and Spain met in Riobamba (Ecuador) and adopted a Charter of Conduct stressing the need for peaceful settlement of disputes and undertook to set in motion the implementation of the principles of the Declaration of A-

yacucho. Together with these declarations, the Cartagena Mandate, which was set up at Cartagena (Colombia) in
1979 by the Member States of the Andean Group and which
established political machinery for co-operation on the
basis of a pluralist approach to regional peace and integration, represents a central factor in building confidence in Latin America.[6]

While all these agreements and declarations have
established mechanisms to resolve or avoid conflicts in
the region, it must be admitted that they have not been
sufficiently used on an overall regional scale. In particular, serious disputes such as those between Argentina and Chile, and Nicaragua and El Salvador, have not
been settled within the inter-American system.

On the other hand, a series of military confidence-
-building measures are being carried into effect through
bilateral or multilateral arrangements involving certain
Latin American countries. Thus, for example, the Council for Central American Defense, set up in 1962, has
among its other tasks the duty to organize joint military manoeuvres. The Argentinian and Brazilian navies
conduct joint naval manoeuvres while Panama and Venezuela conduct joint manoeuvres of land, sea and air forces.
Brazil and Uruguay conduct joint anti-submarine warfare
exercises and a group of Latin American countries conduct air force manoeuvres. Also some Latin American
navies have been participating in extracontinental naval
manoeuvres (for more detail, see Table 5.1).

In addition, representatives of neighbouring states
are often invited to observe manoeuvres carried out in
other areas (as in the case of the Mexican land manoeuvres in 1980, to which high Guatemalan officers were
invited). Visits of naval units and exchanges of military missions among Latin American states are common
events. In addition, military academies are frequently
attended by officers from other countries. Finally,
the commanders-in-chief of the army, navy and air forces
of regional states hold annual conferences in different
capitals.

PROBLEMS AND PRACTICAL SUGGESTIONS

Confidence-building measures in the military field,
which are only now taking shape on a very modest scale
in Europe, have been in force for quite some time and
on a much larger scale in Latin America. However, one
of the impediments to achieving the goals of confidence-
-building measures is that in a number of important undertakings participation is not restricted to Latin
American states. In particular, joint manoeuvres with
US or Soviet armed forces unavoidably assume the appear-
ance of military bloc exercises, minimizing the importance of confidence-building among Latin American states
themselves.

Superpower participation in regional security systems is seen to serve only their own interests, and it
is feared that Latin American security interests may be
jeopardized. Such apprehension has been expressed, for
instance, regarding the goals and organization of the
Inter-American Military Armies (1973).[7] The exclusion
of Nicaraguan participation from the 14th Conference of
Commanders of American Armies held in Fort MacNair,
Washington D.C., in November 1981, should likewise be
interpreted as a lack of confidence from the USA. General Peter M. Dawkins, the Secretary General of the
Conference, explained to Colonel Donald Mendoza, the
military attaché at the Nicaraguan Embassy in Washington
D.C., that "the attendees must share common perspectives
on security and defense issues of mutual interest within
the boundaries of the American hemisphere".[8]

The step-by-step reduction of mistrust and fear and
the development of confidence between states by agreed
rules of military and political behavior could play a
significant role at the sub-regional level, where confidence-building arrangements could perhaps function
more efficiently, than if the initiative were to come
from regional organizations or from individual states
in the region. The viability of possible sub-regional
confidence-building in politico-military policies would
be determined by such factors as: the dominant conflict
formation (north-south, east-west, south-south), the
regional balance of forces, the disparities of power
(e.g., regional stratification), the number of regional
military conflicts and politico-military threats, and
the degree of militarization (level of defense expenditures, numbers of military manpower and military hardware).

Confidence-building measures as a collateral proposal to facilitate the settlement of disputes and conflicts in the region and to reduce the causes for mistrust, fear, tensions and hostilities, could contribute
in the following fields, which may be worthy of further
consideration:

a) mutual exchange of information on military potential and advanced notification of significant
   changes in the size and structure of the armed
   forces;

b) openness regarding military budgets and stan-
   dardized reporting of military expenditures;

c) prior notification of major military manoeuvres
   and movements of troops in border areas under
   agreed criteria;

d) reduction in the arms-trade of sophisticated
   weapons;

e) coordination of programmes for arms acquisitions;

f) multilateral cooperation in conventional arms development and production;

g) improvement of communications between governments and establishment of direct lines to serve in conflict situations; and

h) establishment of a verification agency to deal with these matters, within the already existing regional organizations (SELA or OPANAL).

The above-mentioned CBMs may be quantum sufficit for illustrative purposes. However, the achievement of these goals would require adherence by all the states of the region, and a condition sine qua non would be the adoption by the USA and the USSR of a policy of restraint in the Western hemisphere.

NOTES

1. For the status and implementation of these treaties, see Status of Inter-American Treaties and Conventions (revised to May 8, 1980), Secretaría General Organización de los Estados Americanos, Washington D.C., Series de Tratados No. 5, 1980.

2. World Armaments and Disarmament, SIPRI Yearbook 1976 (Almqvist & Wiksell, Stockholm, 1976), pp. 359-62; UN Document A/36/474, 6 October 1981, p. 11; H. Günther Brauch, Confidence-Building Measures, Regional Security, Arms Control and Disarmament.--Three Examples: Europe, Latin America, Indian Ocean, paper presented at 29th Pugwash Conference, 18-23 July 1979, Mexico City.

3. UN Document A/36/474, 6 October 1981.

4. J. Goldblat & V. Millán, 'Militarization and arms control in Latin America' in World Armaments and Disarmament, SIPRI Yearbook 1982 (Taylor & Francis Ltd., London, May 1982).

5. UN Document A/10044, 28 January 1979.

6. UN Document A/36/474.

7. J. Child, Unequal Alliance: The Inter-American Military System, 1938-1972 (Westview Press, Boulder, Colorado, 1980).

8. 'U.S., Latin Officers meet privately', Washington Post, 6 November 1981.

TABLE 5.1. JOINT MILITARY MANOEUVRES IN LATIN AMERICA IN 1978-1981[1]

Participating countries	Date	Area	Designation	Participating Units
Honduras/Nicaragua	1978	C. America	Operation Speed	Land and air forces
Argentina/Brazil	1978	S. Atlantic	Fraterno I	Naval forces
Brazil/Uruguay	1978	S. Atlantic	Operación Atlántico 1978	Naval forces
Panama/Venezuela	1979	Caribbean		Land, navy and air forces
Peru/Argentina	1979	Pacific	Castor Perú	Test of missiles
USA/Brazil	1979	S. Atlantic	UNITAS	Navy and naval air force
USA/Colombia	1979	Pacific	UNITAS	Navy and naval air force
USA/Venezuela	1979	Caribbean	UNITAS	Navy and naval air force
Argentina/Brazil	1980	S. Atlantic	Fraterno II	Naval forces
Argentina/Brazil/Colombia/ Chile/Ecuador/Peru/Uruguay/ USA/Venezuela	1980	Argentina	Ejercicios Conjuntos	Air force
Argentina and Bolivia/Brazil/Colombia/Chile/Ecuador/ Guatemala/Honduras/Panama/ Paraguay/Peru/Dominican Republic/Uruguay/USA/Venezuela/El Salvador/Nicaragua (Members of the Commission for Inter-American Aeronautic Cooperation)	1980	Argentina	Ejercicios Conjuntos	Air force

(Table 5.1. Continued)

Brazil/Paraguay (annual)	1980		Operativo Ninfa	Land and naval forces
Argentina/Paraguay (annual)	1980		Operativo Sirera	Land and naval forces
Argentina/USA	1980	Argentinian coast	UNITAS XXI-Solidaridad Hemisférica; Defensa Hemisférica	Navy and naval air force
USA/Netherlands/Venezuela/ Colombia/Uruguay/Argentina	1981	Atlantic and Caribbean	REDIX 1-814	Navy and air force
USA/Argentina	Aug. 1981	S. Atlantic	Ocean Venture-81	Naval forces
USA/Argentina	Sep. 1981	S. Atlantic	UNITAS XXII	Naval forces and ASW* (marine landing exercises)
Argentina/Brazil	Oct. 1981	S. Atlantic	Fraterno III	Navy and air forces (ASW)
USA/Brazil	Sep. 1981	S. Atlantic	UNITAS XXII	Naval forces and ASW (marine landing exercises)
USA/Uruguay	Oct. 1981	S. Atlantic	UNITAS XXII	Naval forces and ASW (marine landing exercises)
USA/Venezuela	Oct. 1981	Caribbean	UNITAS XXII	Naval forces and ASW (marine landing exercises)
USA/Colombia	Oct. 1981	Pacific	UNITAS XXII	Naval forces and ASW (marine landing exercises)
USA/Chile	Oct. 1981	Pacific	UNITAS XXII	Naval forces and ASW (marine landing exercises)
USA/Honduras	Oct. 1981	Caribbean	Eagle View-81	Navy and air force (ASW intercept operations)

* ASW: anti-submarine warfare.

[1] Most manoeuvres are attended by foreign observers.

6

The Latin American Economic System as a Mechanism to Control Conflicts

Carlos Moneta

INTRODUCTION

The purpose of this paper is to analyze the Latin American Economic Organization, SELA. Of particular interest is SELA's capacity for dealing with intra-regional conflicts, the methods used and its success in bringing about cooperative attitudes between members. The issues arising within SELA are essentially of a type which allow for negotiation between the parties.[1] Since the majority of cases do not involve a "zero-sum game", where one participant's gain signifies an equivalent loss for his rival, the common aim of the organization is to come up with solutions reasonably satisfactory for all concerned.

Cases examined within the intra-regional context will be related to conflicts arising on the inter-American and inter-continental scene. For purposes of comparison, reference will be made to the structural differences between SELA and other regional entities such as the Organization of American States (OAS) and the Inter-American Development Bank (IDB) and the differences existing in the objectives and methods they apply in dealing with conflicts.

SELA: OBJECTIVES, ORGANIZATION AND FUNCTIONS

On October 17, 1975, 26 countries[2] of Latin America and the Caribbean met in Panama City and signed the Panama Convention constituting the Latin American Economic System. Article 2 of this Convention stipulates that SELA is a regional organization of a permanent nature for economic and social consultations, coordination, cooperation and promotion, which enjoys legal status and is made up of Latin American sovereign States.[3]

Objectives

SELA's basic aims are as follows:

a) to promote intra-regional cooperation with a

view to accelerating the social and economic development of its members; and

b) to promote a permanent system of consultation and coordination for the purposes of adopting common stands and strategies in economic and social matters, both in international organizations and fora and vis-à-vis third countries and groups of countries.[4]

Tasks

In order to achieve these objectives, SELA is called upon to carry out a broad spectrum of activities. For example, in the field of regional cooperation, it aims to increase Latin America's bargaining power for the acquisition and utilization of capital goods and technology, as well as for the exportation of commodities and manufactured goods and agreements with transnational corporations. Related activities include promotion of the processing of raw materials, industrial complementarity and the formulation of a regional food policy. It is also entrusted with promoting the creation of Latin American multinational corporations and better use of human, natural, technical and financial resources and offering support to the processes of Latin American integration and actions aimed at harmonization and convergence. Another vast field of action is SELA's involvement as a mechanism for the formulation of common strategies for the region, in economic and social matters, vis-à-vis the rest of the world.

Organization

SELA comprises three organs: 1) the Latin American Council, 2) the Action Committees and 3) the Permanent Secretariat.

1. The Latin American Council is SELA's supreme organ and is made up of one representative of each member state. It holds regular annual meetings at the ministerial level and can call special meetings. The Council's powers include establishing SELA's policy and its work programs and analyzing the tasks of the Action Committees. The Council also approves the common stands and strategies adopted by the Member States in economic and social matters, both in international organizations and fora and vis-à-vis third countries or groups of countries. Likewise, it considers the proposals and reports submitted to it by the Permament Secretariat and resolves all matters of interest to it in connection with SELA's objectives.[5]

2. The Action Committees are organized in response to the interest of two or more Member States in order to carry out specific studies, programs and projects,

and to determine and adopt joint negotiation positions of interest to the members of the Committee vis-à-vis extra-regional actors.[6] The Committees are temporary in nature, are open to the participation of Member States and have their own Secretariats.

3. The Permanent Secretariat is SELA's technical-administrative organ, with headquarters in Caracas. It is headed by a Permanent Secretary, whose term of office lasts four years and who legally represents the Secretariat and SELA on the conditions stipulated by the respective regulations.

The Permanent Secretary performs the functions entrusted to him by the Latin American Council and implements the latter's decision. The functions of the Permanent Secretariat include that of proposing to the Council programs and projects of institutional interest, including their form of implementation, and any other measure which may contribute to the achievement of SELA's objectives. It can also undertake studies and arrange programs and projects with international, regional and national organizations and institutions.[7]

SELA, POLITICAL OR TECHNICAL MECHANISM?

The interest of member states in maintaining strong control over regional and international organizations, with a view to preventing them from acquiring a growing share of decision-making power which might eventually be detrimental to national sovereignty, is a trend shared by the majority of Latin American governments throughout their history. However, Mexico and Venezuela, the countries which first conceived the idea of creating SELA and later promoted it, thought of it as a structure endowed with the necessary powers to perform effectively its functions aimed at the unification of interests between the countries of the region.

This original idea of SELA as an eminently political forum was strongly opposed by several governments (particularly those of Argentina and Brazil),[8] for fear of its becoming a supranational organization. The original emphasis on political aspects was then modified and an approach subsequently taken which focused on technical aspects.

The present structure of SELA reflects the compromise reached by negotiation between the supporters of these positions. While it is relatively in advance of other organizations in some ways (for example, in its capacity to articulate and aggregate interests), SELA still suffers from considerable limitations as far as the autonomy, authority and representativeness of its organs are concerned--particularly the Permanent Secretariat--and in the human and financial resources available to it to solve the multiple and complex problems faced by the region.[9]

Nevertheless, the organization is finding new formulae to reduce or counteract the impact of these shortcomings, due to a large extent to a capacity for innovation, the careful selection of strategic issues and
the search for favorable political circumstances demonstrated by the Permanent Secretariat.

PROCEDURES FOR THE SETTLEMENT OF CONFLICTS IN SELA

In principle, the Latin American Economic System
lacks specific mechanisms for the settlement of conflicts between its members. However, this function is
accomplished in practice by the system's organs: the
Latin American Council, the Permanent Secretariat and
the Action Committees.

Procedures within the Latin American Council

Article 17 of the Panama Convention stipulates
that all issues connected with the establishment of SE-
LA's general policies must be approved by consensus of
the member countries within the Latin American Council.
Although this article has not yet received a definitive
interpretation (it does not specify the conditions
which are to be met for there to be a "consensus"),[10]
its application up to now has meant that all the member
states have the right to impose a veto in substantive
matters. Consequently, prior negotiation, of an inten-
sive and careful nature, is necessary in matters likely
to create disagreement between the members, for the
purpose of reaching the required consensus in decisions.
While the need for a consensus strengthens decisions
adopted within the Latin American Council, this often
limits the intensity and depth of the resolutions.
Normally, the main negotiating activity takes
place precisely on the occasion of the regular annual
meetings of the Latin American Council, in which the
policies, the international positions of the region and
future work programs are established. Consequently,
the main procedure used to minimize conflicts in SELA's
meetings in which decisions are adopted is that of the
traditional resources of consultation and bilateral and
multilateral negotiation, which are entrusted to the
various Ministries of Foreign Affairs and the Permanent
Secretariat.

Management of conflicts within the Action Committees

The Action Committees enjoy a certain degree of
independence from the Permanent Secretariat in their
activities, despite the fact that the latter often continues to undertake consultations and attempts to reconcile parties involved in disputes. The member countries establish their own methods for the settlement of

disputes and normally consultations take place among
the national authorities in charge of the activities of
the Committee in question. It is to be noted that the
Committee's regulations establish different voting criteria (qualified majority, majority, etc.) for the
adoption of decision.

Evaluation

The existence of the rule of consensus and the
lack of specific organs in SELA to deal with conflicts
limit conflict resolution possibilities to the use of
the traditional resources of establishing contacts between the Ministries of Foreign Affairs and to reliance
on diplomats and the Permanent Secretary as negotiators.
In this system, therefore, the personal characteristics
and aptitudes of the different national representatives
before the Latin American Council and those of the Permanent Secretary are of particular significance in this
respect.

SELA functions as a system which contributes to increasing interactions between the bureaucratic units of
the member countries (particularly between those which
do not maintain diplomatic relations, or are politically isolated). Usually, this increase in interactions
and the personal diplomacy used by some Ministries of
Foreign Affairs and by the Permanent Secretary have not
prevented deep-seated conflicts, unrelated to the organization, from disturbing SELA's activities. But SELA
has often been successful in minimizing such externally-
generated disturbances. The system also provides a relatively "neutral" forum in which adversaries (Chile-
Cuba, for example) can cooperate and maintain a positive
dialogue.

SELA has encountered serious internal conflicts,
but it has usually been able to overcome them. However,
this has sometimes resulted in a considerable reduction
of SELA's capacity and efficiency in the performance of
some of its functions.

CONFLICTIVE FACTORS WITHIN SELA

The conflictive issues which arise within SELA are
associated with different factors, as described below.

Heterogeneity in the possession of resources,
levels of development and economic capacities
of the different Member States

This heterogeneity within SELA tends to repeat situations already seen in the integration mechanisms of
the region, sometimes leading to the formation, around
common interests, of informal nuclei of large, medium-
size and small countries. The degree of integration of

these nuclei varies according to the sub-regional loca-
tion (for example, Central American, Caribbean, Andean
countries and those of the Southern Cone) and political-
strategic affinities and antagonisms.

In this field, SELA's action has been extremely
positive and no major problems have arisen. In those
cases in which problems have arisen, acceptable solutions
were reached in the interest of all concerned.

Diversity of ideological, political and economic models existing in the region

Two major kinds of conflicts are involved: (a) the
heterogeneity of political-ideological models constituting a serious obstacle to the achievement of SELA's
goals, and (b) the difference in economic models in recent years being a fundamental obstacle to progress in
the fields of regional cooperation and integration and
to the adoption of joint international stands by the member countries of SELA.

(a) The military regimes of Latin America and some
civilian governments with conservative tendencies, by
emphasizing the East-West conflict in strategic and
ideological terms, generate considerable resistance to
any association with some--but not all--of those of the
region's cooperative efforts which include socialist
and Marxist regimes. This is the cause of the well-
known tensions which have existed between the governments of the Southern Cone (Argentina, for example) and
certain Central American and Caribbean countries (examples: Cuba, Nicaragua, Grenada). Nevertheless, it is
significant that these differences have never been explicitly and formally manifested within SELA. Likewise,
countries in the south of Latin America took an active
part in the "Action Committee for the Reconstruction of
Nicaragua" (created in 1979), as a result of the civil
strife which ended the Somoza regime.

Related difficulties can be detected with the group
of English-speaking countries of the Caribbean, although,
just as in the previous case, they have not manifested
themselves explicitly. These difficulties are due to
the fact that these new members of SELA have close political, cultural and economic links with organizations
and countries outside the region. Consequently, their
economic and political approaches and interests differ
from those of the Southern and Central American countries as a whole.

(b) Several large and medium-size countries of Latin America have implemented monetary and neoliberal economic models. These give rise to serious difficulties
in the exploration and adoption of cooperative action
in different fields (examples: joint measures vis-à-vis
multinational corporations; transfer of technology; financial policy; foreign debt).

Currently, this diversity of political-ideological and economic models constitutes the major area of tensions, conflicts and obstacles within SELA. It is extremely difficult and sometimes impossible to harmonize positions in these matters. Despite this fact, the SELA strategy of seeking a shared minimum common denominator has often made it possible to minimize the major difficulties, but, as has already been mentioned, at the expense of a significant reduction in the effectiveness of the system. Since it is to be assumed that the existence of considerable political-ideological and economic diversity will be a long-lasting factor, it is of fundamental importance to seek new forms and procedures to reconcile positions and settle differences.

Historical experiences of conflict, competition and mistrust among the Member States

As has already been suggested, SELA's experience has been positive from the point of view of historical conflicts between some of its members. While some old conflicts have not prevented progress within SELA, there has been a greater incidence of temporary bilateral tensions associated with differences between regimes and political-strategic views. For example, we recall the opposition manifested by Argentina and Brazil, on the occasion of the creation of SELA, when those countries viewed this as a project of Venezuela and Mexico destined to confer upon these countries a certain leadership in the region, in addition to the qualms induced in Argentina by the "leftist" political profile of the Mexican regime (Presidency of Echeverría). The same type of situation subsequently arose, but with less intensity and scope, because of tensions existing between the democratic governments and certain military regimes of the Southern Cone (example: deterioration of Argentine-Mexican relations during 1976-1982).

Conflicts connected with disturbances in the international system

In recent years, the world economic crisis, together with the increase in the number of strategic and military conflicts, has gradually obliged Latin America to undertake an analysis of its situation within the world system and the seriousness of the conflicts transmitted by the latter to the region. Unfortunately, the specter of serious short-term situations posed by the world crisis has led the countries in the region to attach more importance in their economic policies to adjustment and adaptation than to structural transformation. Short-term adaptation may be required, but there is a formal majority consensus among the member countries of

SELA about the need for solutions aimed at structural change and not only ad hoc emergency measures.

There are two particularly important cases which illustrate the conflicting aspects of the problems mentioned above and progress made in terms of regional cooperation.

Latin American coordination in economic relations with the United States. In pursuance of a Latin American Council decision, a High-Level Consultation Meeting was held at the end of November 1981 in Panama to deal with Latin America's economic relations with the United States. The Permanent Secretariat presented a document, which formed the basis of the Meeting's work.[11] The document proposed a new strategy for economic relations with the United States, including specific proposals in the fields of trade, commodities, transnational corporations and the transfer of technology and external financing, through the strengthening of Latin America's joint negotiating capacity.

The Panama Meeting therefore represented an effort to arrive at a common negotiating front, embracing all the countries of the region. It also aspired to overcome attitudes which were only capable of viewing existing problems from the bilateral or sectoral angle.

In the view of some of the large countries, that meant restricting their independence of action and their individual negotiating capacity. For other governments, it threatened to jeopardize their cooperative links with the Reagan Administration, thus losing some economic advantages which could have been obtained--depending on the case--in individual negotiations or in negotiations by subregional groupings (the Caribbean Basin, for example). Moreover, a gradual and slow process of strengthening the joint negotiating capacity would have been unable to satisfy immediately the pressing needs of the smaller countries of the region.

Along with the economic interests at stake, there were also strategic factors at work. Such, for instance, is the case of the Argentine military regime, which, in its quest for a privileged relationship with the United States, actively supported the policy of the Reagan Administration in Central America. This regime's posture caused serious tensions in its bilateral relations with the governments of Nicaragua and Cuba.

The topics on which there were serious differences of opinion at the SELA meeting were bound up with these factors. The points concerning the treatment of foreign investments and transnational corporations brought disagreement between those countries (e.g. Andean Group) which were calling for defense of national and subregional industry and control over foreign investments and companies and the monetarist and economically outward-oriented regimes in Argentina, Uruguay, Chile and,

in a different fashion, Brazil. On the other hand,
there was agreement on those issues where national interests were similarly affected by North American economic policy (e.g. closure of markets and protectionism,
financing, and external debt).[12]
    Ideological and political-strategic factors pro-
duced tensions when the vast majority of participating
countries decided to support a resolution on the Panama
Canal (submitted by Panama), which criticized North
American conduct in the observance of the treaties on
the Canal, and a proposal by Nicaragua which indicated,
in very harsh terms, the instances of economic coercion
and pressure to which that country was subjected by the
United States.[13]
    The countries of the Southern Cone, once again led
by Argentina, categorically opposed the approval of
these documents, arguing that they were political in
nature and that it was therefore inappropriate to deal
with them, since the meeting could only address itself
to economic issues.[14] The draft resolution on the Panama Canal was finally approved, but only after the
most critical sections of the document were deleted.
Similarly, the resolution presented by Nicaragua was
not approved in a final working session, thereby giving
rise to a considerable distancing between Argentina,
Brazil, Chile and Uruguay, and the remainder of the SE-
LA member countries.[15]

    SELA and the South Atlantic conflict. Although
historical perspective will be necessary to support
this judgement, available evidence permits the tentative conclusion that the Malvinas conflict was an important milestone in the gradual process of strengthening intraregional cooperation and the coordination of
joint policies by Latin America towards the rest of the
world. As a result of the need for organized channell-
ing of regional solidarity with Argentina and the aim
of fostering conditions of regional economic security,
SELA carried out very important economic and political
actions during the period April-August 1982.

    1. Consultation Meeting of High-Level Government
Representatives to consider the application of coercive
economic measures against a SELA Member State by a
group of industrialized countries. The meeting took
place in Caracas from June 1-2, 1982, and was promoted
and convened by the Permanent Secretariat, in consultation with the Argentine government. As a result of the
discussions held, it was decided; (a) to condemn the
embargo adopted by the United Kingdom, the United
States of America, the European Economic Community and
other industrialized countries; (b) to recommend to
the Latin American Council the formulation and adoption
of a strategy for regional economic security and inde-

pendence, which would include the expansion and intensification of trade and economic complementarity as one of its key elements, and, finally, (c) to entrust the Permanent Secretariat with placing before the Eighth Regular Meeting of the Latin American Council the bases and guidelines of that strategy.[16]

At that meeting, the Constitutive Act of an Action Committee in Support of Argentina was also prepared, and this Committee assumed its functions in July. Its purpose is to coordinate the actions of its 18 member countries in favor of Argentina. It has been engaged in substituting some of the imports from industrialized countries through greater intraregional trade and coordination, inter alia cooperative measures among the member countries in tariffs, insurance, freight and transport.

During the Meeting, Trinidad and Tobago, Jamaica, Grenada, Barbados, Colombia and Chile questioned the degree of support to be given Argentina during the conflict and the terms of the condemnation of the industrialized countries used in the document prepared by the Meeting, in response to the coercive acts carried out against Argentina. These states further doubted the competence of the Meeting to adopt what were considered "political" stances.[17]

In view of the resolute and unwavering support unanimously displayed by the remainder of the participating countries for the agreements reached, the dissenting members held their objections to a minimum. The documents elaborated by the Meeting therefore retained their original tone and scope, being submitted as recommendations to the Latin American Council.

The stances taken by the dissenting countries stem basically, though not exclusively, from their extra-regional links and interests. Such is the case of the English-speaking Caribbean countries' links with Great Britain and the Commonwealth. The Colombian position, based on juridical arguments which had been previously put forward in the OAS, favored a peaceful solution to the conflict and reflected Colombian problems of maritime delimitation in the Gulf of Venezuela as well as the close ties maintained by the Turbay Ayala government with the Reagan Administration.

Chile's dissent, in addition to reflecting its neutrality in the Malvinas conflict, seems to have been a renewed expression of the traditional attitude of the countries of the Southern Cone preventing regional bodies from acquiring greater autonomy in their decision-making capacity. Chile therefore wished to prevent SELA from dynamically engendering new mechanisms to confront totally unforeseen situations for which it did not have the appropriate legal provisions.

2. The Eighth Regular Meeting of the Latin American Council. This initial disagreement lessened gradually over the ensuing months, as events in the Malvinas led in mid-June 1982 to British victory but a postwar stalemate. At the Eighth Meeting of the Latin American Council, held in Caracas at the end of August 1982, the recommendations of the First High-Level Consultation Meeting provided the basis for decisions which were then supported by all the member states, including those which had previously stated reservations. Thus, the Council adopted decisions which: (a) consider the use of coercive economic measures against developing countries as illegal and arbitrary and demand their elimination; (b) establish a mechanism to examine and adopt measures in the event of grave, emergency economic situations which might confront the countries of the region in the future; (c) initiate the formulation of a strategy of regional economic security and independence; (d) endorse the recommendations submitted by the High-Level Consultation Meeting on Latin America's economic relations with the United States of America and establish a work program for this purpose; and (e) lay down conditions for a resumption of the dialogue between Latin America and the EEC.[18]

The Malvinas conflict therefore reveals new elements in the regional setting, which are indications of a breakthrough in intraregional cooperation and in the adoption of more assertive joint positions vis-à-vis external actors. The South Atlantic conflict does not, however, signify a turning point in Latin America's relations with the United States, although it is an important step in that direction.

The tendency among the countries of the region to have differing foreign policies, which predated the conflict, also still persists. Further blurring patterns of interaction are current endeavours by the United States and Western Europe to neutralize the impact of their conduct during the Malvinas conflict and mend the damage done to their relations with the region.

The South Atlantic conflict does show a very positive balance with regard to institutional evolution. SELA is launching mechanisms--such as the High-Level Consultation Meetings--which provide fora of a more appropriate political level for dealing with important topics. The creation of a mechanism for considering emergency situations affecting regional economic security also fills a crucial vacuum, since the region had no exclusive Latin American forum for that purpose. A related result is a more significant role for the Permanent Secretariat as an organ which promotes and engenders actions designed to coordinate progressive positions in pursuance of SELA's objectives.

SELA AND REGIONAL AND INTER-AMERICAN BODIES

When SELA was created, the role which this new body should play in the promotion of regional cooperation was perceived as a potential source of conflict with other integration mechanisms.[19] The experience of SELA's seven years of life renders these fears unfounded. SELA has succeeded in forging excellent working relations with all the subregional integration agencies and has signed consultation and cooperation agreements with the majority of them. Similarly, links between SELA and CEPAL (Economic Commission for Latin America) are growing and strengthening notably, including cooperation and consultation agreements between both institutions.

SELA and the OAS: competition or cooperation?

There are many differences between the OAS and SELA in terms of: (a) objectives and strategies; (b) composition of membership; (c) functions and competence; (d) mechanisms for the settlement of disputes; and (e) prospects.

(a) In practice and beyond formal structures, the core objectives of the two organizations are quite distinct. The OAS model bases itself on the assumption that there exist wholly common and coincident, permanent interests between the United States and Latin America. Strategic security aspects are emphasized by the power in the North, while Latin America favors aspects relating to its economic and social development. An ever-widening gap is evident between Washington and a large number of Latin American governments with respect to their assessment of the importance and nature of security problems, both intra- and extraregional.

Thus, the dominant power's concept of the role of the OAS is framed within a criterion of isolation of Latin America from the rest of the world. It is based on the notion of a sphere of influence which, by and large, has lost its validity, since Latin America has considerably increased its participation in international affairs and diversified its links with other actors in the world system.

In contrast, the SELA model embraces precisely those factors which are rejected or de-emphasized by the OAS. SELA's premise is the existence in the region of specific vital interests which are shared by its Latin American members. These interests are notoriously distinct from those of the United States in the majority of substantive issues.[20] It likewise posits that an inter-American concept of cooperation, with the United States as a key element in building up relations with Latin American states, is misguided, since it is based upon an assumed identity of interests between

both, which is non-existent in a wide variety of important areas.

SELA instead advocates negotiation with the United
States in a climate of mutual and mature recognition of
these differences and willingness to cooperate in solving them.[21] Similarly, it views the United States as
an actor of paramount importance but not as the sole
object of Latin American attention, since regional action and concerns are increasingly comprehensive, and
cannot be restricted to a single actor, regardless of
the latter's importance.

(b) Membership of the OAS includes Latin America
and a growing number of Caribbean states, in addition
to the United States, but in practice excludes Cuba.
The superpower is not a member of SELA, which embraces
twenty-six Latin American and Caribbean states, among
which Cuba is a full and active member.

(c) Both organizations share the same purpose of
promoting cooperation, but in the case of the OAS, it
is a matter of cooperation between the countries of the
region and one superpower, while in SELA, this cooperation is restricted exclusively to the intraregional am-
bit.   Another significant distinction between SELA and
the OAS relates to the identity of the external actors
with respect to which each of these bodies fosters the
adoption of common postures and strategies.   For the
OAS they are actors external to the inter-American system; for SELA they are the United States and other industrialized countries as well as third countries and
regional and international organizations.   Finally, the
OAS possesses competence in political, strategic and
economic issues.   SELA's task, in contrast, is limited
to the terrain of economic and social development.

(d) With regard to the settlement of disputes, the
objectives of the OAS include keeping the peace and
maintaining the security of the continent, as well as
ensuring the pacific settlement of disputes among its
members.   The OAS Charter clearly establishes the organs through which the organization performs its functions in this field (e.g.: the Permanent Council).   As
was stated above, the essential purposes of SELA do not
include the settlement of disputes, so that specific
organs for that purpose have not been established.

The 1982 South Atlantic conflict produced diametrically opposite consequences for SELA and the OAS with
regard to their functions as direct or indirect mechanisms for the settlement of disputes.   For the Latin
American Economic System it signified a reaffirmation
of its role and a breakthrough in its capacity for har-
monizing, coordinating and strengthening common positions.   On the other hand, in the case of the OAS mechanisms and the Rio Treaty, it connoted a serious setback.

From the viewpoint of most Latin American countries, the Malvinas conflict throws into striking re-

lief the gradual loss of validity and the ineffectiveness
of the inter-American institutions--as they are currently fashioned and operating--entrusted with safeguarding
peace and order with justice. This situation is reflected in a gradual loss of credibility of the inter-
American security system. The inter-American concept of
a community of interests between the United States and
Latin America, while retaining some validity until recently, has now been discredited. The "war of the Malvinas", as dealt with by the mechanisms of the inter-
American system, accentuated disaccord between most of
the Latin American members and the United States.

(e) While the future of the OAS is uncertain, particularly its conflict resolution mechanisms, its prospects are enhanced by a relative abundance of resources.
SELA has a budget of approximately US$4 000 000, which
amounts to a mere 5 to 10 per cent of the total OAS budget. In turn, the total SELA staff does not exceed 50
persons, of which a mere 18 comprise its professional
cadre. In comparison, the Press and Publicity Unit of
the OAS in Washington alone has the same budget and a
larger staff than SELA as a whole.

While a prognosis of competition between both organizations, to their mutual disadvantage, is not im-
plausible, it is possible to differentiate roles and
dovetail activities between the OAS and SELA. The latter should act as the region's forum for coordinating
positions, thereby facilitating the organization of a
Latin American bloc for negotiation with the United
States. This negotiation could be carried out through
the OAS.

However, some countries have still not fully committed themselves to launching this alternative and
still maintain ambiguous or dual positions. In particular, they simultaneously support SELA while not allowing
it to act as promoter of a regional bloc, and they maintain their interest in continuing close bilateral links
with the United States and retaining the OAS as a forum
for individual negotiation without previously harmonized
positions. The positive nature of the suggested division of tasks between both bodies nevertheless seems
gradually to be asserting itself, and has already been
explicitly recognized by the Executive Secretaries of
both entities.[22]

THE INTER-AMERICAN DEVELOPMENT BANK, SELA
AND THE OAS: OPERATING GUIDELINES IN
HEGEMONIC AND NON-HEGEMONIC STRUCTURES

The Inter-American Development Bank (IDB) is another body whose functions are gaining in importance,
both for SELA and for the OAS. A distinguished scholar
noted that "the Inter-American Development Bank has
functioned within a hegemonic structure, in which the

United States possessed the dominant proportion of national power capabilities", but that "they [US policy-
makers] were not very concerned with tight control of
routine IDB activities" so that "the developing-country
members have secured both influence and resources".[23]

The experience of the IDB (and of other regional
multilateral development banks) suggests that these
bodies allow developing countries leeway to exert some
influence and access to financial resources, as long as
the most important objectives pursued by the dominant
power are not prejudiced. As the number of challenges
by the countries of the region to the United States hegemonic power increases, it may be expected that there
will be an increased number of situations of conflict
between Latin America and the United States over resource distribution (economic, political, etc.) in both
the OAS and the IDB.

SELA, for its part, will have to face, in the financial field--as in other areas, as has been pointed
out--another type of tension, since in this case there
is no hegemonic actor. This involves tension and friction between centripetal forces which strive for the
coordination of Latin America's positions and centrif-
ugal ones, which favour bilateral negotiation with the
industrialized powers.

The critical level of the region's external debt
illustrates such problems. SELA's Permanent Secretariat
is attempting to coordinate a regional position, especially among the countries accounting for two-thirds of
the region's total debt (Mexico, Brazil, Argentina and
Venezuela), whereby their joint negotiating potential
would be optimized. This does not involve dealing
jointly with the extension of terms and interests,
since each situation has its peculiarities, but seeking
an overall solution which modifies the terms of the existing system of relations between creditors and debt-
ors.[24] Nevertheless, the majority of debtor countries
is still seeking to negotiate solutions--now clearly
unattainable in the framework of the present rules of
the game--on an individual basis.

This type of dilemma is likely to be less acute as
regional states become more aware of their individual
vulnerability and of the possibilities offered by concerted action.

CONCLUSIONS

Various tentative conclusions may be drawn regarding the topics examined in this paper:
(a) The growth of Latin America and the important
changes occuring in its form of participation in the
international system, particularly greater differentia-
tion and diversity in its links with the rest of the
world, alter the historic mold of its relations with

the United States and tend to increase considerably the
number of conflicts between that country and the region.

(<u>b</u>) In the inter-American system (or in multilateral bodies such as the IDB), which links developing
with industrialized countries and which is marked by
imbalance in the distribution of power and relative capacities, the dominant actors are prepared to concede
the developing countries leeway to satisfy to varying
degrees such of their aspirations (influence, financial
resources, etc.) as do not affect those interests considered important by the hegemonic actors.

(<u>c</u>) As there is a strengthening of the joint capacity of the countries of Latin America to assume a more
dynamic and assertive role in the international system,
matched by continuing United States' application of
traditional concepts of power relationships, the inter-
American system is growing increasingly inefficient in
finding solutions to conflicts arising both in interaction with the United States as well as at the intra-
regional level.

(<u>d</u>) SELA, on the contrary, is displaying increasing effectiveness in the management and harmonization
of the diverging interests of its members, as well as
in limiting the effect of bilateral or multilateral intraregional conflicts which, pertaining to other levels
(the political/ideological, strategic, etc.), have a
less telling impact within SELA.

(<u>e</u>) The interests of some of the larger countries
in Latin America, which are striving for special cooperative relations with the present North American administration, and the differences and heterogeneity existing among the countries of the region in terms of
their varying degrees of international viability, all
contribute to conflict and intraregional tension. Despite this, as disturbances external to the region increase, there is a lessening of differences between opposing Latin American positions, giving rise to a
greater will for intraregional cooperation for resolution or neutralization of conflicts.

(<u>f</u>) The inter-American system should be thoroughly refashioned, as early as possible, and be geared to
respond to new situations and requirements (e.g. its
principal function should be that of a forum for negotiation rather than cooperation, thereby modifying the
assumptions and the rules of the security sustem). Parallel to this, it is necessary to undertake the rapid
coordination and implantation of endogenous Latin American systems for harmonization in the political and security fields, and to strengthen that already existing
in the economic field (SELA).

(<u>g</u>) The challenge for the Latin American countries
is to participate in a shared political project to at-
tune their foreign policies to a rapidly changing and
increasingly complex international system, which offers

multiple systems of linkage entailing the interplay of cooperative and conflictive factors. To that extent, the nations of the region will be able to reap greater benefits by coordinating their actions in multiple fora, thereby enhancing their negotiating capacity and minimizing intraregional conflicts and tensions.

NOTES

1. Thomas C. Schelling, The Strategy of Conflict (Harvard University, Cambridge, Massachusetts, 1980), p. 5.
2. The following are the SELA member countries: Argentina, Barbados, Bolivia, Brazil, Colombia, Costa Rica, Chile, Cuba, Dominican Republic, Ecuador, El Salvador, Grenada, Guatemala, Guyana, Haiti, Honduras, Jamaica, Mexico, Nicaragua, Panama, Paraguay, Peru, Surinam, Trinidad and Tobago, Uruguay, Venezuela.
3. Panama Convention Establishing the Latin American Economic System (SELA), Art. 2.
4. Ibid., Art. 3.
5. Ibid., Art. 15.
6. Ibid., Art. 20.
7. Ibid., Art. 31.
8. Francisco J. Alejo y Héctor Hurtado, El SELA, un mecanismo para la acción (Fondo de Cultura Económica, Mexico, D.F., 1976), pp. 24-25.
9. Patricio Chaparro, 'El Sistema Económico Latinoamericano (SELA) como instancia de mediación, representación y acción política ¿destinada al fracaso?', Estudios Internacionales 49 (1979):427-428.
10. See Section VII 'Debates on Voting' of the Regulations of the Latin American Council, in Decisions of the Latin American Council, Vol. 1, Nos. 1 to 10 (SELA, Caracas, 1977).
11. Final Report of the High-Level Consultation Meeting on Latin America's Economic Relations with the United States of America (SELA, Doc. RC/AL-EU/C/DF No. 1, Panama, December 1, 1981).
12. Edgardo Silberkasten, 'El SELA: ni éxito ni fracaso', El Nacional (Caracas, 11 Diciembre 1981); 'Intereses políticos trabarán los Acuerdos de Panamá', El Diario de Caracas, December 4, 1981.
13. 'Acuerdo de última hora superó crisis política en el SELA', El Mundo (UPI, Panama, December 2, 1981).
14. Ibid.; 'La delegación argentina obstaculiza las posibilidades de un acuerdo', El National (Caracas, December 1, 1981). See also note 15.
15. 'Una reunión multilateral de planteamientos individuales', El Nacional (Caracas, December 1, 1981); 'Se vió amenazada la formación de un organismo negociador frente a Estados Unidos', El Mundo (Panama, December 3, 1981); 'Grave crisis política supera el SELA', UP Press Report (Panama, December 2, 1981); 'Concluyó la Reunión del SELA', El Universal (Caracas, December 3, 1981).
16. Rapporteur's Report of the Meeting of High-Level Government Representatives convened to consider the coercive economic measures applied against a Member State by a group of industrialized countries (SELA, doc. SP/CL/VIII.O/DT No. 35, Caracas, August

6, 1982), pp. 57-58.

17. Ibid., pp. 4-12.

18. Decisions Nos. 112, 113, 114 and 116 of the Eighth Regular Meeting of the Latin American Council (SELA, doc. CL/VIII.O/DF No. 1, Caracas, August 25, 1982).

19. Alejo y Hurtado, p. 27.

20. Latin America: towards a new approach in economic relations with the United States of America (SELA, doc. SP/RC/AL-EU/I/ DT No. 1, Caracas, September 16, 1981), pp. 74-75.

21. Ibid.

22. Boletín de Prensa conjunta SELA-OEA (SELA, Secretaría Permanente, Caracas, 14 Julio,1982) No. 208, p. 1.

23. Stephen D. Krasner, 'Power structures and regional development banks', International Organization 35(1982):304. Also see Lars Shoultz, 'Politics, economics and US participation in multilateral development banks', International Organization 36(1982): 572-574.

24. 'El SELA propone solución global a deuda externa regional" (AP Press Report, Bogota, November 9, 1982).

7
Proliferation of Weaponry and Technology

Michael A. Morris and Martin Slann

ARMS PROLIFERATION TRENDS

There is a gradual but very definite trend toward militarization in Latin America. This trend is highlighted by the proliferation of both conventional arms and military technology, and is amply encouraged by numerous foreign suppliers as well as by the regional arms recipients themselves. Such a pattern poses quite complex obstacles for controlling weaponry proliferation and conflicts.

Proliferation in Latin America is two-fold: the all-familiar proliferation which involves the transfer of conventional weaponry, much of it quite sophisticated, and the diffusion of military technology, both conventional and nuclear. The transfer of conventional weaponry involves an attempt by Latin American governments, including all of the major ones, to modernize their military capabilities. Expansion of military capabilities is also a goal in a number of instances, as in the case of Mexico, whose relatively small military establishment is being expanded as well as modernized. And, secondly, the proliferation of military technology involves the development of national armament production as well as the development of indigenous nuclear energy programs that, while ostensibly for peaceful purposes, have at least partial military application with results that are far from predictable.

The convergence of recipient demand and supplier-fed demand for weaponry has led to an escalating pattern of militarization. Most states in Latin America are experiencing a clear move from smaller to larger military budgets and from imports of less to more sophisticated weaponry. A few states in the region are moving from arms imports to domestic production of some arms, and, in the foreseeable future, from national self-sufficiency to arms exports; and, finally, perhaps inevitably if current tension continues, from conventional to nuclear weapons.

Each of these elements of the pattern has a self-contained dynamic or rationale toward greater militarization, and all of the elements together tend to be mutually intensifying. There has been in recent years, for example, a steadily rising arms expenditure by most states in the region (as exemplified by the leading countries in Tables 7.1 and 7.3). And the governments of

117

several major Latin American spenders, notably Argentina and Brazil, are substantially encouraging the growth of a national arms industry. Brazil, for example, has even begun to export nationally produced arms in substantial quantities, as Tables 7.5 and 7.6 graphically illustrate. Also impressive is the growth of national nuclear power industries (Table 7.8), particularly those of Argentina and Brazil with attendant proliferation of nuclear technology. These, however, have been quite dependent upon external expertise and assistance, with the notable exception of Argentina and more recently of Brazil as well.

Of course, this escalating pattern of militarization can be observed throughout the Third World. Latin America, however, stands out for several reasons. 1) The quantity of arms imports, while much smaller than that of the Middle East (Figure 7.1), is larger than that of other Third World regions, save North Africa. 2) The potential for increased militarization is also substantial in relation to other Third World regions. Overall Latin American military spending is still moderate with respect to other Third World regions (Tables 7.1 and 7.2), although Latin America's position as a middle income region permits considerably heavier military burdens to be shouldered. There is no apparent relationship between military burden and the six spending categories, except that only a few Latin American states appear to be straining national resources in sustaining the existing military establishment (Table 7.10). 3) Latin America is increasingly a conflict-prone area as old disputes flare up and new ones emerge. 4) While the region has been relatively isolated from the Cold War in modern times, with the notable exception of Cuba, by the early 1980s ideological and political polarization was increasing. 5) Latin America is a quite significant arms producer and exporter itself, at least in the context of the Third World (Tables 7.5 and 7.6). 6) At least two of the region's most important rivals, Argentina and Brazil, are generally agreed to be on the threshold of nuclear weaponry potential.

The trend toward increased militarization is shared by most countries in the region, but is dominated by the larger countries (Table 7.3). Obviously, the larger and/ or wealthier states are the ones that can afford to pursue large-scale militarization and these are the ones that are doing so. For example, the seven states in categories 1 and 2 have been spending more than 85 per cent of the regional total and have imported more than 80 per cent of the weaponry in value terms (Tables 7.3 and 7.4). The spending gap between these regional leaders and the remaining states in categories 3-6 is dramatized in Table 7.3 by horizontal double lines separating the upper and lower ranks. States in categories 3-4 likewise spend considerably more than those in categories 5-6, so the gap between them is similarly emphasized by

horizontal double lines. It should be emphasized that
the six categories of 19 states exclude about a dozen
mini-states in and around the Caribbean basin, whose military establishments are negligible for all practical
purposes.

Motives for the escalating pattern of militarization
particularly include recipient demand and supplier-fed
demand. There are ample supplier rationales for promoting sales of conventional arms. 1) There are no international treaties that prohibit either the manufacture
or purchase of conventional arms. 2) Industrialized
states, both western and communist, have found the arms
trade to be profitable, so that they are generally economic competitors. 3) These states have comparatively
less reluctance to sell or provide conventional arms
technology than nuclear technology. 4) Smaller arms
suppliers are especially eager to market their products,
in order to maintain a viable national arms industry.
5) The proliferation of conventional arms does not out-
wardly seem to threaten the collapse of the international
system, as nuclear proliferation implies. 6) In fact,
the two superpowers have regarded conventional arms exports and associated military ties as an important tool
in their Cold War arsenals for influencing Third World
states.

The major Western European powers have felt free to
compete in the highly lucrative trade of selling nuclear
technology for peaceful purposes, and US policy during
the Reagan administration has been more permissive in
this respect as well. While there are restraints on the
proliferation of nuclear technology for peaceful purposes,
they are often vague and uncertain.

All of these rationales have special application to
Latin America. While the United States was the major arms
supplier to the region during the early part of the postwar period, especially because of sizable transfers of
surplus weaponry, by the mid-1960s recipient demand for
more sophisticated weaponry was increasing. US policy
at the time discouraged purchase of new, high-technology
weaponry by Latin American states, so, as a result, an
arms vacuum for relatively sophisticated weapons was
created that the United States was unsuccessful in discouraging other supplier-countries from filling. In view
of recurring US arms restraints and embargoes, there was
also an understandable desire on the part of states in
the region to diversify their arms supplies away from the
traditional regional hegemon. Latin America is accordingly a region of special interest because of the great
diversity of and competition between arms suppliers, both
for sophisticated conventional weaponry and arms technology as well as for technical assistance in the development of peaceful nuclear research and installations.

Both the United States and Western European countries,

such as West Germany, Britain, and France compete with one another, as well as with the Soviet Union and even Israel, to become the primary suppliers of expensive arms and technical assistance (Tables 7.4 and 7.8). Brazil, too, has targeted its own region as a key market for its burgeoning arms industry, which exported about $1 billion globally in 1981. This diversity of suppliers, with many suppliers providing in at least one or two countries in Latin America, contrasts with a more prominent superpower role in the Third World as a whole as arms suppliers (Figure 7.2).

Countries in Latin America also tend to be interested in acquiring nuclear technology for reasons of national pride and prestige, as well as for the possible contribution to national energy needs. While there are yet no nuclear powers in Latin America, there is a proliferation of nuclear technology to the region, and the two regional leaders in the field, Argentina and Brazil, have been reluctant to endorse nuclear arms control measures, both regional and global (Tables 7.8 and 7.9). Moreover, Argentina was militarily defeated in 1982 by a nuclear power, Britain, and alluded at the time to the potential need in the future to exercise a nuclear option.

This context clearly indicates a desire on the part of both Argentina and Brazil to possess a nuclear weaponry option, although their actual development of nuclear weaponry is not necessarily inevitable. The desire to possess a nuclear capability option is really quite consistent with what has already become an escalating conventional arms race in Latin America.

The more advanced and larger countries of Latin America are tending to follow an emerging Third World pattern with respect to arms suppliers even more rapidly than elsewhere in the developing world -- those few countries willing as well as able to do so are intent on becoming self-sufficient in arms and will attempt to utilize outside resources to that end in the hope of eventually becoming independent of these resources. A related impetus to both arms acquisition and self-sufficiency (and, for some, nuclear capability) has to do with disputes with extra-regional states. Argentina's conflict with Britain over the Malvinas in 1982 has been mentioned, as has the gradual deterioriation of inter-American ties between the United States and several Latin American states. Also the trend toward ideological and political polarization, either directly through heightened involvement of the Soviet Union in the hemisphere or via Cuba as a proxy state, constitutes a further motivation for regional militarization and resulting national military autonomy.

Rivalries among Latin American states themselves are perhaps an even more widespread motivation for militarization. Argentina, for example, in addition to its dispute with Great Britain, has a protracted dispute with Chile, which in turn involves it in the west coast dispute between Chile, Bolivia and Peru. Moreover, Argentina and Brazil have been traditional rivals for leadership in South America.

Rather than catalogue current Latin American disputes, both extra- and intra-regional, we may instead note that these disputes involve states in all 6 spending categories (Table 7.3). As for the top-ranking states in categories 1 and 2, their disproportionate share of spending and arms imports has been noted and all seven states in these two categories are involved in extra-and, or intra-regional disputes. Even disputes involving states in the lower, modest spending categories, such as El Salvador in category 4, obviously can have serious international implications.

Another unsettling factor is that several major countries in the region are increasingly eager to take their places as prominent, powerful members of the international system. And, to compound an already complex situation, the United States is no longer fully able to impose a pervasive amount of hemispheric order. The potential for conflict and resulting militarization in Latin America, then, is substantial.

What the data emphatically make clear is that the proliferation of conventional arms and nuclear technology is intricately linked, and threatens to aggravate an already conflict-prone milieu. Thus, the arms control implications of one can hardly be fully considered without the other. Any effective strategy for controlling proliferation of armaments and technology in Latin America must consider both conventional and nuclear proliferation in tandem. Obviously, this dual-pronged proliferation makes arms control more difficult to achieve, yet recognition of the urgent need to halt further militarization in the region will be a first step toward an effective strategy for controlling the sources of armaments.

CONVENTIONAL ARMS CONTROL

Greater attention has been paid to nuclear technology proliferation in Latin America and more success has achieved in controlling it than in the case of the conventional arms buildup in the region. While the Treaty of Tlatelolco has achieved a certain measure of success in constraining nuclear technology proliferation, recurring talks involving both recipient and supplier restraints on conventional arms have had meager results (Table 7.7).

As for recipient restraints, the bulk of the regional arms buildup has occurred among states in the upper two spending categories, so restraint must naturally begin there. The signatories of the 1974 Declaration of Ayacucho do include most of the big spenders in the

region, with the exception of Brazil, but another chapter
in this volume demonstrates that these states have con-
tinuously built up their conventional military arsenals
in the interim (Chapter 9).

Brazil's military spending and arms imports have
been moderate in view of its considerable economic potential, although sizable resources have been absorbed
by the national armaments industry. Since this thriving
industry has been extremely costly to develop (according
to one estimate, $5+ billion)[1], the extent of the over-
all national military buildup has been considerable.
Moreover, the emergence of Brazil as an alternative regional arms supplier considerably complicates arms control efforts. Were the multi-billion dollar West German-
Brazilian nuclear power contract included as well, mili-
tary-related expenditures would swell still more. It is
accordingly imperative that Brazil become associated more
closely with the recurring, although sporadic, regional
talks about conventional arms control.

States in the lower spending categories may not be able
to sustain sizable military modernization programs, but
they may still be able to acquire sufficient weaponry to
provoke widespread destabilizing effects. This is most
evidently the case in Central America, where a relatively limited arms buildup by small, contiguous states has
contributed to an international crisis. The October
1982 Declaration on Democracy in Central America, which
has an important arms control thrust, is encouraging.
However, it occurred only after unprecedented militarization and polarization of the region had been accelerating over several years (Table 7.7).

Regional states have tended to shirk responsibility
for controlling their own arms buildup by emphasizing the
need to control the far more impressive conventional and
nuclear buildup of the great powers. As Latin American
states become more autonomous in their international dealings, especially the larger ones, such rationalizations
become less convincing, since numerous regional initiatives in conventional arms control are feasible. A variety of confidence-building measures in the military field
would help provide a more propitious setting for regional
initiatives in conventional arms control (Chapter 5).

There is, for example, a need to enforce existing
arms restraint guidelines, especially those of the
Declaration of Ayacucho. Past arms control efforts could
also be reinforced by extending regional talks about conventional arms control to all states in the region on a
regularized basis. This in turn would facilitate elaboration of additional arms restraint guidelines.

Similar restraints also need to be developed for
national military production and related exports. The
rapprochement between Argentina and Brazil, the two leading arms producers in the region, could be a positive

development for regional peace. At the same time, important aspects of bilateral cooperation, especially plans
for joint military production and nuclear energy development, may promote weaponry development more than arms
control.

There is likewise a need to relate conventional arms
restraints to conflict resolution mechanisms, particularly since chronic, unresolved disputes, such as the
Malvinas/Falklands crisis, trigger arms buildups (Chapter
10). Finally, conventional arms restraints need to be
coordinated with controls on the proliferation of nuclear
technology.

While such restraints will be difficult to negotiate,
several existing restraints should be emphasized. The
region has been fairly moderate in Third World terms
both with respect to overall military spending and fre-
quency of conflicts, and ultimately regional self-
restraint is responsible for this moderation. Of course,
the on-going Central American crises, the 1981 Ecuadorian-
Peruvian conflict, and the 1982 Falklands war all point
toward increased militarization and strife in the region.

Money is another restraint that will continue to
limit conventional arms acquisitions by Latin American
states in all spending categories. For example, the
three largest and most developed Latin American states,
Argentina, Brazil, and Mexico were all experiencing severe financial crises in 1982 and 1983. In spite of
financial restraints, the regional arms buildup has nonetheless continued. Accordingly informal and circum-
stantial restraints on regional arms buildups urgently
need to be reinforced through formal, enforceable arms
control agreements.

The United States did make some conventional arms
control initiatives during the Carter Administration,
but the overall record of supplier restraint has been
poor (Table 7.7). The reluctance of other suppliers to
restrain their conventional arms sales to Latin America
in fact contributed to a reversal of US policy during
the Reagan Administration. The proliferation of arms
suppliers to Latin America, with Brazil as a new regional
entrant to the market, threatens to complicate supplier
controls even more than before.

Nonetheless, a new setting, with distinctive opportunities and obstacles for supplier restraint, may be
emerging. Latin American states have long been resentful
of various kinds of US arms embargoes and restraints,
and they have become even more wary of foreign arms
sources since the US and Western European arms embargo of
Argentina during the 1982 Falklands war. The result promises to be greater emphasis on regional arms production
and greater reliance on regional arms exporters. While
more locally produced arms may simply reorient the source
of regional militarization, the tradition of regional

military moderation might have a greater impact if arms acquisition were to depend less on extra-regional sources.

It would be ironic if the developed state arms suppliers, who fancy themselves as more responsible than Third World recipients, would only be restrained because of recipient-imposed controls. In any event, jointly developed and coordinated recipient and supplier arms control guidelines offer greatest promise. Until formal, conventional arms control agreements can be forged, with an enforcement mechanism at least as developed as that of the Treaty of Tlatelolco, supplier-recipient relations might be restrained through existing regional and hemispheric institutions (Chapter 6).

There are some powerful incentives for arms control guidelines on the supplier side, although other incentives naturally pull suppliers toward sales as well. Most of the major suppliers have a considerable stake in Latin American stability, so that the destabilizing potential of unrestrained arms sales policies may of necessity lead to greater interest in developing arms control guidelines.

For example, the large US stake in Latin American stability is well known and recent US policy toward Central America, at least, appears to be emphasizing political conciliation more and militarization of the conflict less than previously. The United States likewise has responded imaginatively to the 1982-1983 financial crises in Argentina, Brazil, and Mexico and to this extent may be coming to regard economic problems as more threatening to regional stability than military problems.

Soviet aims in Latin America differ from those of Western suppliers. However, the Soviet Union still might be induced to cooperate in observing guidelines for arms control in the region were similar guidelines accepted for other Third World regions. Internal US bureaucratic squabbles in the late 1970s in fact undermined this apparently reasonable approach to regional arms control, which President Carter had himself previously approved, and constituted one factor contributing to the collapse of the US-USSR CAT talks (Table 7.7).[2]

CONTROL OF NUCLEAR TECHNOLOGY PROLIFERATION

Latin America is currently the only populated nuclear-free zone in the world. (Antarctica is also a nuclear-free zone, but understandably lacks a permanent population.) Most Latin American states are full adherents to the Treaty of Tlatelolco, which is a pioneer in the area of regional nuclear arms control (Table 7.9). In the decade and a half since the Treaty was first promulgated, no nuclear programs of overt military significance have been undertaken by any Latin American governments and several regional states, particularly Mexico,

have consistently advocated arms control. All of the
world's nuclear powers (plus The Netherlands) have signed
and ratified Protocols I an II, with the exception of
France. France has not ratified Protocol I, principally
because it considers the remaining French possessions in
the Caribbean to be part of France with the prerogative
to move or establish nuclear devices on those portions of
French territory if and when it so wishes. (India has
not signed the Protocols, but is not considered a nuclear
power with any direct interests in Latin America.)

A nuclear free zone in Latin America should be eas-
ier to sustain than elsewhere in the Third World. Latin
American states, as noted above, enjoy a qualified tradition of moderation in military affairs. Moreover, nuclear
weapons have yet to become a part of the security posture
of any country in the region. The opposite may well be
the case in the Middle East and in South Asia where several countries either have already acquired nuclear weapons, such as India, or have expressed a serious interest
in doing so. Israel in particular is widely, and probably accurately, suspected of having the capability of
quickly assembling nuclear weapons.

While the intensity of the Arab-Israeli and Indo-
Pakistani rivalries appears sufficient to escalate to
the acquisition of nuclear weaponry by the key actors,
militarization in Latin America has occurred in a less
explosive context. Argentina and Brazil, the two leading nuclear weaponry candidates in the region, would be
politically and militarily significant without becoming
nuclear powers. While these two Southern Cone powers
have historically been rivals, in modern times the rivalry has been low-key. Moreover, since 1980 there has
been a trend toward rapprochement between these two
neighbors, including nuclear energy collaboration (Table
7.8).

Most Third World countries, including those of Latin
America, appear genuinely reluctant to acquire nuclear
weapons because of the cost involved and the reasonable
desire to avoid becoming a target for another state's nuclear weapons. This reluctance remains a strong regional
incentive to avoid proliferation. A nuclearized Latin
America, it appears to all concerned, would be considerably less stable than the present situation.

The extent of nuclear arms control in Latin America
will ultimately depend on the policies of Argentina and
Brazil, the two regional powers with greatest potential
for developing nuclear capabilities in the near future.
Their approaches to the Treaty of Tlatelolco have in
some respects not been encouraging (Table 7.9), although
the regional nuclear-free zone does appear to have influenced their policies. While both states have decidedly
kept their nuclear weaponry option open, neither state
has rejected the treaty approach and neither has made a

concerted drive to achieve nuclear weapons as soon as
possible. In part, as suggested, this restraint is due
to self-interest, since neither state desires to reactiv-
ate the historical bilateral rivalry, which would surely
occur should either go nuclear. The role of lesser Latin
American states has been a restraint as well, since many
have heartily endorsed the Treaty. The support of the
nuclear powers for the Treaty has constituted another
restraint.

Nonetheless, developed state suppliers have willing-
ly, and at times enthusiastically, supplied both Argentina
and Brazil with nuclear technology that has potential
military application. The Carter non-proliferation restraints proved impotent in such a permissive milieu,
and the Reagan guidelines for nuclear technology transfers have themselves been fairly permissive.

While outside suppliers have supported Latin
America's status as a nuclear-free zone through their endorsement of the Treaty of Tlatelolco, restraints must
extend to their nuclear technology transfer policies as
well. Full-scope safeguards already exist, as administered by the International Atomic Energy Agency, and
should be observed unequivocally by both suppliers and
recipients.

Since Argentina is generally considered to have the
potential to develop nuclear weapons by the mid-1980s
and Brazil shortly thereafter, renewed attention to nuclear technology proliferation in the region is imperative. Even as both states move toward the nuclear weaponry threshold, it is not inevitable that the region will
become nuclearized. Direct and indirect approaches involving both conventional and nuclear arms control should
be emphasized.

An indirect approach to nuclear arms control could
occur through lower-level conflict containment, particularly conventional arms control and resolution of specific regional conflicts. An increasingly militarized and
conflict-prone Latin America threatens to heighten the
probability that a regional state will eventually go
nuclear. The 1982 Falklands Islands conflict is a case
in point (Table 7.8). A direct approach is required as
well because of the distinctive dynamics and potential
destabilizing effects of nuclear technology proliferation.
Failure to curb this proliferation process short of nuclear weaponry would significantly contribute to regional
militarization and tension. Because of linkages between
conventional and nuclear arms control, it is all the more
important to reinforce the region's nuclear-free status
and develop significant controls on nuclear technology
proliferation to the region.

128

NOTES (of appendix)

1. See Michael Brzoska, "Arms Transfers Data Sources," The Journal of Conflict Resolution: Research on War and Peace between and within Nations, 26, (March, 1982), 78. For a brief but quite useful comparison of the three sources see Edward T. Fei, "Understanding Arms Transfers and Military Expenditures: Data Problems," in Stephanie G. Neumann and Robert E. Harkavy, Arms Transfers in the Modern World, (New York: Praeger, 1978), pp. 42-43.

2. Fei, 43.

3. Ibid., 42.

TABLE 7.1
Military Expenditure Summary (in Constant 1979 Price Figures) in Six Developing Areas, 1972-1981

	1972	1973	1974	1975	1976	1977	1978	1979	1980	1981
1) Middle East										
Total	12,320	17,249	24,909	30,784	34,037	33,043	33,432	(34,918)	(36,396)	[43,950]
Egypt	1,788	3,297	3,642	3,536	3,074	3,218	[2,041]	[1,714]	[1,539]	--
Iran	2,891	3,982	8,801	11,230	12,178	9,867	9,165	[5,080]	[4,040]	--
Israel	2,531	(3,577)	(3,632)	(3,868)	(3,866)	(3,862)	(3,437)	(3,540)	[2,462]	--
S. Arabia	2,700	3,447	(4,248)	(6,497)	(8,747)	(9,447)	[11,717]	[15,587]	[18,474]	[22,458]
2) South Asia										
Total	4,601	4,154	3,969	4,356	4,931	4,774	4,969	5,037	[5,480]	[5,587]
India	3,455	3,029	2,839	3,195	3,695	3,508	3,654	3,690	(3,988)	(3,991)
Pakistan	1,070	1,000	998	1,003	1,006	1,025	1,081	1,095	1,212	1,307
3) Far East*										
Total	7,875	8,733	9,680	10,815	12,360	13,470	15,074	15,232	15,812	17,193
Indonesia	[952]	[1,221]	[1,333]	[1,659]	[1,663]	1,608	1,729	1,650	1,261	1,426
N. Korea	1,428	1,418	1,771	2,120	2,341	(2,410)	2,667	2,915	3,128	3,424
S. Korea	1,108	1,120	1,428	1,652	2,373	2,819	3,515	3,300	3,477	3,519
Thailand	564	531	499	679	738	828	842	972	949	1,036

*Japan's figures, while included in SIPRI totals for the Far East, are excluded from this table since its high level of economic development argues against its inclusion in Third World analyses.

4) Africa										
Total	6,519	6,795	8,525	(10,219)	(11,250)	(11,358)	(11,468)	[11,690]	[12,450]	[13,600]
Nigeria	1,805	1,987	2,185	3,265	2,786	2,662	2,095	1,845	1,869	--
S. Africa	830	1,015	1,360	1,670	2,066	2,336	2,250	2,153	2,108	2,254
5) Central America										
Total	1,094	1,152	1,226	1,366	1,647	1,950	2,085	2,158	2,134	2,299
Cuba	337	341	356	(412)	--	886	992	1,064	1,026	1,065
Mexico	472	527	562	612	641	625	633	565	704	782
6) S. America										
Total	4,737	4,854	5,645	5,159	7,240	7,193	7,249	7,351	[6,512]	[6,352]
Argentina	1,600	1,248	1,471	[814]	2,702	2,255	2,339	2,641	2,126	2,241
Brazil	1,496	1,778	1,806	1,799	2,149	2,033	2,089	1,785	1,265	1,234
7) Third World Total (Total of #1 through 6 above)										
	37,144	42,737	53,454	62,699	71,465	71,788	73,677	76,386	79,784	88,981

Source: Adapted from World Armaments and Disarmaments, SIPRI Yearbook, 1982 (London: Taylor and Francis Ltd., 1982) pp. 143 ff.

Notes: ( ) = SIPRI estimates
         [ ] = Imputed values, with a high degree of uncertainty

TABLE 7.2
Military Expenditures of Middle East and Latin America as Percentage of Third World, 1972-1981

	1972	1973	1974	1975	1976	1977	1978	1979	1980	1981
Middle East	33	40	47	49	48	46	45	46	46	49
Latin America	16	14	13	11	12	13	13	12	11	10
	—	—	—	—	—	—	—	—	—	—
Total	49	54	60	60	60	59	58	58	57	59

Source: Derived from entries 1, 5 and 6 in Table 7.1.

TABLE 7.3
Latin American Military Expenditure Hierarchy

Category	Annual Range	Hierarchy	Annual 1977-1981 Mean (in Millions)		Group Share of Regional Spending (in %) (rounded from column 4)
			By Country	By Category	
1	$1 billion or over	Argentina	$2320	$1690	57
		Brazil	1680		
		Cuba	1070		
2	$550-900 million	Chile	$861	$695	31
		Venezuela	713		
		Mexico	652		
		Peru	555		
3	$100-225	Columbia	$226	$169	8
		Ecuador	190		
		Uruguay	150[1]		
		Dom. Rep.	109[2]		
4	$70-90	Bolivia	91[3]	$83	3
		Guatemala	87[3]		
		El Salvador	70		
5	$35-50	Paraguay	48[3]	$42	1
		Guyana	37[1]		
6	$21-30	Honduras	32[1]	$27	1
		Jamaica	28[4]		
		Costa Rica	22		

Source: Derived from SIPRI Yearbook, 1982, pp. 144-145.

[1] 1977-78 only.
[2] Excludes 1981.
[3] 1977-1979 only.
[4] 1977 only.

TABLE 7.4
Latin American Arms Suppliers and Recipients by Category

Category	Country	Value of Arms Imports 1975–1979 (constant 1978 dollars)	Leading Arms Suppliers 1975-1979 (in %)
1	Argentina	934	France (27.70)
	Brazil	777	United Kingdom (54.01)
	Cuba	885	Soviet Union (100.00)
		2,596 (45.99%)	
2	Chile	394	United States (28.95)
	Venezuela	422	Italy (26.83)
			United States (26.83)
	Mexico	79	United Kingdom (57.14)
	Peru	1,157	Soviet Union (59.01)
		2,052 (36.35%)	
3	Colombia	85	West Germany (57.14)
	Ecuador	599	France (48.70)
	Uruguay	35	United States (25.00)
	Dom. Republic	0	
		719 (12.74%)	
4	Bolivia	105	United States (9.1)
	Guatemala	57	United States (40.00)
	El Salvador	37	France (75.00)
		199 (3.53%)	

5	Paraguay	15	United States (25.00)
	Guyana	$\frac{0}{15}$ (.003%)	United Kingdom (50.00)
6	Honduras	64	United States (20.00)
	Jamaica	0	---
	Costa Rica	$\frac{0}{64}$ (.011%)	---
Total		5,645	

Source: Columns 1 and 2 are from Table 7.3 of this article. Columns 3 and 4 are derived from World Military Expenditures and Arms Transfers, 1970-1979, (Washington, D.C. U.S. Arms Control and Disarmament, Agency, 1982), Tables II and III, pp. 85 ff. and 127 ff.

TABLE 7.5
Six Largest Third World Major Exporting Countries, 1979-80

Exporting Country	Percent of Total Third World Exports
1. Brazil	45.6
2. Israel	21.1
3. Libya*	12.3
4. South Korea	8.2
5. Egypt	6.2
6. Saudi Arabia*	1.6
Others	5.0

Source: Adapted from SIPRI Yearbook, 1982, p. 188.

*Arms exports of Libya and Saudi Arabia are almost exclusively re-exports from developed states rather than indigenous arms production.

TABLE 7.6
Orders of the Two Leading Third World Arms Exporters, 1981

Exporter	Developed Countries	Developing Countries
Brazil	A = 46	A = 38 AV = 872 W = 10
Israel	A = 4	A = 46 W = 6 M = 108

Source: Adapted from SIPRI Yearbook, 1982, Appendix 6.B., pp. 194 ff. Abbreviations: Letters stand for the following:
A - aircraft
AV - armoured vehicles
M - missiles
W - warships

Note: These figures are for one year only. The overall trend of diversification of weapons exports is reflected in both cases but not bilateral military relationships.

Table 7.7.
Analytical Chronology of Conventional Arms Control Measures in
Latin America

Recipient Restraints:
  1967: Declaration of Punta del Este - presidents of Latin
American states express their intention to avoid expenditures that
are not indispensible for the performance of their armed forces.
  9 December 1974: Declaration of Ayacucho - the parties to the
Declaration (Argentina, Bolivia, Chile, Colombia, Ecuador, Panama,
Peru, and Venezuela) agree to promote and support the building of
a lasting order of international peace and cooperation, and to create
conditions permitting an effective limitation of armaments and
putting an end to their acquisition for offensive purposes.
  22 June 1978: Declaration of Washington - Ayacucho signatories
reiterate the need to promote establishment of conditions conducive
to an effective limitation of armaments in order that all possible
resources be devoted to economic and social development in Latin
America. The Declaration is welcomed by the Carter Administration,
since it echoes the arms control policy of the U.S. government in
the Third World.
  21-24 August 1978: Mexico City conference deals with the problem of conventional arms control in Latin America with twenty governments represented, including Cuba (the main exception being
Brazil).
  1979: Cartegena Mandate - Andean countries establish political
machinery for a pluralistic approach to cooperation for regional
integration and peace.
  September 1980: Adoption of Charter of Conduct - stresses the
need for peaceful settlement of disputes and to begin the implementation of the principles of Ayacucho.
  4 October 1982: The Declaration on Democracy in Central America
calls for various arms limitation measures (signed by Belize,
Colombia, Costa Rica, the Dominican Republic, El Salvador,
Honduras, Jamaica, and the United States).
Supplier Restraints:
  13 May 1977: Carter Administration statement of arms control
guidelines emphasizes multilateral cooperation among both arms suppliers and recipients to deemphasize and restrict conventional arms
transfers to Third World countries. However, this arms control policy could only be tested unilaterally in view of the lack of both
supplier and recipient restraint, and was consequently implemented
in selective, erratic fashion.
December 1978: A meeting in Mexico City between American and
Soviet delegates, as part of the abortive CAT (Conventional Arms)
talks, explores ways of subjecting arms transfers to arms control
considerations. The United States' attempts to focus this meeting
on arms transfers to Latin America and sub-Saharan Africa are
unsuccessful.

(Table 7.7   Continued)

8 July 1981: Reagan Administration statement of arms control
guidelines substantially reverses the policy of the Carter Administration by emphasizing arms transfers to enhance the ability of
friendly governments to deter aggression and internal unrest (El
Salvador being the most obvious case in point in Latin America).
While this policy rejects unilateral restraint in the transfer of
conventional weapons abroad, multilateral restraints will be
considered.

138

Table 7.8
Analytical Chronology of Proliferation of Nuclear Technology to
Latin America

1950: Argentina is the first Latin American country to create
its own nuclear program.

1 July 1968: Treaty on the Non-Proliferation of Nuclear Weapons (NPT) opened for signature. To date Argentina and Brazil have
refused to sign the NPT, which they consider to be discriminatory
against non-nuclear (but would-be) nuclear powers. Other non-
signatories in Latin America include Chile and Cuba. None of
these states adhere fully either to the Treaty of Tlatelolco
(Table 7.9).

11 February 1971: Sea-bed Treaty prohibiting any nuclear
weapons on the seabed beyond a twelve-mile limit.

3 September 1971: Argentina and Brazil sign Sea-Bed Treaty,
but reaffirm sovereign rights over extensive offshore areas.

January 1974: Argentina's first nuclear power plant begins
operating at Atucha. This is based on natural-uranium technology,
which relieves Argentina from dependence on an external source of
enriched-uranium fuel since Argentina has the largest
known reserves of uranium ore in Latin America. Subsequent measures have been taken by Argentina toward the completion of an independent nuclear fuel cycle based on natural uranium.

27 June 1975: Long term, multi-billion dollar contract announced for West Germany to provide Brazil with a large, self-
contained nuclear power industry with the potential for the manufacture of nuclear weapons. The agreement includes provisions for
the transfer of technology on an incremental basis for a complete
nuclear fuel cycle, which at the time envisaged the largest transfer by far of nuclear technology to the Third World.

29-30 March 1978: President Carter visits Brazil amidst continuing bilateral differences regarding U.S. nuclear nonproli-
feration policy. Brazil reiterates its resentment about U.S.
criticism of its plan to build a uranium reprocessing plant with
West German help that might be used to produce ingredients for
atomic weapons.

1979: Peru contracts to receive an Argentine-built research
reactor.

January 1979: Termination of Argentine and Brazilian nuclear
involvement with Iran after the fall of the Shah.

October 1979: Argentina gives nuclear reactor contract to
the Federal Republic of Germany (West Germany), highlighting long
years of assistance from Germany to both Argentina and Brazil in
nuclear development.

February 1980: Argentina and South Korea (a country on the
"threshold" of nuclear development) sign an agreement for sharing
nuclear power development information.

18 May 1980: Argentina and Brazil sign agreement for nuclear
cooperation and the sharing of information following a state
visit to Argentina by the Brazilian head of government (15 - 17
May).

(Table 7.8   Continued)

August 1980: Argentina and Brazil state specifics of nuclear
cooperation and sharing of information, including the leasing of
uranium concentrate to Brazil by Argentina for Brazil's first nuclear reactor.   In part, this helps overcome Brazil's dependence
on other external uranium sources.

April - June 1982: Press reports claimed that some British
ships operating in the Falklands area during the conflict with
Argentina carried nuclear depth charges, in which case Great
Britain would have been in violation of both Protocols I and II of
the Treaty of Tlatelolco (see Table 7.9).   Great Britain neither
refuted nor confirmed these reports.

2 May 1982: During the Falkland/Malvinas conflict Argentina
suffered its most serious naval casualty of the war when a British
nuclear-powered, hunter-killer submarine torpedoed and sank the
cruiser General Belgrano about 30 miles outside a 200-mile exclusion zone around the islands.   This was the first ship sunk by a
nuclear submarine and, while this was achieved by conventional
torpedoes, a new destabilizing precedent was established.

3 July 1982: Following the Falkland Islands conflict, the
admiral heading the Argentine Atomic Energy Commission indicated
that national security needs might require acquisition of nuclear
submarines and development of nuclear weapons.   This may have been
a statement in the heat of the moment, but it does suggest that an
upward spiral of tension will tend to increase incentives to develop nuclear weaponry.

TABLE 7.9
Analytical Chronology of the Treaty for the Prohibition of Nuclear
Weapons in Latin America (Treaty of Tlatelolco)

Antecedents of the Treaty of Tlatelolco

March   1962:   Mexico declares itself to be a one-nation nuclear
free zone.

29 April 1963:   Joint Declaration of Bolivia, Brazil, Chile,
Ecuador, and Mexico that they are prepared to sign
a multilateral agreement whereby their countries
would not undertake to manufacture, receive, store,
or test nuclear weapons or nuclear launching
devices.
This Declaration is a precursor of REUPRAL (Preliminary Session on the Denuclearization of Latin
America), a larger conference that met the next
year.

November   1964:   REUPRAL meets and creates an ad hoc organ,
COPREDAL (Preparatory Commission for the Denuclearization of Latin America), "to prepare a preliminary draft of a multilateral treaty for the
denuclearization of Latin America,. . . to conduct any prior studies and take any prior steps
that it deems necessary."

March   1965:   COPREDAL has its first session in Mexico City. Three
additional sessions over the next two years coordi-
nated by COPREDAL's Preparatory Commission prepares
the text for the Treaty of Tlatelolco.

Treaty of Tlatelolco

12 February 1967:   Treaty for the Prohibition of Nuclear Weapons
approved by the Preparatory Commission and
opened to signature.

22 April 1968:   Treaty entered into force. The Treaty prohibits
the testing, use, manufacture, production or acquisition as well as the receipt, storage, installation, deployment and any form of possession
of nuclear weapons in Latin America.

June   1969:   Preliminary meeting of OPANAL, an agency established
by Article 28 of the Treaty for the Prohibition of
Nuclear Weapons in Latin America. The purpose of
OPANAL is "to ensure compliance with the obligations"
of the Treaty of Tlatelolco.

(Table 7.9   Continued)

Additional Protocol I: Designed for states with territories in the
                         Treaty zone - France, Great Britain, the
                         Netherlands, and the United States. These
                         states on ratifying agree to "undertake to
                         apply the statute of denuclearization in
                         respect to their territorial possessions."

Additional Protocol II: Designed for nuclear weapons states
                         (China, France, Great Britain, the Soviet
                         Union, and the United States). These
                         states on ratifying agree not to use or
                         threaten to use nuclear weapons against
                         parties to the Treaty.

Protocol I

20 December 1967: Great Britain signs; ratifies 11 December 1969.

15 March 1968: The Netherlands signs; ratifies 26 July 1971.

26 May 1977: United States signs; ratifies 23 November 1981.

2 March 1979: France signs, but has yet to ratify.

Protocol II

20 December 1967: Great Britain signs; ratifies 11 December 1969.

1 April 1968: United States signs; ratifies 12 May 1971.

18 July 1973: France signs; ratifies 22 March 1974.

21 August 1973: China signs; ratifies 12 June 1974.

18 May 1978: Soviet Union signs; ratifies 8 January 1979.

Status of Signature and Ratification of Selected Latin American
    States

14 February 1967: Chile signs Treaty; ratifies 9 October 1974.
                   However, Chile has not waived the requirements
                   for entry into force of the Treaty laid down in
                   Article 28. Thus, the Treaty is not yet
                   binding for Chile.

9 May 1967: Brazil signs Treaty; ratifies 29 January 1968. Like
             Chile, Brazil has not waived the requirements for entry
             into force of the Treaty laid down in Article 28.
             Thus, the Treaty is not yet in force for Brazil.
             Brazil also understands Article 18 to give signatories
             the right to carry out nuclear explosions for peaceful
             purposes, including explosions which involve devices
             similar to those used in nuclear weapons.

27 September 1967: Argentina signs Treaty but does not ratify.
                    Argentina, like Brazil, understands Article 18
                    to recognize the right of signatories to carry
                    out explosions of nuclear devices for peaceful
                    purposes, including explosions which involve
                    devices similar to those used in nuclear
                    devices.

(Table 7.9. Continued)

Current Status

Twenty-five of the region's governments have signed the Treaty; of these 24 have ratified (the exception being Argentina). Cuba is not a party to the Treaty. All of the world's nuclear powers have signed and ratified both Protocols I and II with the exception of France's failure to ratify Protocol I. (India has not signed the Protocols, because it does not consider itself a nuclear power.)

TABLE 7.10
Selected Indicators of Military Burden

Category	Country (by Hierarchical Category)	Mil. Exp. as % of GNP	Milt. Exp. Cer. Govt. Exp. %	Arms Imports Total Imports %	Armed Forces per 1000 People	Economic-Social Standing (of 141 States)
1	Argentina	2.5	17.0	7.9	5.7	44
	Brazil	0.8	4.3	1.0	3.8	59
	Cuba	7.6(1978)	NA	5.2	21.4	34
2	Chile	2.6	12.0	2.8	10.3	47
	Venezuela	1.3	6.4	1.0	3.8	47
	Mexico	.4	2.8	0.0	2.2	58
	Peru	3.9	20.3	5.5	7.3	72
3	Colombia	0.8	10.3	0.5	2.3	68
	Ecuador	1.8	12.0	9.2	4.5	64
	Uruguay	2.2	14.8	0.4	9.7	45
	Dominican Republic	2.0	10.9	0.0	3.4	70
4	Bolivia	2.0	16.6	6.9	3.8	91
	Guatemala	0.9	7.2	0.6	2.1	86
	El Salvador	1.5	9.1	2.9	2.3	82
5	Paraguay	1.2	12.2	1.9	4.8	71
	Guyana	3.2	5.8	0.0	8.8	66

6	Honduras	1.7	8.2	1.2	3.9	92
	Jamaica	2.1	2.1	0.0	0.5	53
	Costa Rica	–	0.0	NA	1.4	52

Sources: Data for this table refer to 1979 and are derived from World Military Expenditures and Arms Transfers, 1970–1979 (Washington, D. C.: U. S. Arms Control and Disarmament Agency, 1981), with the exceptions of the 1978 Cuban figure cited from SIPRI Yearbook, 1982, p. 152, and the economic-social standing for 1979 from Ruth Sivard, ed., World Military and Social Expenditures, 1982 (Leesburg, Virginia: World Priorities, 1982), p. 30. The 1979 economic-social ranking by Ruth Sivard is based on GNP per capita, education, and health of 141 countries.

Figure 7.1

Percent of Arms Imports by Developing Area, 1981

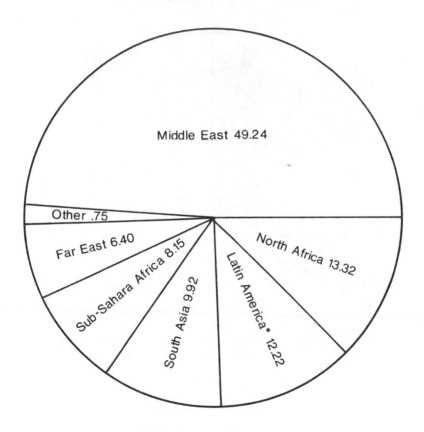

Middle East 49.24

Other .75

Far East 6.40

Sub-Sahara Africa 8.15

South Asia 9.92

Latin America* 12.22

North Africa 13.32

Source: Adapted from

SIPRI Yearbook 1982, p. 191

*The percentage of imports to Central America is 3.77 and to South America 8.5

Figure 7.2
Percent of Arms Exports by Supplier to Third World, 1981

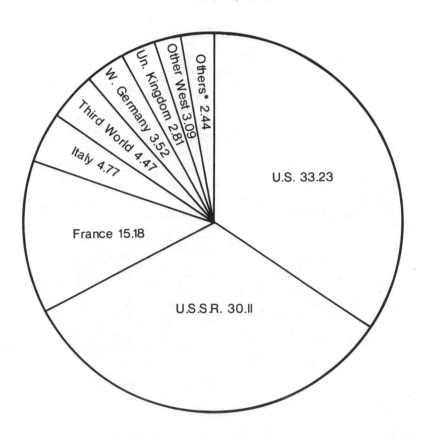

Source: Adapted from

SIPRI Yearbook 1982, p. 193
*Primarily, China and East Europe

8
Naval Arms Control in Latin America

Michael A. Morris

NAVAL ARMS CONTROL

Naval arms and conflicts are distinctive in some important ways so that conflict management of this environment, to be effective, must be adapted to these peculiarities.[1] As for arms, there has been rather steady, if uneven, naval buildup and modernization throughout Latin America over the past decade. This buildup has generally occurred later than that of the other armed services, and has varied in nature and extent from state to state. Increasing divergence in regional navies, with some having undertaken impressive buildups while others have remained weak or impotent, is expressed through a regional naval hierarchy (Table 8.1).

Distinctive aspects of the Latin American naval hierarchy are evident when contrasted with the Latin American military expenditure hierarchy (Table 7.3 and Chapter 7 passim). For example, Cuba's overall military buildup is much more impressive than its naval buildup. Conversely, Argentina has been able to remain on comparable naval terms with Brazil while falling behind in most other areas of military competition. While Argentina's extensive, conflict-prone maritime interests contribute to this distinctive pattern, the prominence of land-based threats vis-a-vis maritime threats help explain the contrasting Cuban force structure.

Uneven, belated naval development has been accompanied by rising interest in control of extensive offshore areas, including exploitation of offshore resources. This has often led to new sources of maritime dispute which have been added to, and at times have accentuated, long-standing maritime disputes. The regional naval buildup consequently threatens to aggravate an already conflict-prone maritime setting, both in the Caribbean basin and in South America.

Several approaches to regional naval arms control -- treaty and non-treaty, explicit and implicit -- have been tried, but with mixed results.

The Tlatelolco Treaty on a regional nuclear-free zone encompasses naval arms control in part, but with very limited results in the ocean sphere so far. Other arms control treaties extending in whole or in part to regional naval affairs (i.e., Seabed Treaty, Antarctic Treaty) have not played a significant role either in halting naval expansion or attenuating maritime disputes in Latin America.

National enclosure can have an arms control impact, and applies to all coastal states in the region as well. This involves mutually agreeable extensions of offshore jurisdiction, including the EEZ (exclusive economic zone), as expressed in the 1982 law-of-the-sea convention. In particular, circumscribed naval expansion for enforcement of widely recognized rights of resource protection can be stabilizing. At the same time, national enclosure has conflictual aspects. As elsewhere, the EEZ itself generates disputes over boundaries and resources in Latin America (see Table 12.2).

Finally, hemispheric defense co-operation has included implicit arms control measures, as well as military measures to enhance defense. For example, international disputes which may arise between member states are to be submitted to the procedures set forth in the Charter of the Organization of American States for the maintenance of continental peace and security.

However, the inter-American system has been characterized by uneven political relations and this has distorted arms control measures. In particular, the United States has traditionally been able to rely on its hegemonial position in the hemispheric defense network to promote its preferred designs of both military co-operation and arms control. As for naval arms control, the United States has relied on the multilateral system of military co-operation to curb local naval arms races, prevent local naval conflicts, impose settlements on naval conflicts once they erupt, ban sophisticated naval arms transfers to the region, encourage ceilings on naval expenditures, and promote preferred missions for regional navies through training of personnel and other measures. In essence, this amounted to unilaterally imposed naval arms control.

Such paternalistic US policies towards the region have been declining rapidly in effectiveness, since the declining US hegemonial position in the hemisphere has tended to limit US influence on Latin American states in this and other matters. The United States has still made continuing attempts to play a hegemonial role in the region, even as its own military and naval involvement there has tended to decline and involvement of extra-regional states has increased.

Rising Latin American determination and ability to charter a more autonomous course in the naval and other spheres has contributed to reduced US ability to impose

its policy preferences on the region. Increasing national military capabilities, alternative arms sources,
and decreasing dependency on the United States all contribute to enhanced regional ability to pursue more autonomous national security policies. In recent years,
the hemispheric defense relationship has accordingly been
characterized as much by tension as by co-operation.

The new strategic setting in the Western Hemisphere
does not imply that Latin American states will either
cease to co-operate with the United States in the naval
sphere or reject naval arms control measures involving
the United States out of hand. But unilaterally imposed
naval arms control measures, like other paternalistic US
policies, are less viable. Latin American states insist
with increasing effectiveness that hemispheric defense
co-operation be in a new, less paternalistic mold, including freedom to determine on their own what appropriate naval arms control measures might be taken.

While a new setting is emerging for naval co-operation and arms control, it would be incorrect to conclude
that US paternalistic policies ever did result in effective regional naval arms control. After all, the main
purpose of hemispheric naval co-operation has not been
arms control but rather deterrence and opposition to any
potential extra-hemispheric aggression by an outside power, especially the Soviet Union. This central military
aim of the inter-American defense relationship has always
meant that unilaterally imposed naval arms control was of
secondary priority for US policy. Of primary importance
was how Latin American naval structure and roles would
best complement the US global military posture.

An uneasy balance therefore existed in US policy between encouragement of and contribution to Latin American
naval development appropriate to hemispheric defense and
unilateral imposition of arms control measures when considered necessary. On the one hand, effective Latin American participation in anti-submarine warfare (ASW) and related high seas defense of sea lanes and convoys have been
the regional naval contributions most preferred by the
United States. Annual UNITAS naval exercises between the
USA and selected Latin American navies have been designed
towards that end. On the other hand, a variety of arms
control and other considerations led the United States to
limit assistance for buildup of naval capabilities in this
area.

As matters stand, US policy has encouraged development of potent coastal defense navies in Latin America
without forging viable naval arms control measures. On
their own, the larger regional navies have often stressed
antisurface warfare capabilities in order to prepare a-
gainst hostile neighbors. Lower-ranking navies with none
of these capabilities have been limited by resource constraints rather than by arms control considerations.

Absent from either the US or Latin American approaches to naval development has been consistent emphasis on naval arms control.

However naval roles and naval structure of regional navies are to evolve, this increasingly depends on local decision-makers, not on the United States. This does not mean that an unrelenting naval buildup will result, since both external and internal naval trends are ambivalent. External powers on occasion have accentuated co-operative, as well as conflictual, aspects of local naval relations, and some important co-operative initiatives have been made in the naval sphere by local powers, in addition to more hostile measures.

In such a complex, changing setting, reassessment of possibilities for naval arms control is necessary. The new context of offshore jurisdiction is a case in point. In the traditional context until at least the 1970s, the United States opposed the national enclosure movement, most particularly as practiced in Latin America, and tried to impose its interests on Latin American states in the naval and other spheres. Faced with these policies and pressures of the hegemonial power of the hemisphere, it was understandable that Latin American states resented US policy while still co-operating willy-nilly in the defense sphere. In contrast, US acceptance of the EEZ and declining US paternalism in the 1970s may contribute to a milieu more propitious for naval arms control in the 1980s. In particular, since some reconciliation and accommodation of US and Latin American EEZ interests has been occurring in recent years, restraint in naval growth may become more palatable for both sides. While the United States has traditionally supported coastal defense roles for regional navies more ambitious than some Latin American states might have chosen on their own, US relative disengagement from regional defense ties tends to lessen this longstanding stimulus for naval growth. The EEZ consensus also reconciles the United States more easily to autonomous Latin American naval development. Latin American navies, for their part, may be attracted to relatively modest EEZ protection roles both to consolidate offshore resources and to adapt to budgetary constraints.

Navies emphasizing coastal patrol/enforcement of the EEZ, rather than coastal defense, would be more compatible with naval arms control. Coastal patrol/enforcement navies set rather clear limits for expansion of navies and of naval roles, and complement the consensus in law on many coastal and foreign state rights and duties out to 200 miles. In contrast, coastal defense navies are better armed and oriented towards more ambitious roles, and tend to be drawn towards ever more open-ended, conflict-prone roles.

Of course, in the new setting, regional ocean

rivalries and disputes pose formidable obstacles for naval arms control. A conflict-prone regional setting propels local states towards naval expansion, and there are few precedents for locally-generated naval arms control.

Naval arms control measures, to be viable, would also need to be integrated with more general arms control approaches restraining overall military developments including land-based as well as maritime conflicts. Such a comprehensive approach is not sketched here although a sectoral approach is, which is complementary to a more general approach. The whole is made up of its parts, so that progress in naval arms control might well contribute to more comprehensive approaches for controlling conflicts. Moreover, a focus on naval conflict and naval conflict resolution in Latin America provides a necessary supplement to the usual East-West naval analysis.

Implications of the Latin American naval milieu for arms control may be specified further by subregion. Table 8.1 subdivides the Latin American naval hierarchy into three subregions (South America, Central America and Caribbean, and South Atlantic), which, while overlapping, are the key arenas for naval arms control. In particular, Caribbean basin and South American navies operate in distinctive geopolitical contexts, have different naval structures, and are distributed differently in the naval hierarchy. Naval arms control measures which adapt to these subregional differences are likely to complement regional arms control approaches.

THE CARIBBEAN BASIN

Until the past several decades, neither naval competition nor naval buildups by local powers troubled politics in the Caribbean Basin. The United States was the predominant external power and local navies were all small and weak and in any event co-operated with the United States through the Inter-American Military System. A 1923 arms control convention between the Central American Republics was a rare instance in which local states set arms limits among themselves, including a ban on acquisition of warships except coastal craft. This treaty unfortunately had no verification or control system and fell into disuse by World War II.

For a variety of reasons, the Caribbean Basin has emerged as a particularly volatile region in the Third World with many potential sources of conflict. Cuba's shift to the Eastern bloc and the increase in Soviet military and naval activities in the Caribbean Basin have contributed to the polarization of regional politics. In the past few years several other regional states have appeared to be potential candidates for a bloc shift as well. For its part, the United States has consistently objected to the extension of Cuban or Soviet influence in the Caribbean Basin, but only in the past several years has it begun to forge a unified regional response on the economic, political and military fronts. The emergence of many new, weak states has also contributed to instability and great power competition in the Caribbean Basin. Finally, a few leading Caribbean Basin states, in addition to Cuba, have recently begun to pursue their own political objectives in the region. As part of more vigorous defense and foreign policies, they have placed greater emphasis on naval development as well. All these factors together tend to aggravate existing maritime disputes and stimulate new areas of naval competition.

There are also some promising co-operative relationships involving Caribbean Basin states in the naval/maritime sphere. For example, with some important exceptions, Caribbean Basin states have made considerable progress in resolving maritime jurisdictional and resource disputes peacefully, with the United States, with US/European territories, and among themselves. Many Caribbean Basin states also supported the 1972 Santo Domingo patrimonial sea declaration, and there was subsequently an active Caribbean role at the law-of-the-sea conference in promoting the patrimonial sea and the related EEZ proposal. Some joint military maneuvers, including naval exercises, have been held between Caribbean Basin states without US participation (i.e., Panama/Venezuela in 1979).

However, these co-operative maritime and naval relationships between Caribbean Basin states are not as important as those between South American states, which reflects greater autonomy and self-sufficiency in South America. Nor are Caribbean Basin co-operative naval relationships as important as conflictual relationships within the area. Moreover, increased co-operation in some instances is specifically oriented against the opposing bloc, and therefore contributes to polarization of regional politics. The Soviet alliance relationship with Cuba, including maritime and naval affairs, is the most prominent example. Cuba itself has given limited security assistance to several Caribbean Basin states, and has provided some technical assistance in fisheries as well but not yet naval assistance.

Constructive naval and maritime co-operation between Caribbean Basin states is nevertheless of increasing importance. This may contribute to resolution of local disputes and help limit great power polarization of regional politics. Both larger and smaller local states may contribute to regional stability without reliance on outside powers, and Mexico and Venezuela indeed aspire to such a role. Even a small state, Panama, in association with other powers, has been able to contribute to regional stability through responsible management of the canal.

In their totality, such co-operative measures may assist
the emergence of a more stable, mutually acceptable regional order.

Moreover, the modest coastal patrol and defense emphasis of all Caribbean Basin navies is compatible in
principle with nonprovocative, mutually acceptable EEZ
enforcement. National enclosure as arms control can result if Caribbean Basin states can continue to abstain
from ambitious naval arms buildups and naval arms races.
In this respect, the prospect for arms control is less
optimistic in South America, where large coastal defense
navies continue to expand along ambitious lines and naval
arms races recur.

SOUTH AMERICA

Practically all of the Southern Cone countries have
a conflict-prone maritime setting. Old maritime disputes
and rivalries continue and have even been aggravated by
extended ocean zones; ocean security interests have been
expanding; and the means to sustain maritime conflict
have been escalating. Shifting patterns of involvement
of outside powers contribute to the fluidity of the maritime setting. The interlocking nature of on-going disputes further complicates attempts to contain and resolve
disputes. Consequently, conflictual naval relationships
in the region overshadow co-operative ones.

There are nevertheless developments and approaches
which can promote containment and management of regional
naval disputes. In particular, there is an impressive
variety of co-operative maritime and naval relationships.
For example, bilateral co-operation includes Argentine-
Brazilian joint naval exercises, River Plate development,
and limited co-operation between indigenous armaments
industries. Chile, Ecuador, and Peru also have longstanding coordination of law-of-the-sea and offshore resource policies, with military implications. Another co-
operative example is CAMUS, which is a shipping control
organization to keep track of shipping in the western
half of the South Atlantic (Argentine, Brazil, Paraguay,
and Uruguay) loosely related to the Inter-American
System.

Similarly, the fluidity of the maritime setting opens
the opportunity to strengthen co-operative relationships,
even though change also threatens to trigger conflict.
South American co-operative naval relationships with the
great powers and between local states will be considered
in turn.

South American co-operation with the United States
has traditionally involved strategic dependence of regional navies and militaries on the hemispheric great
power, which particularly rankled fairly sizable, developed South American states. In order to lessen dependency,

most South American states and navies have been moving towards more assertive foreign and naval policies insofar as resources and an altered international context have permitted. While this process of dependency reversal inevitably involves friction and has led to a decline in bilateral and multilateral security ties with the United States, key links such as the Rio Treaty have not been severed. Redefinition and reshaping of hemispheric security relationships, while difficult, may accordingly lead to a more equal and hence mutually satisfactory new context.

Brazil's evolving military and naval relationships with the great powers point towards such a satisfactory reshaping of the traditional context, and constitute a particularly constructive example for other regional states since Brazil is the most prominent regional power (Table 12.4 and Chapter 12 passim). Some other regional states have unfortunately pursued a more conflict-prone path in redefining military and naval relationships with the great powers, such as Peru's shift to Soviet arms in pique at US policy and Argentina's reliance on force in seizing the Falkland Islands in 1982.

As for prospects for naval co-operation between South American states, Brazil again figures large as the most prominent regional power with a rank 1 navy. Brazil's maritime setting has remained the least conflict-prone of all major Southern Cone countries, and its careful, pragmatic course of maritime and naval expansion has constituted an important contrast with the conflictual relationships characterizing much of the rest of the continent. On the east coast of the continent, the emerging Argentine-Brazilian accommodation could give a major impetus to co-operative maritime/naval relationships. On the west coast, Spanish-American fears of Brazilian encroachment into the Amazon and of Brazilian designs on a Pacific port have appeared exaggerated. Argentina, Brazil, Chile, and the United States, as the four guarantor nations of the 1942 Rio de Janeiro peace agreement, in fact, helped settle the 1981 Ecuadorian-Peruvian conflict.

Brazil's naval/maritime expansion does augur problems for regional competitors, but it is not likely to lead to regional hegemony. Brazil has been outdistancing its traditional competitor, Argentina, as well as all other regional states, in naval affairs and other aspects of national power. Argentina has nonetheless been able to maintain its rank 1 naval status in spite of the growing overall power differential, and numerous other regional states have undertaken substantial naval expansion. The traditional Argentine-Brazilian edge over all other regional navies combined has accordingly been narrowing. This could simply intensify naval competition along both coasts of South America, but it also might contribute to

a more stable, autonomous regional order in which many
fairly strong local navies reinforce coastal defense.
Whether the emerging regional order is to tip more towards co-operation or towards conflict will depend on reactions of both local and external powers to regional
naval expansion.

Regional arms production, in which Argentina and
Brazil are leaders, involves similar alternatives. National military production may contribute to regional
militarization if existing disputes and rivalries are
not resolved, but if military production occurs in an
increasingly co-operative, autonomous regional context,
including projected Argentine-Brazilian joint ventures,
restraint could be encouraged. For example, in NATO
joint military production has been encouraged as an important way to cut waste and free resources for other
purposes. In South America, national and joint military
production has been encouraged to lessen traditional dependency on external powers and thereby better promote
legitimate goals of self-determination and self-defense.

Future South American naval structure will be a
touchstone in determining whether regional order is to
be primarily co-operative or conflictual in orientation.
South American navies continue to rely heavily on major
warships as they have in the past, and current naval expansion plans indicate that this emphasis will be projected into the future. The evolution of national military production industries is also towards manufacture
of increasingly larger, more potent warships, and during
the 1980s both Argentina and Brazil aspire to produce
nationally designed submarines. Both states also face
the major decision of whether to replace their aging
aircraft carriers, and both have debated the merits of
acquiring nuclear submarines and other nuclear-powered
warships. This kind of ambitious naval expansion tends
to escalate in expense, spur neighbors towards
similar expansion, and thereby heighten tensions. For
example, Chile's projected purchase of a fairly new aircraft carrier from Great Britain, if culminated, would
likely trigger yet another round of naval spending by
neighbors. The 1980s then threaten to lead to a new
stage of regional naval expansion, intensified local arms
races, and aggravation of multiple maritime disputes.
Greater emphasis on coastal patrol and enforcement of
the EEZ is more compatible with naval arms control and
restraint, and would constitute a particularly constructive alternative for South American navies.

A tradition of regional military restraint, while
generally tacit and partial in nature, may contribute to
more binding or explicit kinds of naval arms control
agreements.

. . . based upon percentage of gross national
product, Latin America spends less on armaments than any other populated world region.

NOTES

1. Ken Nolde, "Arms, Arms Manufacturing, and Arms Limitations in Latin America," a paper presented at the Latin American Studies Association, Bloomington, Indiana, October 17-19, 1980, p. 6.
2. Andrew J. Pierre, The Global Politics of the Arms Race (New York: Princeton University Press, 1980), pp. 288-289, 302.

METHODOLOGICAL APPENDIX 7A

The data analyzed in this essay on military expenditures and conventional arms transfers are primarily derived from the publications of the Stockholm International Peace Research Institute (SIPRI). This source for arms data has been checked against those published by the other major surveyor of arms transfers and military expenditures, the United States Arms Control and Disarmament Agency (ACDA). Another source of information on arms transfers and military expenditures is, of course, the International Institute for Strategic Studies (IISS). But this third source is not considered to be as exhaustive in its investigations as SIPRI and ACDA, mainly because the IISS does not generally try to offer its data in aggregate form for better and more informative comparisons.[1]

Basically, differences occur when estimates are determined by different sorts of data. For example, SIPRI usually goes along with a government's announced arms or defense budget. ACDA, on the other hand, tries to measure the amount of (or changes in) the resources that are allocated in a government's arms budget.[2] Nevertheless, ACDA and SIPRI frequently come up with quite similar conclusions, at least in most years. Sometimes they do not, as in the 1972-1974 period.[3]

The present study relies principally but not exclusive on the SIPRI data mainly because the data are better organized and more comprehensive than the other sources, while being consistent and generally accurate. The SIPRI data are also generally more current. The ACDA and IISS materials have, however, been examined and are integrated into the text where pertinent, as are data from yet other sources on related issues. All three of these sources are useful, but arms transfers and military expenditures are unusually complex activities. The data, as general estimates, are necessarily of limited application. They should be considered with the understanding that they are reliable only in a relative fashion. The data nevertheless do suggest rather definite directions and trends of arms transfers and military expenditures that frequently suggest impressive if tentative conclusions.

> During periods of intense competition,
> Latin American nations have also had the
> maturity to voluntarily restrict naval
> armaments by international agreement. In
> 1904, Argentina and Chile signed the Pacto
> de Mayo, halting a naval arms race.[2]

The Declaration of Ayacucho of 1974 for limiting armament,
including naval weaponry, and subsequent related measures
by the signatory states have likewise been South American
initiatives.

THE SOUTH ATLANTIC

Both the South Atlantic and Antarctica have been
relatively isolated from the Cold War, and regional arms
races and conflicts have been quite restrained. But both
areas are increasingly conflict-prone, and each threatens
to become militarized. In part, this is due to the increasing prominence of disputes involving both great powers and local states. Co-operative arrangements involving great powers and local states, including arms control
agreements, have not contained the proliferation and escalation of disputes and in some cases have even contributed to this.

Some co-operative arrangements are too often adversarial in nature, and to this extent do not promote long-
term stability between states with diverging interests.
This is the case of the Rio Treaty, which includes portions of the South Atlantic and Antarctica, as well as
the proposed SATO (South Atlantic Treaty Organization)
pact for the South Atlantic and adjacent Antarctic waters.
Heightened Cuban and Soviet involvement in Africa, including co-operative maritime and naval arrangements with
African littoral states, also tends to be adversarial in
nature.

The Antarctic Treaty is a genuine arms control agreement which has helped stabilize the region and is not primarily adversarial in nature, at least as far as the
great powers are concerned. But its exclusive nature has
led to disputes between signatories and non-signatories,
and its arms control provisions have not resolved disputes between claimants and nonclaimants nor those between
claimants. Military power and technological expertise
have accordingly continued to shape the larger context
of the Treaty regime.

Protracted negotiations have also not been able to
resolve important disputes, particularly the Beagle Channel and Falkland Islands disputes. The 1982 Falkland
Islands conflict, which is linked to both the South Atlantic and Antarctica, illustrates the risks of allowing
fundamental divergencies in interests to continue unabat-
ed (Chapter 11). Moreover, two major mechanisms for resolving disputes in Latin America, while already in decline, were further undermined by the Falklands conflict.

Conflict resolution in the hemisphere was traditionally encouraged in a variety of ways by the United States and by peaceful settlement procedures set forth in the Charter of the Organization of American States. Strains in inter-American ties caused by the Falklands conflict have contributed further to decline of these two peaceful settlement procedures, particularly in the first case by the abortive US mediation effort and in the second case by the failure to invoke the Rio Treaty against the UK or at least to involve the inter-American system in mutually acceptable peaceful settlement efforts.

It may be concluded that numerous naval relationships, including many co-operative relationships, in the South Atlantic and Antarctica are unstable and threaten to lead to militarization and conflicts in both areas. Some aspects of the status quo are nevertheless constructive and can help contribute to development of a more stable regime in which mutually acceptable arms control arrangements are more prominent.

The Inter-American military system, which has been strained most recently by the Falklands conflict, may still provide a viable framework for US-Latin American co-operation but only if mutual respect and accommodation of interests is stressed. On the one hand, a number of South American states cancelled their participation in the 1982 UNITAS naval exercises with the United States because of differences over the Falklands conflict. On the other hand, these same concerned states participated in the annual Inter-American Naval Conference in October, 1982, in order to try to resolve differences. Both sides accordingly continue to value hemispheric naval co-operation, so that the current crisis may help encourage resolution of underlying differences and provide a stronger basis for constructive co-operation.

Local states may contribute to a more stable, constructive ocean regime in other ways as well. Expansive coastal state security interests have contributed to disputes with great powers (Falkland Islands) and with other local states (Beagle Channel), and need to be tempered. While it is not realistic to expect that such expansive aspirations will be renounced, efforts to halt further militarization of competing claims are realistic. Domestic political currents in Argentina coincide with this goal, since force did not succeed in achieving expansive claims to the Falkland Islands and its dependencies and domestic public opinion now favors a quick transition to civilian government. Flexible responses or concessions from the UK and the international community would help reinforce domestic trends steering Argentina towards a peaceful course in pursuing its claims. For example, the UK has indicated some willingness to compromise by considering a transition to some kind of international peacekeeping force on the Falkland Islands.

Moderate, legalistic responses of Latin American states to the Falklands conflict indicate that the rich legal tradition of the region can likewise make a significant contribution to building a more viable regional order. Law was used to reinforce their view that decolonialization in the Falklands would promote a more stable regional order as well as to emphasize that this order should evolve through generally recognized modes of peaceful change rather than through the use of force. While Latin American states supported the Argentine claim of sovereignty over the Falkland Islands and were critical of the UK and the USA during the conflict, their general disapproval of Argentina's unilateral recourse to force in advancing its claim tempered their material support for Argentina during the conflict. In addition to widespread regional respect for legal norms, the impressive regional record of restraint in military spending and limited reliance on armed force also augur well for halting further militarization of competing claims.

Latin American EEZ implementation can also constitute a crucial element of a strategy for regional conflict containment in the South Atlantic and Antarctica. Latin American states played a central role in promoting the EEZ concept before and during the law-of-the-sea conference, and gained decisive support for their cause when African littoral states joined the EEZ bandwagon. Latin American influence on African states is likely to continue as lessons are derived about EEZ implementation. Influence through example will likely occur as African states observe how Latin American states relate naval structure and EEZ implementation, particularly since all leading local navies in the South Atlantic are South American. On the one hand, were South American leaders such as Argentina and Brazil to continue to expand towards deep-water navies and to favor militarization and territorialization of their EEZs, and extension of influence beyond the EEZ, leading African states such as Nigeria may be expected to follow a similar course. Indications are that such a process has already begun. On the other hand, were the South American leaders to curb their proclivity to militarize and territorialize their EEZs and instead to place greater emphasis in their naval structures on EEZ patrol duties, their example could be expected to have a beneficial impact on African states on the opposite side of the ocean basin.

The South American impact on Africa is likely to be more direct as well, particularly in the case of Brazil. Brazil has been emerging as a significant trading partner and arms supplier to numerous Black African states, including the regional leader, Nigeria, and aspires to expand commercial and arms sales markets there further. The Brazilian campaign to expand commerce and arms sales with Black Africa is influenced in the maritime sphere by Brazilian naval and EEZ practice, which could accordingly make a significant contribution towards either African restraint or militarization. On the one hand, a key African state such as Nigeria could follow the Brazilian lead in militarizing and territorializing its EEZ, including imitation of the Brazilian naval structure emphasizing large, modern warships. It is in fact within the Brazilian potential to supply large warships to Africa, and Brazil's proclivity for arms-for-oil deals, which have included oil-rich Nigeria, tends to intensify such militaristic relationships. On the other hand, Brazil not only could set an example of restraint in implementing its own EEZ, but could reinforce this restraint by supplying EEZ patrol craft, as it has already done in the case of Chile.

South American restraint in EEZ implementation and naval armament would also tend to have a beneficial impact on traditional regional rivalries. Most particularly, the longstanding Beagle Channel and Falkland Islands disputes were significantly worsened by changes caused by the EEZ. In each case, Argentina felt that an EEZ controlled by a traditional adversary in its own purported sphere of influence would constitute a direct threat to vital interests. Expansive coastal state security interests then directly contributed to militarization and territorialization of EEZs. General restraint in EEZ implementation is therefore all the more important for resolving these EEZ-linked disputes.

South American EEZ practice can have an important impact, either positive or negative, on Antarctic disputes as well. Overlapping claims of Argentina, Chile, and the UK have been complicated by both continental and offshore disputes, and the divisive issue of Antarctic EEZs has loomed larger as offshore resource wealth has been verified and steps have been taken to exploit this wealth. Moreover, claimant states such as Australia have followed the South American lead in making and enforcing offshore Antarctic claims. Brazil, as the premier South American power, would further complicate a conflict-prone situation by making its own claim, which would probably trigger additional South American Antarctic claims as well. In all these cases, South American restraint in claiming and enforcing EEZs could have a significant arms control impact.

There is considerable evidence that the great powers would respect coastal state initiatives involving restraint in EEZ implementation and naval armament. The great powers have recognized that militarization and territorialization of South American EEZs is a source of potential conflict, but they have still responded with restraint when restrictions have been placed on their warships and fishing vessels which they consider beyond the purview of the law. All of the great powers have also adhered to the Treaty of Tlatelolco, a Latin American arms control initiative whose nuclear-free zone includes a considerable portion of the South Atlantic.

There are also some indications that the great powers will continue to restrain competition among themselves. The Antarctic Treaty was primarily undertaken as an initiative of the great powers to prevent the extension of their military competition to the cold continent. While the Treaty has important defects, such as its exclusivity, the great powers still appear committed to the goals of demilitarization and denuclearization of the Treaty. In the South Atlantic, great power competition is tending to escalate, but less rapidly than had been generally expected. As long as great power competition remains at a relatively low level in the area and their interests remain of secondary importance, prospects for controlling further militarization are enhanced.

Finally, the relatively small number of important actors in the South Atlantic and Antarctica, including both great powers and coastal states, facilitates efforts to forge a more satisfactory order. But the trend is towards proliferation of influential actors and militarization of both areas. Hence, it is all the more important to respond constructively now to destabilizing aspects of the status quo before disputes escalate.

Notes

1. For a description of the Latin American naval setting, including both conflictual and cooperative trends, see a monograph by Michael A. Morris, Expansion of Latin American Navies, (Stockholm, Sweden: Institute of Latin American Studies of the University of Stockholm, Research Paper Series, Paper No. 25, 1980).

2. R. L. Scheina, "South American Navies: Who Needs Them?," US Naval Institute Proceedings 104 (February 1978):66.

Table 8.1. The Latin American Naval Hierarchy (1980)

VARYING COASTAL DEFENSE AND COASTAL LAW ENFORCEMENT CAPABILITIES

LIMITED COASTAL LAW ENFORCEMENT CAPABILITIES ONLY

Categories of Navies	Regions — South America	Central America and Caribbean	South Atlantic
1. REGIONAL NAVIES	Brazil Argentina		(Brazil) (Argentina)
2. SUB-REGIONAL NAVIES	Peru Chile		
3. OFFSHORE NAVIES	Venezuela Colombia	(Venezuela) (Colombia) Mexico	(Venezuela)
4. COASTAL NAVIES	Ecuador Uruguay	Cuba Dominican Republic	[South Africa] (Nigeria) (Uruguay) (Ghana)
5. CONSTABULARY NAVIES			(Guinea-Bissau) (Gabon) (Guinea)
6. TOKEN NAVIES	Surinam Guyana	Guatemala (Surinam) Bahamas Costa Rica Trinidad & Tobago Haiti El Salvador Panama Nicaragua Honduras Barbados (Guyana) Jamaica St. Vincent St. Lucia Grenada Belize St. Kitts	(Mauritania) (Senegal) (Zaire) (Angola) (Surinam) (Ivory Coast) (Congo) (Cameroon) (Liberia) (Benin) (Guyana) (Cape Verde) (Sierra Leone) (Gambia) (Equatorial Guinea)
LANDLOCKED NAVIES	Bolivia Paraguay		
	12	19 (23)	(24)

Notes to Table 8.1:

This Latin American naval hierarchy is derived from an article by this author, "The Third World Naval Hierarchy," in The 8th Annual Third World Conference Proceedings, ed. Roger K. Oden (Park Forest South, Illinois: Governors State University, 1983), pp. 303-339. Both quantitative and qualitative considerations were taken into account in developing the hierarchy, and are described in detail in this article. States are ranked hierarchically within as well as between ranks. States are listed without parentheses for their main region and with parentheses for regions they overlap. South Africa is the only littoral state considered to be a developed state and is included in brackets for purposes of comparison.

9
Monitoring Latin American Arms Control Agreements

Max G. Manwaring

INTRODUCTION

Since the wars for Latin American independence, the peace of the area has been disrupted by numerous interventions, insurrections, civil wars, and wars between two or more of the Republics. In that period, various regional and global attempts have been made to establish some sort of security system. As early as 1826, Simon Bolivar called a conference at which it was hoped-- among other things--that machinery could be established to arbitrate disputes between Latin American States and to provide for collective security.[1] Since then other attempts have been made to demilitarize frontiers,[2] prohibit certain methods of war,[3] limit armaments,[4] prevent subversion,[5] prohibit military use of certain geographic regions and space,[6] prohibit proliferation of nuclear weapons,[7] create a nuclear free zone,[8] limit armaments in order to devote resources to economic and social development,[9] and support general disarmament.[10]

The general ineffectiveness of these much-heralded efforts is related, at least in part, to the fact that verification has always been left to national discretion; consequently, no viable enforcement machinery has ever been established. This paper, then, will propose an empirical approach to conflict control in Latin America providing the basis for future verification clauses and final clauses of general arms-limitation measures. A model designed to accomplish the unobtrusive monitoring of governmental actions pertaining to the development of relative military capability is outlined, and examples provided which indicate what might be done in looking beyond the words of an integrated arms-control measure to actual deeds.

Through the fusing of this information, this chapter aims to present a picture of the reality and present status of arms control measures in Latin America; and, hopefully, will make a small contribution to promoting more effective verification of such measures.

163

RELATIVE MILITARY CAPABILITY:
A MODEL FOR THE UNOBTRUSIVE MONITORING
OF GENERAL ARMS CONTROL AGREEMENT

The arms control treaties now in force have little
or no effect on general military capability of states.
These agreements tend to deal piecemeal with particular
types of weapons systems or type of warfare[11] and with
specific parts of the world or of space.[12]

One major type of systemic aggression with which
the world must contend is the expression of explicit
military hostility.[13] This type of aggression is exemplified by war, threats of war, and the general spectrum of overt military violence between actors. The
potential for this kind of conflict is operationalized
and assessed through the concept of 'Relative Military
Capability' (RMC). The RMC, which is described in detail in the Methodological Appendix, aims to measure
the total integrated war-making potential of a state,
rather than specific aspects of this potential. It can
also be an effective indicator of adherence to general
arms-limitation agreements.

The elements that might constitute the military
capability concept are numerous. However, using the
Statistical Package for the Social Sciences (SPSS) Factor Analysis, the problem is reduced to manageable proportions and the variables most closely related to military power capability are identified.

Instead of a clear-cut, single military-capability
factor emerging, the SPSS factor analysis indicated
that this concept consists of three principal components: (1) actual and potential military forces (Armed
Forces Strength); (2) the ability to project force over
distance (Reach); and (3) the ability to maintain and
increase forces and reach (Infrastructure).

Armed Forces Strength (AFT)

The principal component called AFT is best explained by two variables: (1) the number of armed forces
personnel in a given country (AFT), and (2) the theoretical capacity to produce a given number of 20-kiloton (KT) bombs per year (NUC). These indicators represent projectable power.

Thus the first indicator records the number of
soldiers, sailors, and airmen immediately available for
engaging in military hostilities. Wars, regardless of
the level of intensity, are fought by people. Territory, airspace, and critical sea lanes must be physically controlled. As a rule, the more individuals in
the armed forces of a given state, the better that
state's fighting capability in relation to that of another.

Because of the seriousness of even the possibility of the use of nuclear weapons, the NUC indicator measures the output of electric power currently produced by thermal reactors in operation, under construction or planned and indicates the total theoretical capacity for 20-KT atomic bomb production. As a rule, the greater the capacity to produce energy by means of nuclear reactors, the greater the ability to make nuclear weapons; and, the greater the capacity to make and deliver nuclear weapons, the greater a state's capability and influence in relation to that of another.

Reach (RE1 and RE2)

The factor identified as Reach is also best explained by two 'indicator-variables': (1) the merchant marine (RE1), and (2) the number of passengers flown on domestic airlines per year (RE2).

The size, and even quality, of an armed force may alone have little significance in the context of world affairs. The indicators labeled RE1 and RE2 are intended to measure a country's capability to project and sustain its armed forces into international security affairs. In this connection, the airlift capacity of a state, in terms of number of passengers carried on domestic and international routes in a given year by its airlines, and the capacity of a country to move bulk cargo, in terms of the tonnage of its merchant marine, are examined. Civil air and sea transport are used as indicators of Reach simply because they are considered an integral part of the military infrastructure of virtually all the countries of the world and would be employed to supplement military and naval capability to move and support troops and equipment. Moreover, small numbers of aircraft and troops can be deployed to most parts of the world within hours of notification, given a secure airbase and adequate fuel. Sustaining even a small force over a period of time, however, is complex and cumbersome. The most readily identifiable means of accomplishing the tasks associated with projecting and sustaining power over long distances is airlift and sealift. Again, the greater the capacity, the greater the relative advantage.

Infrastructure

The component called Infrastructure is composed of three variables: (1) defense expenditure per capita (DEP), (2) arms exports (AEX), and (3) government revenue as a percent of Gross Domestic Product (GRP). These indicators not only measure the ability of a state to sustain and increase Armed Forces Strength and Reach, but each one suggests something more. For exam-

ple: the DEP variable qualifies the capability of the
armed forces of a given state. Firstly, it indicates
the scope of operations of a military organization.
Secondly, and less reliably, it provides a qualitative
measure of armed forces strength. In these terms, in-
sufficient funds imply deficiencies in training, equipment, and supplies. The size of a country's population
has a great impact on this statistic. For example, the
DEP for Argentina in 1977 was $28; Brazil's DEP was
about half of this, at $13. Nevertheless, total de-
fense expenditures in the same year were only $722 mil-
lion (in constant dollars) for Argentina, and twice as
much, $1536, for Brazil.[14] Thus, more accurately, the
DEP indicator measures the degree of commitment a government has made--the priority it has given--to the
quality of its armed forces. An adequate index for measuring the degree of a state's exploitation of military
capability to its international advantage would include
this variable.

The capability to produce arms for export (AEX) is
an important asset in the projection of influence in a
world that is buying arms at record rates.[15] In addition, should the need arise, this capability can be
immediately channeled to meet national requirements.
It would also be an important asset for projection and
staying power in international security matters. On
the other hand, if a country must import war materials,
as well as spare parts for old equipment and arms, it
is dependent on the exporter or exporters and cannot
project or sustain itself on the international scene
any longer than its inventory and supplier will allow.
Clearly, the larger the quantity of a nation's exports
of nationally-made armaments, the more independent it
is. In these terms, arms exports can provide an independence of action that is absolutely necessary in order to exploit military capability to the national advantage.

The GRP indicator is an important dimension of a
notion suggested by Knorr ('putative power') and more
fully developed by Cline, and by Organski and Kugler.[16]
They argue that recent important miscalculations in
reading a comprehensive estimate of the military capability of nations have been the result of the failure
to take into account the idea of 'will to fight'. Organski asserts that 'will' per se is not the vital difference that allows one state to prevail over another
in international conflict. Rather, it is the capacity
to penetrate effectively a society and extract resources
from it. Revenue data provide good, strong indicators
that can measure that capacity. The better a government's performance in extracting resources from a society, the more successful it is in penetrating and
controlling it. The better the control, the better the

capability to fulfill tasks imposed by the international
environment and to generate the 'will' to sustain a
fight. Thus, GRP suggests a level of capability to ad-
minister, coordinate, and sustain political and military goals across the conflict spectrum in the contemporary world.

After weighting the variables, each nation's Relative Military Capability score was computed according
to the following equation: $RMC = (P_{AFT_{aw}} + P_{NUC_{aw}}) \times (P_{RE1_{aw}} + P_{RE2_{aw}}) \times (P_{DEP_{aw}} + P_{AEX_{aw}} + P_{GRP_{aw}})$. Each
of the principal components was multiplied because mul-
tiplication implies nonsubstitutability. That is to
say, a country with a relatively high level of Armed
Forces Strength but little or no Reach and/or Infrastructure cannot be considered to have the capability
to project and sustain military force over distances.
The same applies to a country with a high level of Infrastructure and Reach, but a small number of armed
forces. Thus, a viable military capability requires
relatively high scores in all three principal components.

Accordingly, the model was applied to identify and
clarify the relative military capabilities over time of
23 Latin American republics. As has been suggested in
the Methodological Appendix, the ranking part of the
analysis is concerned with military capability at a
given point in time. The longitudinal analysis demonstrates patterns of behavior in terms of unilateral development of relative military capability from 1970 to
1981.

This type of analysis is useful for macro-level
problems. The results will enable one to answer the
following questions in general terms: "Is country X
living up to its commitments in terms of a given arms
control agreement?" "What is country X's capability/
vulnerability in relation to country Y, or in relation
to countries Y and Z?" "In what direction are capabil-
ities/vulnerabilities moving for a specific country or
potential alliance of countries?" In short, this type
of analysis can be applied to the problem of verification of general arms control measures.

Verification refers to the process of assessing
compliance with provisions contained in conflict control
measures. It is an essential element in the enforcement
process. Thus, verification clauses of an arms control
agreement should include procedures for acquiring information regarding adherence to obligations and for enforcement. For example, Article III of the 1972 Seabed
Treaty (Treaty on the Prohibition of the Emplacement of
Nuclear Weapons and Other Weapons of Mass Destruction
on the Seabed and the Ocean Floor and in the Subsoil
Thereof) provides that a Party which has a reasonable
doubt concerning another Party's fulfillment of obligations assumed under the Treaty may use its own means,

the help of others, or appropriate procedures within the framework of the United Nations to observe and inspect activities beyond the 12-mile limit. If a serious question is raised regarding compliance with the Treaty, a Party may refer the matter to the Security Council, which may take appropriate enforcement action.[17]

A variety of methods and procedures may be employed in the verification of arms control agreements. What type or combination of means is used depends primarily on the character of the restrictions. Procedures dealing with specifics and highly sophisticated weaponry--such as quality and quantity of re-entry vehicles in a missile--are beyond the scope of this paper. What we are interested in here is general arms-limitation agreements. That is to say, the methodology and model set forth above are designed to determine compliance with measures which call for limitations on a country's ability to conduct viable military aggression.

Monitoring of this kind of general agreement by accepted methods of overt data collection has a number of important advantages. For example, it is not necessary to operate in the territory of the parties being monitored; it does not compel the formal acceptance of a foreign presence by any of the parties to an agreement; it does not require elaborate stipulations for reciprocity or for ensuring the needs of observer teams; it does not require sensitive technologies or a large staff; and it is inexpensive.

Quantitative verification at the macro-level, like other forms of verification, is subject to different limitations. In this context, this method must be regarded primarily as a supplement to other means of verification designed to collect data on specific activities at a micro-level. Nevertheless, analysis of the macro-level can, and does, provide adequate indicators of movement towards or away from compliance with international obligations. In this context, this type of analytic monitoring of agreements can be the basis of at least four things which serve the prospects for international well-being. Firstly, information gathered may be the basis for calling a review conference. Such a conference could examine the operation of a given measure and determine whether or not its purposes are being realized. Secondly, putting an agreement and the related activities of its Parties to a degree of careful scrutiny may generate constructive amendments which otherwise would never be proposed. Thirdly, knowledge that activities prohibited by an agreement are not taking place can create an environment of confidence, which is helpful in creating security and peace. Finally, from a negative point of view, a government may be deterred from violating an international commitment if it fears detection and a possible response from another Party or an international organization.

STATE BEHAVIOR WITH REGARD TO GENERAL
CONFLICT CONTROL MEASURES

Introduction

Actual behavior is the key to understanding a
country's attitudes regarding an arms-control agreement. It is also a key to determining compliance.
In order to analyze the actions of Latin American
governments in connection with general conflict control
measures, we measure RMC over time in two cases. First,
we examine the military capabilities of the eight parties to the Declaration of Ayacucho--Argentina, Bolivia,
Chile, Colombia, Ecuador, Panama, Peru, and Venezuela.
This 1974 agreement obligated the parties to "the effective limitation of armaments and an end to their acquisition for offensive purposes so that all possible
resources may be devoted to the economic and social development of every country in Latin America".[18] Prior
to Ayacucho, the various arms control measures in force
had little or no effect on the military potential of
Latin American states. The measures were either considered irrelevant, the activities and weapons banned
were of little or no relevance in the Latin American
context, or it was perceived that the agreements had
been stipulated by the "Super Powers" as a means of
maintaining their relative power in international security affairs and/or a means of denying important technology to developing nations.[19] On the other hand, the
Declaration of Ayacucho was a positive statement imply-
ing quantitative and qualitative limitations on a large
package of items that in fact make for military power--
limitations and gradual reduction of armed forces, gradual reduction of military budgets, and the limitation
of all types of international transfer of conventional
weapons. In this sense, the Ayacucho Declaration is a
general, integrated conflict control measure to which
eight nation-states ascribed. They also set themselves
up as examples for the rest of Latin America and the
world as leaders in the effort to maintain progress toward general and complete disarmament. It is for these
reasons that we also measured the RMC of the parties to
the agreement in an attempt to see how well they have
complied with the letter and the spirit of their own
declaration.
In the second case, we examine the military capability of 23 Latin American states, who supported the
Final Document of the 1978 Special Session on Disarmament of the United Nations (UN) General Assembly. A
good part of the Final Document reiterates the general
principles and goals of general and nuclear disarmament
as defined by various UN resolutions adopted during the
past 30 years, and since 1969, when the UN declared the
1970s to be the 'Disarmament Decade'.[20] As such, it is

a more-or-less integrated approach to general disarmament, as opposed to obviously piecemeal arms control
measures. And, since the Final Document focuses on the
1970s, we measure RMC for the Latin American republics
over the period 1970-1981. Thus, we may see how seriously the governments of these countries took the 'Decade of Disarmament'.

Patterns examined lead to the general conclusion
that the military behavior of the various Latin American governments over the period 1970-1981 has been
guided less by international agreement than might have
been hoped. There has been a general proliferation of
military capability, a diffusion of power among a growing number of states, and, thus, a general weakening of
mutual security in the Latin American region.

The Military Capability of the Parties to
the Declaration of Ayacucho, 1974-1981

An analysis of the data produced by the principal
components model outlined above reveals that six of the
eight 'Ayacucho' countries have maintained their relative rankings over the years 1974-1981 (see Table 9.1).
Argentina has enhanced its position as a relative "Super Power" within the group. Peru has replaced Chile
as the second ranking power. Chile slipped to fourth
position, and Venezuela, Colombia, Ecuador, Bolivia,
and Panama retained their third, fifth, sixth, seventh,
and eighth positions, respectively.

Argentina greatly improved its position, relative
to the other 'Ayacucho' countries, by virtue of significant increase in its Armed Forces Strength and Infrastructure. Within each of those principal components,
it was the development of the potential for nuclear
weaponry and the Argentine arms export industry which
made the greatest contributions to a relative increase
of military capability by approximately 30 times. Peru
increased its Armed Forces Strength, Reach, and Infrastructure to double its RMC. However, even though Peru
bypassed Chile, Argentina's spectacular relative power
increase in fact provided all the other parties to the
Declaration of Ayacucho a net relative loss (see Tables
9.1 and 9.2).

Close examination of the data suggests that are
large gaps between the various countries, and that
those gaps have increased over the years. Ranking, per
se, means very little in this kind of analysis. What
is important is the number of points one nation-state
has as opposed to another. For example, in 1981, Argentina had 30,630,896 points to Peru's 308,994. Consequently, even through Peru is ranked number two within the 'Ayacucho' community, the gulf between it and
Argentina is significantly large. At the same time,

the gap between Peru and Chile has reversed itself to
the point where--in relative terms--Peru has about $1\frac{1}{2}$
times the military capability of Chile. Another significant gap is that which exists between the top four
or five countries and those ranking at the bottom of
Table 9.1. In this context, even though Ecuador, Bolivia, and Panama have increased their relative military
capability anywhere from about $1\frac{1}{2}$ to 5 times over the
short period examined, the gap between them and the
other parties to the Declaration of Ayacucho is so
great as to appear unbridgeable.

Clearly, the parties to the Declaration of Ayacucho have not been reducing military capacity in favor
of economic and social development. Moreover, the military imbalance that existed at the time of the Ayacucho Declaration is currently even greater.

Implications for arms-control measures in the 'A-
yacucho' community revolve around the potential for
conflict in the area. There are at least three extremely volatile disputes--the Beagle Channel, the Marañón
Region, and the Atacama Desert--which threaten the peace
and security of that part of the Hemisphere.

These issues affect countries with uneven RMCs.
Chile (212,252) would be no match for Argentina
(30,632,896) if the Beagle Channel dispute were to develop into armed hostilities. Peru (308,994) could
easily expedite a confrontation with Ecuador (21,925)
over the Marañón Region, and a brief war indeed occurred in 1981. Normally, this kind of unstable imbalance portends conflict, and the issue normally is resolved in favor of the strongest. Fortunatelly, however, this has not happened, except in the case of the
Ecuadorian-Peruvian war in which Peru clearly had the
upper hand. The Atacama Desert problem, which involves
Bolivia, Chile, and Peru, is one in which the major
protagonists--Chile (212,252) and Peru (308,994)--are
not well matched. Bolivia (7,434) could not enhance
either Peruvian or Chile power enough to be decisive in
any conflict. Even though the power gap between Chile
and Peru is not nearly as great as that between Chile
and Argentina, this kind of situation also portends
conflict. A miscalculation or some irrationality on
the part of one government or another could easily res-
urrect the War of the Pacific.

One apparent result of this imbalance between potential conflicting parties is a perceived regional or
international "balancer" or set of "balancers". In addition to the Balance of Power concept inhibiting the
use of force in any of the disputes noted above, it may
be that the 'Ayacucho' countries are alarmed about the
potential social, political, and economic costs of
armed hostilities. If that in fact is the case, these
states should be more concerned with resolving the

shared problems of economic, political, and social development.

Putting this principle into practice means accepting the reality that the days of strictly military solutions to security problems are gone. It also means
that the appropriate responses must be made to situations before they reach crisis proportions. Finally,
it also means that a whole new set of institutions must
be established to develop meaningful dialogue on substantive issues of security. At a minimum this would
require a new Declaration of Ayacucho which: (1) includes all of Latin America; (2) sets forth a package
of measures including qualitative and quantitative re-
ductions of important military power components such as
armed forces, military budgets, and production and
transfer of weapons; and (3) promotes cooperative, verifiable, and enforceable approaches to the problem of
conflict control in the region.

The Military Capability of 23 Latin American Republics,
1970-1981 (representing supporters of over 40 resolutions that make up the Final Document of the 1978 United
Nations Special Session on Disarmament)

Patterns determined by the principal components of
RMC and their indicator-variables discerned above lead
one to infer--public rhetoric notwithstanding--that the
various arms control measures set forth in the Final
Document have failed to reduce general military power
in Latin America.

To be sure, in overall regional terms, eight countries have in fact lost ground with respect to their
Relative Military Capability over the period of the
Disarmament Decade. They are: Argentina, Venezuela,
Chile, Colombia, Trinidad-Tobago, Guatemala, and Paraguay. In each of these countries, armed forces per se
have not been reduced; rather, Reach and Infrastructure
have not expanded with sufficient rapidity to prevent a
loss of capability relative to the other countries examined.

At the same time, 12 countries have increased
their relative military capability; some of them sus-
tantially. As Tables 9.3- 9.5 indicate, Brazil, Cuba,
and Mexico lead in this field. An examination of the
specific variables that make up Relative Military Capability indicates that the numerical strengths of the
armed forces have generally increased; the nuclear
variable has become important; airlift and sealift have
been enlarged; and the growth of domestic arms indus-
tries--especially in Brazil--is becoming increasingly
important.

Despite the general increase of relative military
strengths in Latin America, three points should be em-

phasized. First, Brazil's move from 293,874 RMC points
in 1970 to 11,751,112 in 1981 has--in relative terms--
increased the gap between itself and the rest of the
countries of the region. In this context, the other 22
republics have sustained a net relative loss. Consequently, Brazil is the "Super Power" of Latin America.
Although Argentina ranks second to Brazil, Brazil's RMC
is significantly larger. Tables 9.3- 9.5 show that
disparity.

Second, although Brazil's RMC has risen considerably over the past 10 years, it should be noted that
Cuba, Mexico, and Peru have also registered significant
gains. In so doing, these countries appear to be emerging out of the main body of Latin American states to
join Argentina as powers to be reckoned with. The primary arms-control implication of the emergence of new
power brokers in the Hemisphere is that any solution to
a conflict in the region could and should include input
from one or all of these states. Indeed, these coun-
tries--including Cuban activity in Africa--perceive
much larger roles for themselves in Latin America and
the world. Unfortunately, this same trend may also
lead to the proliferation of regional actors in local
conflicts.

Third, while countries such as Brazil, Cuba, and
Mexico have been increasing their relative military
potential at the rates indicated, those other countries
whose RMC has not been growing at similar rates have
become correspondingly less advantageously situated
with respect to all levels of aggression. The decrease
in capability and corresponding increase in vulnerability in regional terms is most notable for Argentina
(1,146,114 to 403,293), Venezuela (20,790 to 15,318),
and Chile (25,982 to 14,475). These countries, along
with any of the 16 other republics at the bottom of the
ranking list on Table 9.3, would be potential targets
for stronger states with aggressive notions. Moreover,
the gap between the top and lower ranks is so great
that any likely increase in RMC on the part of the last
16 ranking countries could not bridge the difference.

The financial commitment to the armed forces--
measured by Defense Expenditures per Capita--clearly
illustrates the problem. For example, DEP for Brazil
in 1979 was $13. DEP for Uruguay was considerably
higher at $39. Yet Brazil's military expenditures that
year were $1,580 million as compared to Uruguay's $115
million.[21] Obviously the size of a country's population has a great impact on this statistic. Thus, the
DEP indicator measures the current degree of commitment
or priority a government has given to the quality of
its military establishment. It does not indicate real
expenditure. Uruguay could never match Brazil in this
regard--to say nothing of catching up.

All this having been said, it must be remembered that we are measuring <u>Relative</u> Military Capability within the Latin American context. This part of the world does not exist in a vacuum. What might appear as a suggestion of some kind of gigantic arms build-up taking place in the Hemisphere is, of course, not the case. In global terms, the Latin American nations are spending considerably less on military and arms pur- chases than other parts of the world.[22] For example, Brazil's military expenditures for 1980 were only 0.7 percent of Gross National Product.[23] No other major country was spending so little.[24] In these terms, low levels of defense spending imply deficiencies in train- ing, supplies, facilities, equipment, maintenance, and general scope of operations. This severely limits the possibility of any large-scale conflict, and diminishes the argument that Latin America is in some kind of un- controlled arms race.

Nevertheless, the trends that have been demons- trated in the empirical portion of this paper suggest a new dynamism for Latin America. It is not--as one might hope--a cooperative effort to balance force structures and regulate armaments so as not to upset existing power relations and world hierarchies. Rather, there has been a general proliferation of military capability and dif- fusion of power among a growing number of states.

With the accumulation of increasingly sophisticat- ed weapons--conventional and possibly nuclear--the se- curity of all states has been weakened. This, coupled with a tendency toward a more multi-polar world, sug- gests several possible sources of conflict. They would include: (1) the resurgence of traditional rivalries and border tensions; (2) a growing competition for re- sources and markets; (3) a general frustration with the inability to influence other governments significantly through the use of economic or political pressures; and (4) a resulting increase in the credibility of the idea of military--even nuclear--power as the guarantor of influence in the regional and international systems. Faced with a series of possible simultaneous confronta- tions, governments are likely to become trapped in a series of contradictions irresolvable through on-the- spot negotiations. Moreover, as the strategic impor- tance of Latin America becomes more and more obvious, outside actors are likely to take a more active role in exploiting the vulnerabilities of the area to their own ends. This, in turn, could lead to: (1) heightened instability; (2) left or right wing insurgency triumphs; and/or (3) some sort of warfare in particularly vulner- able target countries.

However, if the potential for conflict is real, the opportunities for its control are also real. In this connection, arms control measures can be made more effective by including verification clauses and final clauses which provide--among other things--machinery to monitor compliance with obligations. As these devices are improved, they reduce the risk of conflict as a result of accident or miscalculation; and, bit-by-bit, pave the way towards a more secure and peaceful world. The challenge is to rethink, improve, and revitalize such machinery before any given dispute reaches crisis proportions.

NOTES

1. The Congress of Panama.

2. Examples are the 1829 agreement between Peru and Colombia to reduce frontier forces to those absolutely necessary for maintaining control of common borders; and the 1881 agreement between Chile and Argentina not to fortify the Strait of Magellan.

3. For example, the Geneva Protocol of 1925 on Chemical and Biological Warfare.

4. For example, the 1923 Central American Convention on Arms Limitation.

5. Through the creation of the Emergency Advisory Committee for Political Defense in 1947.

6. For example, the Antarctic Treaty and Outer Space Treaty (1961 and 1967).

7. The Treaty of Tlatelolco in 1968.

8. Ibid.

9. The Declaration of Ayacucho of 1974.

10. For example, all the Latin American countries consistently supported the various measures proposed in the 1978 United Nations' Special Session on Disarmament.

11. For example, the Treaty of Tlatelolco pertains to nuclear weapons, and the Biological Warfare Convention is concerned with that topic of warfare.

12. For example, the Seabed and Antarctic Treaties obligate parties only in those particular geographical areas, and the Outer Space Treaty prohibits specific activity and weapons systems there, but not on earth.

13. See, for example, Ivo K. Feirabend with Rosalind L. Feirabend and Betty A. Nesvold, 'The Comparative Study of Revolution and Violence', Comparative Politics (April 1973), pp. 393-424; and Steven Jackson, Bruce Russett, Duncan Snidal, and David Sylvan, 'Conflict and Coercion in Dependent States', Journal of Conflict Resolution, 22 (December 1978): pp. 627-657.

14. World Military Expenditures and Arms Transfers, 1968-1977 (USACDA, Washington DC., 1979), pp. 33, 35.

15. World Armaments and Disarmament, SIPRI Yearbook 1978 (Taylor & Francis Ltd., London, 1978), Part II, pp. 133-297.

16. Klaus Knorr, 'Notes on the Analysis of National Capabilities', J. Rosenau, V. Davis and M. East, editors, The Analysis of International Politics: Essays in Honor of Harold and Margaret Sprout (Free Press, New York, 1972); Ray S. Cline, World Power Assessment: A Calculus of Strategic Drift (Georgetown University Center for Strategic and International Studies, Washington D.C., 1975); and A.F.K. Organski and Jacek Kugler, 'Davids and Goliaths: Predicting the Outcomes of International Wars', Comparative Political Studies, 11 (July 1978): p. 175.

17. A copy of the text of the Seabed Treaty is found in Jozef Goldblat, Arms Control: A Survey and Appraisal of Multilateral Agreements (Taylor & Francis Ltd., London, 1978, Stockholm International Peace Research Institute-SIPRI), pp. 90-92.

18. A text of the Declaration of Ayacucho is found in Jozef Goldblat, Arms Control: A Survey. . ., p. 121.

19. For example, see The Outer Space Treaty, The Biological Warfare Convention, and The Nuclear Non-Proliferation Treaty, in Jozef Goldblat, Agreements for Arms Control: A Critical Survey (Taylor & Francis Ltd., London, 1982, Stockholm International Peace Research Institute-SIPRI).

20. World Armaments and Disarmament, SIPRI Yearbook 1979 (Taylor & Francis Ltd., London, 1979), pp. 490-523.

21. World Military Expenditures and Arms Transfers, 1970-1979 (USACDA, Washington, D.C., 1982), pp. 51, 81.

22. The Military Balance, 1981-1982 (IISS, London, 1981), p. 112. See also Chapter 7 of this volume.

23. Ibid.

24. Ibid.

METHODOLOGICAL APPENDIX 9A

The concept of military capability is more than a quantitative and qualitative evaluation of military forces in being.

As a result, the elements that might constitute military power capabilities are numerous.[1] However, in the interest of parsimony and manageability, it is necessary to determine which indicator-variables are best.

I chose to identify empirically the variables most closely related to military power capability, rather than determine them a priori.

Consequently, I submitted 16 variables to the SPSS (Statistical Package for the Social Sciences) Factor Analysis.[2]

Instead of a clear-cut, single military capability factor emerging, the principal components analysis indicated that military capability consists of the ability to sustain and increase military strength, the ability to project force over long distances, and actual military forces.

More specifically, the factor analysis indicates the following.

First, the principal component called Armed Forces Strength is best explained by two variables:

1. The number of armed forces personnel in a given country (AFT); and
2. The theoretical capacity to produce a given number of 20-kiloton (KT) bombs per year (NUC).

These indicators represent projectable power.

Second, the factor identified as Reach is also best explained by two indicator-variables:

1. The merchant marine (RE1); and
2. The number of passengers flown on domestic airlines per year (RE2).

Third, the component called Infrastructure is composed of three variables:

1. Defense expenditures per capita (DEP);
2. Arms exports (AEX); and
3. Government revenue as a percent of Gross Domestic Product (GRP).

These indicators measure the ability of a state to sustain and increase Armed Forces Strength and Reach.

Graphically, the model is as follows:

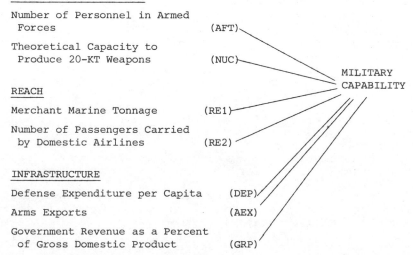

ARMED FORCES STRENGTH

Number of Personnel in Armed
  Forces   (AFT)

Theoretical Capacity to
  Produce 20-KT Weapons   (NUC)

                                         MILITARY
                                         CAPABILITY
REACH

Merchant Marine Tonnage   (RE1)

Number of Passengers Carried
  by Domestic Airlines   (RE2)

INFRASTRUCTURE

Defense Expenditure per Capita   (DEP)

Arms Exports   (AEX)

Government Revenue as a Percent
  of Gross Domestic Product   (GRP)

After the factor analysis compressed the original
16 variables into 7 that best explain a 3-component military capability, it remained to devise a suitable tech-
nique for aggregating the data and producing a single
index for a given point in time. As a preliminary step,
each country's score on each variable was rescaled and
expressed as a percentage of the sum of the scores on
that respective variable for all the nation-states examined. This was done in order to establish a single
basis from which to measure and compare relative stand-
ings and to eliminate the problem of measuring inflation. With the data rescaled, the indicators were combined into a single index.

Common sense and factor analysis suggest some sort
of weighting of the variables. Consequently, weights
were assigned to the variables on the basis of the factor loading scores that resulted from the factor analysis.[3] These figures were squared and multiplied by 100.
The resulting numbers were set to equal to unity, and
the total number of units was set at one million. Then,
each nation-state's Relative Military Capability score
was computed according to the following equation:

$$RMC = (^P AFT_{aw} + ^P NUC_{aw}) \times (^P RE1_{aw} + ^P RE2_{aw}) \times$$

$$(^P DEP_{aw} + ^P AEX_{aw} + ^P GRP_{aw}).$$

RMC: Relative Military Capability
P : Percentage
aw : Adjusted Weight

Finally, each country's RMC score was multiplied by 10,000 to produce the final score, which allows for whole member ranking and categorization of the countries examined. Each factor was multiplied because multiplication implies nonsubstitutability. That is to say, a country with a relatively high level of Armed Forces Strength, but little or no Reach and/or Infrastructure, cannot be considered to have the capability to project and sustain military force over distances. The same applies to a country with a high level of Infrastructure and Reach, but a small number of armed forces. Thus, a viable military capability requires relatively high scores in all three principal components.

Accordingly, the model was applied quantitatively to identify and clarify the relative military capabilities over time of 23 Latin American republics. It was applied again for the same purpose for the eight parties to the Declaration of Ayacucho. The ranking analysis is concerned with the relative military capabilities of the various Latin American countries at a given point in time. The longitudinal analysis demonstrates patterns of behavior of these governments in terms of unilateral development of military capability.

NOTES TO APPENDIX

1. A list of a few of these indicators would include quality and quantity of supplies, equipment and training, civil and military transportation and communications, facilities, morale, population, raw materials, GNP, industrial capacity, technical and administrative skills, tax revenue, capability of an intelligence service, ease of making and implementing governmental decisions, generalship, and military reputation.

2. Factor analysis is a relatively straightforward method of transforming a given set of variables into a new set of composite variables. These 16 variables are armed forces manpower, total defense expenditure, defense expenditure per capita, defense expenditure as a percent of GNP, arms exports, GNP, territorial area, population, total foreign trade, merchant marine, domestic airlines, theoretical capability to produce 20-KT nuclear bombs, government revenue, government revenue per capita, and military reputation.

3. It is assumed that variables that correlate highest (load high) with a given factor or dimension are more important than those that load lower as determinants of the phenomenon in question. The final indicators and factor loading scores are as follows:

(Note 3 Continued)

	Factor 1	Factor 2	Factor 3
AFT	-0.10000	-0.00785	0.59017
NUC	0.55048	0.51582	0.64264
RE1	0.01290	0.92327	0.05480
RE2	0.09681	0.94496	-0.18660
DEP	0.96375	0.11050	-0.11534
AEX	0.81244	0.20081	0.34977
GRP	0.72851	-0.04006	-0.13266

SOURCES FOR TABLES 9.1, 9.2, 9.3, 9.4, and 9.5

World Military Expenditures and Arms Transfers, 1970-1979 (USACDA, Washington DC., 1982), pp. 49-81.

The Military Balance, 1981-1982 (IISS, London, 1981), pp. 92-113.

World Armaments and Disarmament, SIPRI Yearbook 1981 (Taylor & Francis Ltd., London, 1981), pp. 315, 196, 91, 93, 97.

UN Statistical Yearbook, 1980/81 (UNO, New York, 1981), p. 392.

UN Statistical Yearbook, 1977 (UNO, New York, 1978), pp. 595-597, 544.

Economic and Social Progress in Latin America (Latin American Development Bank, Washington DC., 1980-1981 Report), p. 412.

TABLE 9.1. THE AYACUCHO COUNTRIES: 1974 AND 1981 RMCs COMPARED

RMC (1974)		RMC (1981)	
1. Argentina	1,248,338	1. Argentina	30,630,896
2. Chile	524,824	2. Peru	308,994
3. Venezuela	252,473	3. Venezuela	236,610
4. Peru	153,734	4. Chile	212,252
5. Colombia	114,618	5. Colombia	121,142
6. Ecuador	15,327	6. Ecuador	21,925
7. Bolivia	3,473	7. Bolivia	7,434
8. Panama	52	8. Panama	283

TABLE 9.2. THE AYACUCHO COUNTRIES: 1974 AND 1981 RMC BREAKDOWNS

	$(P_{AFT_{aw}} + P_{NUC_{aw}})$	×	$(P_{RE1_{aw}} + P_{RE2_{aw}})$	×	$(P_{DEF_{aw}} + P_{GRP_{aw}} + P_{AEX_{aw}})$	=	RMC (1974)
1. Argentina	2.27		14.51		3.79		124.8338
2. Bolivia	.27		.59		2.18		.3473
3. Chile	1.36		4.25		9.08		52.4824
4. Colombia	.91		8.87		1.42		11.4618
5. Ecuador	.52		1.31		2.25		1.5327
6. Panama	.12		.02		2.15		.0052
7. Peru	1.36		3.60		3.14		15.3734
8. Venezuela	.75		4.58		7.35		25.2473
							(1981)
1. Argentina	11.16		13.12		20.92		3063.0896
2. Bolivia	.31		1.09		2.20		.7434
3. Chile	1.17		3.08		5.89		21.2252
4. Colombia	1.18		6.71		1.53		12.1142
5. Ecuador	.44		1.65		3.02		2.1925
6. Panama	.11		.10		2.57		.0283
7. Peru	1.53		4.89		4.13		30.8994
8. Venezuela	.60		7.17		5.50		23.6610

TABLE 9.3.   23 LATIN AMERICAN COUNTRIES: 1970 AND 1981 RMCs COMPARED

	RMC (1970)		RMC (1981)
1. Argentina	1,146,914	1. Brazil	11,751,112
2. Brazil	293,874	2. Argentina	403,293
3. Cuba	59,577	3. Cuba	167,234
4. Chile	25,982	4. Mexico	128,856
5. Mexico	21,242	5. Peru	20,943
6. Venezuela	20,790	6. Venezuela	15,318
7. Peru	15,868	7. Chile	14,475
8. Colombia	10,632	8. Colombia	7,491
9. Ecuador	767	9. Uruguay	1,622
10. Uruguay	600	10. Ecuador	1,474
11. Bolivia	299	11. Bolivia	503
12. Honduras	145	12. Jamaica	205
13. Guatemala	102	13. Honduras	142
14. Trinidad & Tobago	56	14. Trinidad & Tobago	33
15. Nicaragua	52	15. Nicaragua	29
16. Jamaica	27	16. Guatemala	26
17. Costa Rica	14	17. Costa Rica	17
18. Paraguay	14	18. Dominican Republic	14
19. Dominican Republic	13	19. Guyana	8
20. Haiti	5	20. Haiti	5
21. Panama	3	21. Paraguay	5
22. Guyana	2	22. El Salvador	4
23. El Salvador	1	23. Panama	3

TABLE 9.4. 23 LATIN AMERICAN COUNTRIES: 1970 RMC BREAKDOWN

	$(P_{AFT_{aw}} + P_{NUC_{aw}})$	×	$(P_{RE1_{aw}} + P_{RE2_{aw}})$	×	$(P_{DEP_{aw}} + P_{GRP_{aw}} + P_{AEX_{aw}})$	=	RMC (1970)
	(ARMED FORCES)		(REACH)		(INFRASTRUCTURE)		TOTAL
1. Argentina	.95		7.11		16.98	=	114.6914
2. Brazil	2.55		9.85		1.17	=	29.3874
3. Cuba	.95		2.17		2.89	=	5.9577
4. Chile	.48		2.09		2.59	=	2.5982
5. Mexico	.55		4.71		.82	=	2.1242
6. Venezuela	.30		2.25		3.08	=	2.0790
7. Peru	.55		1.77		1.63	=	1.5868
8. Colombia	.30		4.27		.83	=	1.0632
9. Ecuador	.11		.64		1.09	=	.0767
10. Uruguay	.12		.40		1.25	=	.0600
11. Bolivia	.11		.27		1.01	=	.0299
12. Honduras	.04		.55		.66	=	.0145
13. Guatemala	.09		.12		.95	=	.0102
14. Trinidad & Tobago	.01		.40		1.40	=	.0056
15. Nicaragua	.04		.12		1.09	=	.0052
16. Jamaica	.01		.33		.82	=	.0027
17. Costa Rica	.01		.29		.51	=	.0014
18. Paraguay	.14		.01		1.00	=	.0014
19. Dominican Republic	.11		.01		1.27	=	.0013
20. Haiti	.08		.01		.63	=	.0005
21. Panama	.03		.01		1.05	=	.0003
22. Guyana	.02		.01		1.38	=	.0002
23. El Salvador	.02		.02		.69	=	.0001

TABLE 9.5. 23 LATIN AMERICAN COUNTRIES: 1980 RMC BREAKDOWN

	$(P_{AFT_{aw}} + P_{NUC_{aw}})$	×	$(P_{RE1_{aw}} + P_{RE2_{aw}})$	×	$(P_{DEP_{aw}} + P_{GRP_{aw}} + P_{AEX_{aw}})$	=	RMC (1980)
	(ARMED FORCES)		(REACH)		(INFRASTRUCTURE)	=	TOTAL
1. Brazil	6.99		12.88		13.69	=	1175.1112
2. Argentina	1.92		5.47		3.84	=	40.3292
3. Cuba	1.68		1.84		5.41	=	16.7234
4. Mexico	2.84		5.97		.76	=	12.8856
5. Peru	.64		2.20		1.62	=	2.0943
6. Venezuela	.25		2.96		2.17	=	1.5318
7. Chile	.49		1.29		2.29	=	1.4475
8. Colombia	.49		2.73		.56	=	.7491
9. Uruguay	.13		.60		2.08	=	.1622
10. Ecuador	.18		.70		1.17	=	.1474
11. Bolivia	.13		.44		.88	=	.0503
12. Jamaica	.05		.38		1.08	=	.0205
13. Honduras	.05		.37		.77	=	.0142
14. Trinidad & Tobago	.01		.23		1.65	=	.0037
15. Nicaragua	.06		.04		1.23	=	.0029
16. Guatemala	.07		.06		.62	=	.0026
17. Costa Rica	.02		.23		.37	=	.0017
18. Dominican Republic	.14		.01		1.07	=	.0014
19. Guyana	.05		.01		1.63	=	.0008
20. Haiti	.09		.01		.57	=	.0005
21. Paraguay	.08		.01		.68	=	.0005
22. El Salvador	.07		.01		.66	=	.0004
23. Panama	.04		.01		.91	=	.0003

10
Islas Malvinas or Falkland Islands: The Negotiation of a Conflict, 1945–1982

Rubén de Hoyos

This case study of the control of Latin American conflicts advances the thesis that negotiations can transform a dispute into a crisis unless both sides are convinced that this approach fo conflict resolution is leading to, or at least can lead to, a solution. Negotiation involves, after all, the elimination of alternatives--one after another--in search of a definitive solution. When a solution nevertheless fails to present itself, crisis management can paradoxically produce the crisis that it was intended to avoid. This is so, simply because after expectations are raised by a dialogue and then frustrated, there may be no alternative at hand other than conflict, since all previous hopes have already been eliminated.

This conclusion is obviously not meant to advise against negotiations, but rather to counsel caution in negotiating solutions to disputes. In the case of the Falklands/Malvinas crisis the record is largely negative, involving 133 years without negotiation and then 17 years of UN-mandated negotiations with differing Argentine and British expectations and perceptions. Despite 76 days of bloody fighting following the last negotiating round, which resulted in a military winner and a military loser, a solution is still as remote as it has been for the last century and a half and a renewal of hostilities is even more probable than before. Hopefully, the lessons of failure provided by this case study can suggest how negotiations might play a more constructive role in the control of Latin American conflicts.

THE FIRST STAGE: THE RULES OF THE GAME, 1945-1960/65

In spite of the decolonization movement in the early postwar period, positions regarding the Falklands/ Malvinas remained basically unchanged, with Argentina calling for negotiations and the United Kingdom denying that negotiations were necessary. During the years 1960-1965, the United Nations produced two documents

which radically changed the parameters of the discussion
by encouraging eventual negotiations.

The first document, Resolution 1514, approved by
the XV General Assembly of the United Nations on the
20th of December, 1960, called for decolonization, which
affected the general context of the Falklands/Malvinas
dispute. Paragraph four provided that decolonization
should be achieved on the principle of self-determination of colonial people and paragraph six stipulated
that decolonization should not violate the principle of
national territorial integrity. Five years later, on
the 19th of December, 1965, the XX General Assembly approved Resolution 2065, which was addressed directly to
the Argentine Republic and the United Kingdom on the
issue of Falkland Islands/Islas Malvinas. This resolution squarely dealt with the issue of the islands' final
sovereignty and directed both nations to negotiate terms
and to report back to the General Assembly about their
progress.

The combined effect of Resolutions 1514 and 2065
effectively altered the relative positions of the United
Kingdom and the Argentine Republic. Resolution 2065 established the existence of a dispute, namely that between the UK and Argentina regarding the final ownership
of the islands. Argentina had claimed ownership since
1833, whilst the UK had for a century and a half been
dismissing the claim as "unsubstantiated". The parties
were asked to report to the United Nations which thus
declared itself competent to oversee such a process. Also,
United Nations Resolution 2065 stated that the interests
of the islanders should be considered. Argentina prom-
ised to respect this point whilst affirming that the
dispute should not be decided by the wishes of the Falk-
landers--a position in which the UK seemed to take ref-
uge.

Symbolic of the new developments was the resolution
that the United Nations approved in session 1558, 16 November, 1965, by which, from that time on and until resolution of the dispute, the islands were to be renamed
Falkland Islands/Islas Malvinas, in the official docu-
mentation.

THE SECOND STAGE: A TIME FOR TALKS AND COOPERATION,
BUT LITTLE NEGOTIATION

This stage extended for nearly ten years, from 1966
to 1976. Starting with Resolution 2065 and its call for
a fruitful dialogue, it nevertheless ended with an Argentine warship shooting over the bow of a British survey ship and strained bilateral diplomatic relations.
While the Argentines kept talking of establishing meaningful negotiations, the British preferred to limit the
dialogue to talks.

Two rounds of meetings took place in London, one in

July 1966 and the other in 1970, with the opening of
communications between the islands and continental Argentina occurring in 1969. Until that time, Argentina
had been carrying on an apparently contradictory foreign
policy for many years. On the one hand, all communications with the islands had been cut to express disgust
with their original capture by the British. Yet, Argentina generally maintained excellent economic and political relations with Britain.

In July 1971, a United Kingdom-Argentine Republic
accord on air, sea and postal communication was signed.
During the winter of 1972, Argentine Air Force engineers
opened the first airstrip that the islands have ever had
and regular flights were scheduled between Comodoro Riva-
davia and Port Stanley.

The history of the first airstrip reflected the difficulty of advancing negotiations in an atmosphere of
mutual distrust. The Kelpers (Falklanders) considered
it against their interest to reduce their options to a
sole air linkage with Argentina and pressed, unsucess-
fully, for a larger airstrip able to receive international flights. For economic reasons the United Kingdom
was not willing to foot the bill, especially since the
(peacetime) population of the islands was never more
than 2,200.

In 1974, further accords were signed on trade and
the Argentine oil monopoly (Yacimientos Petrolíferos
Fiscales) assumed charge of satisfying the Kelpers' oil
needs. Argentina also extended medical services to the
Kelpers, and made the Argentine educational system
available through scholarships.

But while the Argentines emphasized their claim of
sovereignty, the Britishers stressed economic cooperation. At first, the Argentine negotiators expected that
discussion of the issue of sovereignty according to Resolution 2065 would be favored by bilateral cooperation.
But even by the early seventies, it appeared that the only reward for cooperation would be further cooperation,
which in fact would primarily assist Britain in exploiting the islands' resources, which even in the seventies
appeared promising.

Further strain was exerted on bilateral relations
by what has been described as "an accident on the high
seas". The survey ship HMS Shackleton was intercepted
by A.R.A. Storni of the Argentine navy, ordered to stop,
shot at when she refused and followed to harbor (Port
Stanley) because of alleged British prospecting for gas
and oil while sailing in Argentine territorial waters.
A few months later, as a consequence of the British Ambassador calling the discussions about sovereignty "sterile", the Argentine government decided that the two nations should recall their respective ambassadors from
London and Buenos Aires.

Overall, once the tension regarding the Shackleton

incident and the recall of the ambassadors receded, the
position of Argentina did seem to be noticeably improved.
Argentina had reestablished its links with the islands
that it claimed to be its own, and had replaced the British connection (one ship per year) with a firm and evolving net of regular weekly services by sea and air. Even
while the shock of the Shackleton incident was still
alarming the islanders, the Argentine Marines landed on
the island--according to arrangement--to put the last
touches on the airstrip, and then left.

Increasing services to the islanders (medical, educational, trade, gas and oil) made the reluctant Kelpers
more dependent on the Argentines. Of course, some Kelpers, especially those linked to the Falkland Islands
Corporation and the Falkland Islands lobby operating in
London, insisted on viewing this as part of a British
Foreign Office plot for selling the islands to Argentina.
More broadly, the Kelpers felt gradually abandoned by
the United Kingdom, which for its part grew more and
more irritated with the refusal of the islanders to accept any compromise. And Argentines and Kelpers shared
a distrust of the British Foreign Office.

THE THIRD STAGE: OPTIONS, BUT STILL LITTLE PROGRESS

This stage started on the initiative of the British
government in 1977, yet ended in a stalemate as the domestic problems of the Argentine government mounted
(1981).

The hardening attitude of Argentina during this
stage seems to have had a softening effect upon the
United Kingdom's previous reluctance to negotiate. In
particular, it was the United Kingdom this time which,
on April 26, 1977, proposed reestablishing political relations, "including considerations /of the issue7 of
sovereignty with regard to the Falkland, South Georgia
and South Sandwich Islands". Talks took place in two
rounds: in New York and in Rome (July 1977), again in
New York (December 1977) and then in Lima, Peru (February 1978).

The content of these and other informal talks
were protected by a well-guarded silence. By November
1980, Mr. Nichols Ridley, Minister of State at the British Foreign Office, presented four possible options regarding the future of the islands:

1. Transfer of the islands' sovereignty to Argentina, with the proviso of an immediate lease-back
   to the United Kingdom for a time to be determined (a variation of the Hong Kong solution).
2. Outright transfer of sovereignty to Argentina.
3. Freeze on the sovereignty dispute for 25 years.
4. Break-off of the talks between Argentina and the
   United Kingdom.

While the British Foreign Office had been insisting that nothing be done without consulting the islanders, it was evident that neither the Kelpers nor the Argentines had been consulted regarding these four options. The Argentines could only accept option number two, while the Kelpers could accept all options save number two.

In March 1981, the Argentines came up with their own version of a sort of option. If sovereignty were transferred to Argentina, they would transform the Malvinas into the country's most favored region, which could retain its distinctive language, culture, and even its legal system. The United Kingdom launched a counterattack of generosity by offering to consider special British citizenship for the islanders.

Some have considered these five options to be an exercise in futility, but at any rate it was the first time that the issue of sovereignty had received direct consideration. In mid-1981, Lord Trefgarne, Parliamentary Undersecretary of State, in addressing the House of Lords, acknowledged the lateness of the hour in negotiating a solution to the issue.

All attempts to secure Argentine agreement to proceed with economic cooperation, while leaving the sovereignty issue on one side, have come to nothing. ...If the Argentines felt that we were no longer prepared even to discuss the issues with them then it could not be ruled out that they would look for other means of obtaining what they want.[1]

The Argentines were at that time certainly frustrated in not reaching their goal, the devolution of sovereignty for the islands, but were effectively discouraging investment of international and British capital in the future of the islands. Even the British did not want to invest in the fish, gas and oil potential available around the islands without first resolving the difference over sovereignty, since Argentina was increasingly disposed to create any type of inconvenience, 'from legal to military' for prospectors. Meanwhile, Argentina approved and finalized contracts for gas and oil prospecting in areas contiguous to the islands (Magallanes Este), and with Poland, the Soviet Union, Spain and Japan regarding the expansion of their fishing industries.

Due to the impasse, even normal British economic relations with Argentina were suffering. For example, the United Kingdom lost a 200 million pound Argentine Navy contract to European shipyards (1980), as Argentina showed her displeasure with the British handling of the Falkland/Malvinas Islands negotiations.

While British commercial interests were suffering, the Falklanders were becoming an increasingly heavy bur-

den for Britain. Their number was diminishing (1,700
estimated in 1981), and they were losing confidence in
the intentions of the Foreign Office policymakers. For
their part, the Falklanders seemed pushed to be--as Lord
Trefgarne put it--the best judges of their own interests
"...in the knowledge that the situation has to change if
the dispute is not to be allowed to stifle all hopes of
development".

THE FOURTH STAGE: A CRISIS IN THE NEGOTIATIONS

This stage started between the unfinished presidency of General Viola (1981) and the beginning of the administration of General Galtieri later that year. A
sort of vacuum was created by the lack of decisiveness
of Viola's administration and permeated the period after
the announcement of the four British options with a
sense of uncertainty. This was characteristic of other
moments in the negotiation of the conflict, when changes
of presidents ritually brought reevaluation of ambassadors and policies.
However, Argentine policy toward the Falklands/Is-
las Malvinas, even if adversely affected by these historical fluctuations, has always had considerable continuity of content and intention. Firmness was lacking
at times, but the new Galtieri government was characterized by self-confidence. Moreover, the ongoing dispute
with Chile over the Beagle Channel seems to have been
given second place by the Galtieri administration and
priority given to the expeditious resolution of the
Falklands/Malvinas Islands affair.
The process of negotiation was also acquiring new
urgency because of its inner dynamics. Once all the
talks had been concluded, all the options had been negotiated and rejected, positions naturally began to hard-
en. This was particularly evident in Argentina's communiqué which resulted from the last round of meetings
(February 26 and 27, 1982). At that time, Argentina
demanded that subsequent rounds of negotiations should
be more frequent (including a monthly meeting with a
fixed agenda), and, after recalling 17 years of incon-
clusive talks in pursuit of the United Nations' recommendations, Argentina alluded to a possible "rupture
with the United Kingdom". At the same time, a wave of
rumors and leaks circulated regarding the possible military takeover of the islands by Argentine forces.

THE CONFLICT

In the first hours of April 2, 1982, two hundred
specially-trained Argentine marines stormed Port Stanley and sent the Falklands' governor back to England,
while eight thousand soldiers fanned out on the islands
to secure them for Argentina. London immediately broke

relations with Buenos Aires.

The conflict, so precariously contained most of the time and dormant at others, had finally become inflamed after 133 years of dilatory manoeuvres on the part of the British and of frustrated expectations on the part of the Argentines. To that should be added 17 years of UN-sponsored "negotiations" (as the Argentines understood them to be) or "conversations" (as the British apparently seem to have decided to treat them).

However each party perceived the discussions, both did cooperate in controlling the dispute. But by April 1982, the dispute was entering the arena of a public crisis, thereby escaping all controls, including even those still desired by the respective protagonists.

Between the time the dispute was still under control and the time it escalated out of control, there was a moment--here called the "trigger moment"--when the process passed definitively from that of an uneasy peace into a conflict which for all practical purposes ignored traditional restraints. The trigger moment then refers to the definitive dividing line before which there was no unrestrained war and after which there was no real possibility of peace. With respect to negotiations, the track recommended by the United Nations during 17 years --that of "peaceful negotiations"--was superseded by hostile negotiations under the aegis first of the United States and then of the United Nations, until finally, open war, free of all restraints imposed by negotiations, resulted. Seventy-six days of undeclared war resulted in fifteen hundred deaths, dozens of airplanes and tens of ships destroyed and put out of commission, billions of dollars expended and far-reaching political implications, including the fall of one political administration (that of President Leopoldo F. Galtieri on June 17, 1982).

A variety of explanations has been offered to explain why the dispute was kept under control for so long, but none has emphasized that the role negotiations played in these process, if at first constructive, were ultimately counterproductive. Cynics might like to point to the military disparity between the antagonists, with a great power (the United Kingdom) on one side and a weaker Third World state (Argentina) on the other. But the disparity did not deter the Argentine take-over on the morning of April 2, 1982.

In fact, relations between the United Kingdom and Argentina were, most of the time, more harmonious than, for example, those between Argentina and the United States. Some have even said that Argentina more than once used the shadow of the British Empire to challenge the hegemony of its great neighbor to the North. The legacy of Anglo-Argentine empathy, reinforced by financial, commercial and cultural linkages, helped control the ongoing dispute and calm momentary outbursts.

Argentine did attempt, for a century and a half, to carry on negotiations with the United Kingdom, not only because the prospects for recourse to force were judged dim against the mighty Empire which ruled the seas and one quarter of the world's land, but also because of the legalistic tradition of Argentina's Chancellery. For example, many of the top functionaries responsible for Argentina's foreign relations had come from university chairs of international law. The conflict was kept under control--from the Argentine perspective--not only because the military alternative was remote, but because of the sincere conviction that a determined legal approach would finally be rewarded by the devolution of the islands to Argentina, with the United Kingdom recognizing the rights of Argentina.

When in the sixties negotiations were finally accepted in principle, successive Argentine administrations stressed public respect for the legal process under way. When disapproval of British attitudes was considered necessary (as in the case of the Shackleton/Storni naval incident, or when the British Ambassador in Buenos Aires, forgetting protocol, called the ongoing negotiations for sovereignty of the islands "nonsense"), the Argentine reactions, while firm, were restrained and the policy was always to keep a door open to compromise. Likewise, any exercise of violent political protest by individuals against the British presence in the islands was severely discouraged, as when, during the Onganía administration, a small nationalist commando force landed in Port Stanley (September, 1966).

British attitudes and approaches to the negotiations contrasted with those of Argentina. The Falklands/Malvinas dispute was kept under control for years simply by the action of British representatives politely denying that there was any need for a solution since they refused to acknowledge the existence of a dispute. When negotiations were eventually imposed upon the UK by public international pressure, their diplomats were successful for 17 years in skillfully deferring the moment of formalizing the so-called "negotiations".

Briefly, one of the ways to keep a conflict under control seems to be to deny that there is a conflict. This seems to work especially well when the proponent (the United Kingdom in this case) has the military force to back it up. From a diplomatic angle, another means of control is to use promises of further concessions, even token ones, to prevent a potential aggressive drive of the complainant. This seems also to have worked, at least for many years, in the Falklands/Malvinas dispute.

When negotiations finally started, Argentine expectations about a peaceful settlement of the conflict escalated, but meager results from protracted negotiations eventually produced bitterness. While negotiations can control a conflict for a certain time while alternatives are being considered, every time an alternative is considered and discarded by mutual agreement, the dispute --which in the last instance provokes the negotiation-- has less and less room to evolve toward settlement. The successful control of a conflict--not necessarily its resolution--seems to lie in the ability to avoid running short of viable alternatives.

By the beginning of March 1982, it had become evident that the negotiations were failing to control the conflict, despite a diplomatically worded joint Anglo-Argentine communiqué after the last bilateral meeting in New York (February 26-27). Subsequent events drew the antagonists closer to the trigger moment.

In the historiography of war, trigger moments tend to be remembered by the spark of certain incidents (the murder at Sarajevo, the bombing of Pearl Harbor, the sinking of the Lusitania or that of the Maine, etc.). But more than dramatic incidents, trigger moments grow out of protracted processes. Retrospectively, the particular trigger moment in the Falklands/Malvinas conflict can be identified as extending from the last days of February to the first days of May 1982. Furthermore, three phases can be distinguished, each with its own typical incidents and contributions to the development of the final crisis and confrontation. The three phases may be distinguished in terms of how the conflict first escaped diplomatic control (Phase I and II) and, once out of the grasp of politically moderating controls, became an uncontrolled war (Phase III).

Briefly, the three stages are:

1. From February 26-27 to March 18. This could be called the South Georgia Affair or the White Card incident, starting with a summons (Argentina's) and ending with a paramilitary landing.

2. The second phase extended from the dispute about the legality of the landing of Argentine merchants on one of the South Georgia Islands (San Pedro) to the landing of Argentine commandos in Port Stanley. This automatically ended direct "peaceful negotiations" between Argentina and the United Kingdom.

3. The third phase started when the United Kingdom and Argentina seemed to accept the role of the United Nations as an intermediary in the dispute. It ended sometime between the day the United States openly declared its support for Britain (April 31) and the day a British nuclear submarine torpedoed the ARA Cruiser Belgrano outside the British proclaimed "exclusion zone" (May 3). This likewise relegated the United Nations' and Peru's mediation efforts to failure.

THE FIRST PHASE: THE SOUTH GEORGIA MISUNDERSTANDING

A key factor, if an unnecessary one, contributing to the escalation of the crisis started in South Geor-

gia when the Argentines landed there. In order to give
perspective to that event, relations between Argentina
and the United Kingdom at that time need to be analyzed.

Both parties got together in New York for yet another round of talks--this time at the invitation of the
British--with the announced purpose of negotiating the
issue of sovereignty and mutual cooperation regarding
the future of the islands (February 26-27, 1982). On
February 27, a terse joint communiqué announced that the
meeting had been conducted and that the representatives
were returning to their governments to inform them. The
tone was moderate and perhaps tinged with a certain op-
timism, but in fact the Argentines used the meeting to
present a triple demand to the British. Argentina, apparently disgusted with the dilatory techniques used by
the British Foreign Office, demanded that subsequent
meetings be conducted monthly on the issue of sovereignty, that they follow an established agenda, and that
they be conducted by high-level functionaries.

A sharp hardening resulted on both sides, with each
perhaps trying to give the other the impression that
they would not be bullied. Nevertheless, other situations had been even more tense than this one (for example, the shelling of HSM Shackleton by the ARA Storni).
Thus, the British press initially devoted little attention to the issue, although the Argentine press started
to speculate about more dramatic options, including
blockading the islands, cutting of economic, medical,
trade and communications links established during the
previous ten years, and severing diplomatic relations.
But the Argentine journalists did not add war to the options. Diplomatic relations between Argentina and the
United Kingdom settled into a significant silence, which
Argentina interpreted as a calculated indifference by
the British.

However, the level of diplomatic exchange between
Argentina and the United States increased in intensity
during this time, and, at least in Argentine eyes,
shared bilateral interests were assuming new importance.
For example, newspapers published in Buenos Aires during
the first weeks of March were laudatory as never before
of the Reagan administration's position against "Marxism
in the Caribbean". There was written speculation as
well, both by independent publications and other newspapers more representative of sectors of the Armed
Forces, about the United States' assumed plan of defense
for the Americas. In it, Argentina would allegedly be
assigned the role of protecting the South Atlantic, including the Falklands/Malvinas.

A caravan of North American personalities sent by
Reagan in those days to Buenos Aires added credibility
to those speculations, culminating with the visit of Assistant Secretary of State for Inter-American Affairs,
Thomas Enders (March 6-8). His speeches emphasized the

common inter-American heritage and the nurturing of an
already established line of friendship between the USA
and Argentina. The optimistic perception in Argentina
of bilateral relations, strengthened by visits, declarations, and special US recognition of Argentina as "a new
and loyal partner", helps to explain why weeks later
public opinion and behavior swung radically against the
United States.

By mid-March, the Argentine chancellery was still
waiting for the British answer to the "summons" of February 27. "We expect the /British7 answer to be positive, otherwise we shall address the issue to the United
Nations", said Foreign Minister Nicanor Costa Méndez on
March 19. Public expectations, likewise, were high. It
was in this charged context that the South Georgia incident took place.

Already in the first phase, positions were becoming
polarized and compromise becoming more difficult for each
side. Expectations, rewards and confidence in each
other's intentions--all traditional incentives for the
control of conflicts--were all being vitiated.

In the next phase, antagonistic military and diplomatic moves and countermoves would escalate rapidly.

THE SECOND PHASE: THE LANDING OF ARGENTINE TROOPS

This phase starts with the landing of Argentine
civilians on the South Georgia Islands (March 18, 1982)
and ends with the landing of Argentine commandos in Port
Stanley (April 2) only fifteen days later.

On March 18 forty Argentine civilians (scrap-iron
workers) landed with the purpose of removing an old iron
whaling station, which was long out of use. The Falkland Islands' governor, Rex Hunt, immediately denounced
the operation as illegal and London later supported his
accusation.

According to Argentina, the Argentine workers had
a duly legalized contract signed in London (September
19, 1979) and presented to the British Embassy in Buenos Aires, where it had been approved (March 9, 1982).
The Argentines saw the British denunciation as a unilateral abrogation of the Anglo-Argentine First Joint
Agreement on Communications (August 1971) and particularly of its clause regarding the White Card. By this
clause both countries agreed on an ingenious way to
solve communication problems without surrendering their
alleged sovereign rights to the islands. Argentines
were to accept the permit (White Card), given by the
British to their subjects, the Kelpers, as a document
sufficient for travel to and on the Argentine mainland.
The British were likewise supposed to accept the Carta
Blanca (White Card)--given by Argentina to its own citizens and written in Spanish--as the only document required to allow lawful entrance and exit to the islands.

As a matter of fact, this agreement had been followed amicably for nearly eleven years, until March 18, 1982.

The forceful Argentine response reduced possibilities for compromise still further. Photocopies of the contract between London and the Davidoff enterprises (the iron scrappers) were published in the Argentine press, commented on by television and supported by the officers of the Argentine administration. This mobilized public opinion, making it still more difficult to compromise if the demands made on the British were not accepted.

Developments in London were not encouraging. Parliament urged the government to act quickly and decisively, and the Thatcher administration did so with the support of part of the opposition. On March 30, Lord Carrington, the Foreign Minister, announced that his government was considering security measures which could not be publicly disclosed. The British press reported these as including deployment of warships to the South Atlantic.

Toward the end of March it was clear that neither side was going to accept what was perceived as the illegality of the other's action, and that military considerations were overtaking diplomatic considerations. Nevertheless, conflict was still not inevitable. In 1976, for example, the British not only sent a fleet to the South Atlantic, but they positioned it on the horizon of the islands in dispute. The Inter-American juridical Committee of the Organization of American States denounced this at the time as an act of "violent intimidation", but a military confrontation did not ensue.

The last week of seventeen years of attempted peaceful negotiations was about to end. The British had not made a meaningful attempt since February 26-27 to rekindle negotiations, though astutely, they never announced that they were canceling them either. Hostile negotiations were about to start. On April 2, 1982, at dawn, Argentine troops successfully fulfilled their orders to capture the islands and to do so without killing any of the defenders.

THE THIRD PHASE: THE POINT OF NO RETURN

Recurring failure to resolve the conflict ended in a trigger moment. There were two points of no return in the last phase, one for the British and another for the Argentines. The British may have reached their point of no return first, when the islands were taken over by Argentine marines (April 2), but a negotiated settlement of the conflict may still have been possible during the rest of the month. The Argentines reached theirs sometime between the day the United States decided openly to take sides with the UK (April 31) and

several days later when a British nuclear submarine torpedoed the Argentine cruiser, Belgrano, outside the British 200-mile exclusion zone (May 3).

The British had so much at stake (national pride,
and the islands themselves) that there was little incentive for them to negotiate once Argentine troops took
over the islands. For the Argentines, after the US en-
listed openly with the enemy and the British themselves
escalated hostilities, exacting about seven hundred
lives, US mediation no longer could be constructive nor
would further pursuit of an arrangement with the British,
who were showing less interest every day in negotiation
or compromise.

At this third phase of the trigger moment, diplomatic and military trends were ominous. Diplomacy moved
from peaceful negotiations to hostile ones and from direct negotiations to negotiations by proxy. With direct
bilateral communications ended, prospects for accommodation were greatly reduced. On the military front, reliance on force escalated. In the first phase, reliance
on force was absent, while in the second phase it was
limited to intimidation. Moreover, in the second phase
both Argentines and British only relied on force as a
deterrent which--in the mind of the users--might help
avoid the use of more force. However, even if quantitatively the use of force by the two parties was small in
the second phase, politically it was producing a negative reverberation. The same determination was developing on both sides, that of not being cowed by the use of
force. Mobilization of public opinion on each side also
tended to draw each country's leadership into irreversible positions.

The history of the negotiations up to the third
phase, covering seventeen years, has been described as
peaceful but unsuccessful. From the landing of the Argentines on the islands--the third phase--negotiations
could deservedly be called "hostile". These negotiations involved US mediation and UN good offices, and
were conducted in an atmosphere charged with suspicion
and frustration. The British accused the Argentines of
using the negotiations as a screen under which to consolidate their hold on the islands. For their part, the
Argentines argued that Britain was only interested in
negotiations for reasons of military expediency, until
the fleet could reach the islands.

Britain backed and was successful in getting approval by the Security Council of the United Nations of
Resolution 502, by which Argentina was to abandon the
islands, and the two parties were called upon to cease
hostilities and to renew negotiations. This resolution
was variously interpreted. For the British, the ces-
sation of hostilities was conditional on the previous
removal of Argentine troops. For the Argentines, the
resolution's multiple provisions were to be carried out

by both sides simultaneously.

Having gotten into a stage of hostilities, the Argentine administration was anxious to keep the conflict under control, since restraint--they imagined--would demonstrate to the British, as well as the Americans, both their serious stand and their intention of negotiating. The British, meanwhile, viewed escalation of the hostilities as essential, in order to compel Argentina to leave the islands. Particularly after the United States openly sided with the United Kingdom and against Argentina (April 31), there was not much British interest even in hostile negotiation, but rather for increasing hostility as a bargaining tool. The British conducted their first attack on the islands on May 1, one day after the endorsement of the United States and one day before the sinking by a UK nuclear submarine of the ARA Belgrano. All this occurred while the United Nations and Peru were attempting a last-ditch effort to negotiate an end to the conflict.

Sometime between these dates--April 31 and May 2-- the Argentines finally realized that meaningful possibilities for a negotiated resolution were practically exhausted. Until mid-June, when the war ended with the surrender of Argentine troops on the islands, other avenues of peace were explored, but without much hope and with no result.

Negotiations can resolve a conflict, but also can aggravate a conflict situation. If the negotiations are protracted and end in failure, as they did here, they may contribute to military conflict. Moreover, after a military conflict, renewal of constructive negotiations to help resolve underlying problems may be all the more difficult. For example, in the face of recriminations from the Thatcher administration, the United States joined the rest of the United Nations majority to recommend renewal of Anglo-Argentine negotiations (November 1982). Lessons from the past can help lead negotiations in a constructive direction, although the legacy of the past will complicate continuing efforts to control the Falklands/Malvinas conflict.

NOTES

1. Weekly Hansard (1981), House of Lords, No. 1152, June 26- July 2, p. 182.

11
The Containment of Conflict After Revolution: Lessons from Mexico and Bolivia

Susan Eckstein

Governments that come to power by revolution are faced with the immediate, pressing challenge of establishing and maintaining political order. Based on the experiences of Mexico and Bolivia after their respective upheavals, this article will argue that New Regimes are able to institutionalize political order successfully to the extent that they centralize power in a manner that contains demands of elites as well as popular groups. The capacity of the revolutionary-based regimes to accomplish this task is contingent on generating resources with which to coopt and repress opposition. The resource-generating capacity of revolutionary governments, in turn, will be partially determined by the nature of the economy when the Old Order collapsed and by international political and economic constraints.

Power must be centralized in several ways for political order to be established after revolution: through the subordination of regional interests to the central government; through the subordination of different branches of the state apparatus, including the military, to the central government; through the organization of classes under state tutelage; and through the formation of a single or dominant party that can help legitimate the new regime and regulate demands of groups in civil society. The degree of success of the post-revolutionary Mexican and Bolivian governments in accomplishing these tasks will be analyzed after a brief discussion of the origins of the respective sociopolitical upheavals.

BRIEF HISTORICAL BACKGROUND

Both Mexico and Bolivia experienced revolutions that began as liberal middle class reform movements. The reform movements ushered in class and political upheavals because Old Order modes of social control broke down under the New Regimes, and the fledgling new governments could not, as a consequence, constraint demands of "popular" groups. Mexico took longer both to re-

structure class relations and to reinstitute political
order, and the changes occurred only after a much more
violent struggle than in Bolivia. The Porfirio Díaz
dictatorship collapsed when groups pressed for free
elections in 1910, and a civil war ensued until the
1930s when reforms were implemented that transformed
the social and political order. While the Depression
had exacerbated domestic unrest, it also weakened local
and foreign elite resistance to the reforms. The international conjuncture accordingly contributed to the
radicalization of the revolution.

In Bolivia, by contrast, the sociopolitical transformation occurred within less than two years after the
Oligarchy was ousted from power. It occurred more rapidly because the Oligarchy was weaker and therefore less
able to resist middle class, working class, and peasant
pressures, and because foreign resistance to the revolution was minimal. The initial rebellion in Bolivia,
as in Mexico, focused on democratic principles, namely
the right for a party that won a presidential election
to take office. Bolivian demands then escalated rapidly, so that by mid-1953 the largest tin companies were
nationalized and the estates of the latifundistas were
expropriated and redistributed to the peasants who had
worked them. While the Bolivian transformation occurred
during a period of Western economic expansion, when foreign powers were in a position to oppose a local class
upheaval, international resistance was minimal because
there was negligible foreign investment in the country
at the time (unlike in Mexico in 1910). The US government, in fact, chose to support the moderate middle
class led movement, instigated by the Movimiento Nacional Revolucionario (MNR), in order to avert a Communist
revolution.[1]

Despite similar political origins, conditions in
the two countries differed in important respects at the
time of their respective upheavals. Mexico had a more
diversified and developed economy and a more stable polity. The country had been ruled by the repressive Díaz
regime for several decades preceding the 1910 insurrection, under which the economy was modernized. As a result, when Díaz fell from power the country had a substantial network of roads and railroads, industries, an
agricultural base that could support an urban population, and an educated middle class. By contrast, Bolivia, at the eve of its revolution in 1952, had one of
the poorest and least developed economies, and possibly
the most unstable polity on the continent. It had the
second lowest GNP and the third lowest GNP per capita
in South America, and only one other South American
country had a manufacturing sector contributing a
smaller share to the national product than Bolivia's.[2]
A small tin and landed Oligarchy ruled the country,
while most of the population lived humbly off the land.

MEXICO

The Mexican experience supports our thesis that power must be centralized along a variety of dimensions before New Regimes are institutionalized. The anarchy of the Mexican revolution did not begin to give rise to a new political order until institutions were established in the 1930s which served to regulate conflict among groups in civil society, including among elite groups. The new institutions also helped broaden the regime's political base. Postrevolutionary political stabilization came about as well because of astute presidential manoeuvres, plus a propitious international environment. The eventual consolidation of the revolution must be understood in this historical context.

New Regime order is rooted, in part, in the diminution of regionalism. The revolution had actually left the polity territorially fragmented. On the local level caciques and their followers struggled for domination of municipal and state governments. However, after the founding of a territorially based but nationally organized party, and the centralization of the means of violence and budgetary resources, regional conflicts were gradually contained. Through the National Revolutionary Party (PRN) (currently known as the Institutionalized Revolutionary Party, the PRI), which was established in 1929, local governments lost their independent bases of power. While the Party at the time was a loose affiliation of regional and personal parties, it did monopolize patronage. Politicos accordingly became dependent on national functionaries for local appointments. Recalcitrant politicians could thereby either be kept from attaining or from maintaining local office.

Concomitantly, the central government compelled governors to disband their personal security forces, and it began to generate ever larger funds which it could allocate to coopt regions. Central government revenues grew as the country's economic base expanded dramatically and as the central government appropriated an increasingly larger share of public funds. States and municipalities, with a decreasing share of public sector funds, came to depend more and more on the central government for public works, schools, and other social services.[3] Thus, through the control of resources the central government could induce regional conformity.

Meanwhile, the central government reorganized the military and reduced its influence. Both military units associated with the ancien régime and armed groups mobilized in the course of the revolutionary struggle contested for power for two decades after the Porfiriato fell. Armed groups were sufficiently strong through the 1920s to stage major rebellions, although beginning

in the 1930s they lost power. Both the resource base
and the political clout of the military, relative to
that of other groups in the society, declined. Gene-
rals opposed to the New Regime were retired, while officers loyal to the government began to be routinely ro-
tated so that they could not build up independent local
followings. Peasants and workers were also armed, which
deprived the newly constituted armed forces of a monopoly of the means of force. Moreover, President Lázaro
Cárdenas (1934-40) restructured (and renamed) the PNR
in a manner that reduced the military's political clout
by reorganizing the territorially based party along
corporate group lines. The military did become one of
four party pillars in this new corporate structure, but
it had to compete with the other three (peasants, labor
and the middle class) for political patronage. When
the party was subsequently reorganized in the 1940s, the
military sector was dropped altogether. Finally, the
military came to be allotted a progressively smaller
percent of the national budget at the same time as did
local governments. The armed forces' share dropped from
53 percent in 1921 to 3 percent in the latter 1970s.[4]
They now receive a smaller portion of the national budget than in all Latin American countries except Costa
Rica.[5]

While its resource base and influence have declined
dramatically since the revolution, the military still
assume an important role in maintaining domestic order.
The army has, for example, been instrumental in crushing
anti-government student movements, peasant land seizures, and labor protests. It also has tracked down
rural guerrilla and urban terrorist groups,[6] and it has
forestalled the collapse of local governments.[7] In
helping repress movements that challenge the government's claims to rule, the military have helped protect
industry and agrarian property interests against the
very workers who were mobilized in the 1930s to weaken
its power.

The dominant party has, in turn, contributed to
the New Regime's stability. The Party has won all presidential and most other elections since its founding,
and accordingly has helped legitimate the government.
Both the sectoral organization of the Party, and its
populist ideology, convey the impression that its represents interests of non-business civilian groups. In
particular, peasants, labor, and the middle class
(through the so-called Popular Sector) have constituted
the Party pillars since the military sector was disbanded in the 1940s.

However, the Party enjoys no decision-making or
budgetary authority,[8] and it is subservient to the
president who appoints and removes party heads at his
personal discretion.[9] Consequently, although "popular"
groups have received some material benefits from their

affiliation with the Party, they have been incorporated
in a manner that restrains and regulates their demand-
-making capacity. This has been especially true of
peasants who joined the party in the course of receiving
land from the Revolutionary regime.

There are several ways that the Party contains demands of affiliated groups, and in so doing minimizes
class conflict in the society at large. The Party's
nomination procedure, for one, assures elite control.
Second, sectoral leaders do not advance interests of
their constituencies. The Peasant Sector, for example,
wields little influence within the Party for a variety
of reasons: many of its leaders, appointed by the Party's national executive committee, have not been peasants; many of the peasants who have been appointed to
top political positions have been more concerned with
their own advancement than with the interests of the
groups they ostensibly represent; farmers, who compete
with peasants for state resources and land, have been
incorporated into the more influential middle class dominated Popular Sector; and members of Congress and the
Senate from the Peasant Sector do not vote as an interest bloc.[10] For similar reasons, organized labor has
been unable to exercise much political influence
through the Party. It too does not act as an interest
bloc in the legislature, and most of its leadership has
been coopted.

The legislature, in turn, is limited primarily to
legitimization of presidential actions. Although formally independent of the executive branch of government,
it mainly ratifies laws that the president initiates.[11]
As a consequence, neither laws guaranteeing minority
party representation in Congress, nor the PRI's alloca-
tion of its congressional and senatorial seats to groups
affiliated with its respective sectors, provide "popular" groups with institutional means to influence government decision-making; rather, they compel the represented groups to share responsibility for political decisions that they do not make.

The inability of "popular" groups to use formal
institutional powers to serve their own interests is
attributable not merely to the Party's cooptive capacity, but also is rooted in the weak economic power of
urban and rural workers and in the class biases of the
government. Since the 1940s Mexican governments have
subordinated interests of labor to the interests of
business and the public sector. State functionaries,
for example, have restricted peasant access to agricultural resources, harassed peasants through agrarian bu-
reaucracies, prevented a peasant-working class alliance
from forming, and repressed peasant movements that they
could not coopt.[12] Although organized labor has received more benefits than have peasants since the revo-
lution--for example, higher and secure wages, pensions,

medical care, and a share of company profits--the government has deliberately limited labor's collective strength by forcing different groups of workers, such as public sector workers, white collar employees, and farm laborers, to organize into separate unions. While organizational controls and limited material benefits have contributed to peasant and worker quiescence in recent decades, the cutback in "popular" subsidies (under pressure from the IMF) and the dramatic increase in the rate of inflation in the early 1980s may give rise to a new wave of turmoil in the streets and government defeat at the polls.

The party has successfully won elections and contained "popular" unrest in part because politicos have not openly competed for Party offices. Were there open competition, ambitious politicians might mobilize their constituencies on their own behalf, and in so doing incite disorder. There was one major internal party feud in the 1930s, but it was resolved in a manner that strengthened the party's political hegemony.

The conflict centered around the outgoing President Plutarco Elías Calles and the incoming President Cárdenas, and their respective followers. The two groups vied for Party and government control. Cárdenas, who owed his presidential nomination to Calles, sought to establish his own base of power. He accordingly placed loyal followers in key political and administrative posts, expropriated property of Callistas in order to undermine their economic base, and mobilized peasants and workers who previously had been politically marginal. This he was able to do because of the "popular" discontent generated by the Depression and the weakened ability of local elites and the US government to oppose reform at the time.

While Cárdenas incorporated peasants and labor into the party when he revamped the party's organizational base, he concomitantly stripped the institution of much of the informal influence it until then had wielded. Meanwhile, Calles broke with the PNR and attempted to establish his own party, but Cárdenas forced him into exile. Thus, Cárdenas resolved the elite conflict in a way that both broadened the Revolutionary coalition and subordinated the Party to the central government.

Because the government has unequivocally dominated the Party since the 1930s, it has been able to rule primarily in the interests of the potent, yet formally powerless, business class. Business is well represented in governmental decision-making deliberations,[13] representatives of business often sit on government boards, and businessmen are consulted by high level officials. However, post-revolutionary governments have not been the mere pawn of capital, and they have been able to contain business pressure somewhat. For example, businesses must affiliate with economic chambers

which compete for government favor, and government representatives attend chamber meetings.

The relationship between the government and business is nonetheless complex. On the one hand, the two
share common interests. Since the government depends
on the private sector for revenue, they both have a
vested interest in business prosperity. Moreover, high
ranking functionaries tend to develop business interests of their own, while in office and after they retire
from politics.[14] Many of them also get involved in lucrative ventures, including in businesses that provide
goods and services to state enterprises. Commercial
contracts with the government owned oil company, for
example, became a major source of private enrichment in
the late 1970s and early 1980s. On the other hand,
though, business opposes government policies that restrict their profit generating capacity. They are hostile to taxes, to the extension of material benefits to
labor, and to nationalizations (most recently of commercial domestic banks).

Business' ambivalent stance toward the government
has been expressed politically. Although business has
benefited disproportionately from Mexico's post-revolutionary economic growth, including from state subsidies,
the only party that has seriously challenged PRI's hegemony is the conservative, business oriented National
Action Party (PAN). The business community associated
with PAN, centered in the industrial city of Monterrey,
includes the sector of capital least dependent on public contracts. It views the PRI as an unnecessarily
costly political machine, which it does not want to
help finance. The government, to date, has been able
to minimize electoral competition (with limited use of
fraud) from the business based conservative party because the voting majority, the lower and working
classes, supports PRI even though they benefit little
from the regime.

While post-revolutionary governments have managed
to contain most regional and class conflict, the political economy includes internal contradictions that some
day may prove to be problematic. The disjunction between the government's populist ideology and its ine-
galitarian policies, and between the de facto and the
de jure power structures may, for example, evoke unrest.
Groups with only symbolic power may come to demand substantive power, and groups with effective but merely
behind-the-scenes power may come to demand formal power
as well in order to put an end to costly political cor-
ruption and government inefficiency. Concern with administrative reform reflects this tension.

In addition, the interests of local and foreign
capital, and the government, in some respects conflict,
as the 1982 fiscal crisis has highlighted. The cost of
foreign technology and financing has risen faster than

the country's ability to generate export revenues, and has aggravated the already heavy foreign debt. The 1982 economic crisis thus may give rise to a serious political crisis, since foreign creditors who have been willing to help bail out Mexico also have been forcing the government to implement policies that conflict with the interests of most domestic groups.

BOLIVIA

Upon obtaining power the Bolivian Revolutionaries set out to expand and centralize power, in similar ways to their Mexican predecessors. However, they proved to be much less successful in their efforts. They failed because civilian groups were more politicized, because the elite were more divided, because the government commanded fewer resources with which to coopt diverse groups, and because foreign powers had the interests and the means to redirect the course of the revolution.

After 1952 Bolivia established a party much like Mexico's PRI. The Party, the National Revolutionary Movement (MNR), was founded in the 1940s by a group of middle class professionals, but after 1952 it was reorganized as a mass-based corporatist institution. Although middle class interests later came to dominate the party, the military, labor, and the peasantry became the party pillars, as they had in Mexico under Cárdenas. This the Bolivian Revolutionaries took only one year to accomplish while their Mexican counterparts had required twenty years, partly because they could benefit from the Mexican experience.

Despite the similar organizational structure and class biases of the parties in the two countries, neither the Bolivian government nor the MNR succeeded in containing regionally rooted conflict. Bolivia's president in the latter 1950s did attempt to dominate the MNR's territorial units through "interventors", but regional strongmen effectively insisted on local selection of party functionaries. In addition, the government failed in its efforts to control regional militia. Some 40 percent of the national population fell under the hold of two regional caudillos who not only had their own armies but also made laws and dispensed justice within the territories that they commanded.

The MNR leadership initially was more successful in reducing and reorganizing the armed forces, and they did so much more rapidly than did the Mexican Revolutionaries. Immediately after the 1952 upheaval the old officer corps was purged, most military personnel were demobilized, and only MNR members were allowed in the service. Meanwhile, the military share of the national budget dropped from 23 percent in 1952 to less than 7 percent five years later;[15] not until fifty years after Porfirio Díaz fell from power did the military's share

of the Mexican budget drop so low. Moreover, within a
year after the 1952 upheaval workers and peasants were
organized into militia which, along with the armies of
regional strongmen, kept the military from monopolizing
the means of force.

Yet in contrast to Mexico, in Bolivia a newly constituted military gained preeminence within less than a
decade after the collapse of the Old Order. By 1960
the military received about 11 times as large a share
of the national budget and its budget was twice as large
in size, relative to the total population, in Bolivia
as in Mexico.[16] By 1964 the military had become so influential that the Air Force Chief of Staff, René Barrientos, could insist on running as vice president on
the MNR slate, and shortly thereafter he was able to
stage a successful coup d'etat that ousted the MNR from
power.

The military build-up occurred in large part because the central government increasingly turned against
organized labor, with which it had allied in 1952. The
government instead turned to the armed forces to repress
worker demands and enforce anti-labor policies, after
having granted labor a variety of economic and political
concessions in its first years in power. For example,
the Revolutionary regime had awarded labor corporate
status in the government and the Party. Within the MNR,
labor came to control a number of posts on the executive
council, the majority of MNR congressional seats, and
the Party's vice presidential candidacy. Within the
government, labor gained formal power through a system
known as co-gobierno (co-government) allowing it to name
heads of several ministerial posts. Labor participated
in both the government and the Party through a newly
formed labor confederation, the Bolivian Workers Confederation (COB), dominated by miners and the charismatic
mine leader Juan Lechín Oquendo. The mine based COB
was so powerful that it won the right to veto managerial
decisions in the mines, which amounted to a form of
workers' control.

There are two basic reasons why labor gained more
and why it did so sooner after the fall of the ancien
régime in Bolivia than in Mexico. First, miners were
more politicized and they produced a larger portion of
the country's foreign exchange than any labor group in
Mexico. Bolivian miners could paralyze the economy,
which gave them considerable political leverage, especially when the government hesitated to rule through
repression. Secondly, the initially middle class MNR
needed labor support to overthrow the Oligarchy, so that
it had to offer labor benefits in order to get their
backing. The middle class MNR had failed when it tried
to capture power on its own in the 1940s.

The difference in labor gains in the two countries
was not attributable to variances in labor's role with-

in the respective dominant parties, since in neither
Mexico nor Bolivia did the corporatist parties have any
independent base of power. MNR labor functionaries were
primarily national union officers with only a party ve-
neer.[17] Labor accordingly expressed its interests
through its own leaders, not through formal MNR channels.

While the dominant middle class faction of the MNR
and labor shared a common interest in overthrowing the
Oligarchy, their interests in other respects conflicted.
The disjunction between their interests became especially apparent after the introduction of an IMF-US
backed financial stabilization program in 1956, and it
was at this point that the middle class leadership re-
built the military to help undermine labor's power.

The stabilization program reduced real wages and
ended labor subsidies. Although labor formally remained
part of the ruling coalition until the 1964 coup d'etat,
beginning in the late 1950s only unions that supported
the stabilization program were permitted to hold party
and government office. In order to weaken COB's ability to oppose the anti-labor policies, the government
created a rival labor confederation, it forced Lechin
to step down as Minister of Mines, and it deprived the
COB of congressional and party influence.[18] By the
early 1960s, labor also lost its right to participate
in mine management and large numbers of miners were
fired. The newly constituted military, along with armed
peasants, were sent into the mines to curb labor resistance, especially after the 1964 coup. Since then labor
generally has limited demands to wage increases, and
has not pressed for a restoration of their revolution-
ary-won rights to share government power and to participate in mine management.

Labor demands have been limited over the past two
decades largely because military repression has been so
great. The military, who have governed in most years
since 1964, have ruled fairly consistently against labor
interests. Unlike the MNR, the military have relied on
force as well as cooptation to contain worker demands.

MNR relations with the peasant majority differed
somewhat. Peasants had not participated in the 1952
uprising, but in 1953 they allied with the MNR. When
the MNR initially assumed power, peasant defiance
spread. Sharecroppers and tenant farmers opposed land-
lord abuses and refused to work the fields until the new
government implemented an agrarian reform measure in
1953 that granted them land rights. In addition to extending land rights, the Revolutionary government organized peasants in unions affiliated with the MNR. The
proliferation of union locals in the early MNR years
may convey the impression that organized class conflict
stepped up, and that it was incorporated into the Party.
However, the unions served more to regulate peasant de-

mands and to coopt peasant leadership than to advance peasant interests. Peasants gained most when they were defiant, as when the government granted them rights to help restore political order.

New agrarian conflict did erupt after 1953, but this pitted peasants against each other rather than against other classes in the society. By the late 1950s, communities of peasants staged road blocks, engaged in shootouts, and raided and burned towns that rival peasant communities controlled. Around 1960 more than 8,000 peasants in the Cochabamba Valley alone were mobilized, many with arms. The turbulence here (and to a lesser extent elsewhere) was sparked by conflicts among high-level MNR leaders. When MNR elites opposed specific party policies, above all their disqualification for key political posts, they broke away from the party and formed their own political parties. The different political candidates vied for peasant support, and in so doing they fueled the conflicts between neighboring peasant villages.

Although peasants were incorporated into the dominant party as a corporate sector much sooner after the upheaval in Bolivia than in Mexico, the MNR proved less successful at containing peasant conflict. The main internal party feud in Mexico, between Cárdenas and Calles, was resolved in a manner that strengthened the regime's and the party's political base, including in the countryside, but internal party conflict in Bolivia produced splinter parties and it created such unrest that the military could usurp power. The MNF failed both to maintain its middle class support and to oversee political order in the countryside, because it had less resources with which to coopt ambitious politicos and to retire them to the private sector. The agrarian tumult provoked by competing national political candidates was an unintended consequence of government weakness. Thus, the different capacities of similarly structured postrevolutionary political parties to contain conflict on the national and the local levels resulted in good part from the different resource endowments of the two revolutionary rooted regimes.

Military governments since 1964 have been better able to contain agrarian conflict, in part because they have prohibited open conflict among political elites. Barrientos (1964-69) ruled primarily on behalf of local and foreign capital, including on behalf of an agrarian capitalist class that he and his MNR predecessors helped create. While he restored order in the countryside through a combination of cooptation and charisma, subsequent military governments, which also have furthered agrarian capitalist interests, have maintained order more by repression and less by charisma. The military have outlawed peasant unions, they have imposed military "coordinators" on peasant groups, and they have stationed "interventors" in the countryside. Nonetheless, there have been a few significant peasant uprisings under military governments. Peasants have been particularly defiant when governments have blatantly and categorically discriminated against them. In particular, peasants have massively opposed military efforts to impose a land tax on them. They have also opposed government efforts (partly under pressure from the IMF) to raise prices on goods and services that they consume when not concomitantly raising prices of the goods that they produce.

As in Mexico, in Bolivia postrevolutionary governments have allied most closely with capital, although Bolivian governments have come to ally with a somewhat different sector of the bourgeoisie than have postrevolutionary Mexican governments. The MNR initially helped build up a domestically oriented bourgeoisie, both in agriculture and in industry, as had their Mexican predecessors, by offering farmers and manufacturers a variety of direct and indirect subsidies. The 1956 Stabilization, however, compelled the government to end industrial subsidies, including tariff protection which had enabled local firms to compete with foreign imports. Moreover, the devaluation associated with the Stabilization program promoted exports. As a consequence, since 1956 governments in Bolivia have tended to promote enclave business interests, as did prerevolutionary predecessors. Nonetheless, in Bolivia as in Mexico the interests of business and government have not always coincided. The tension is similarly rooted in governmental fiscal concerns. With most of the labor force still absorbed in subsistence production, the government has a limited tax base. Yet, more than in most Latin American countries, business in Bolivia resists taxation; in so doing, it contributes to a severe fiscal crisis. After the Garcia Meza (1980-81) administration attempted to tax business at the same time that it was heavily involved in the narcotics trade, most of the remainder of the business community turned against the armed forces and pushed for democracy. Without business support, the military was so isolated that it relinquished power in 1982.

CONCLUSION

The comparison between Mexico and Bolivia reveals that postrevolutionary regimes may differ in their ability to institute a new political order. They may differ even when they institute similar types of political parties and capitalist economic bases because of differing links to the world economy on the one hand and differing domestic class dynamics on the other hand.

The experience of the two Latin American countries demonstrates that international conditions shape con-

flict containment directly and indirectly. Third World
government options vary with global political and economic conditions. In periods of global economic re-
trenchment, dominant powers are less likely to interfere in the internal matters of other countries. In
periods of global economic expansion dominant powers
are more likely to interfere, especially when they perceive their interests to be threatened by nationalist
revolutionary movements.

The Mexican civil war spiralled into a revolution
in part because the Depression compelled the US government to address its own domestic crisis, despite large
US business interests south of the border. As US business subsequently recuperated from the Depression after
World War II, it helped strengthen the political and
economic role of capital, relative to labor, in Mexico.
This has occurred especially in industry, through ties
that foreign capital has developed with local capital
and the government.

The Bolivian Revolutionaries were able to modify
rural class relations and nationalize the country's
main source of foreign exchange during a peak period of
US world hegemony in part because, in the absence of
significant US investment in the country, the US government perceived no immediate reason to intervene. The
US government also recognized very soon after the upheaval that in assisting the fiscally poor state it
could coopt the revolution and keep the country within
the Western bloc at a time of intense Cold War struggle.
With the support of the IMF, the US government helped
develop a domestic bourgeoisie, but one rooted in an
enclave economy with a small economic base. In addition, the US government helped rebuild and modernize
the military, which, although highly factionalized, has
periodically repressed defiant workers and peasants.

Yet the Mexican and Bolivian experiences suggest
that the capacity of postrevolutionary governments to
contain conflict, and to promote certain group interests
over others, also depends on domestic class relations.
Both postrevolutionary regimes initially attempted to
contain conflict through a populist alliance, but the
Bolivian regime had to award more concessions to labor
to win their support. At the same time, there is no
evidence that the middle class leadership was more committed to labor concerns. Indeed, both postrevolutionary regimes with time increasingly turned against the
"popular" groups with which they had initially allied,
and associated more exclusively with capital. The Mexican regime did allow peasants and labor to retain
formal power, partly because its economic base expanded
sufficiently to coopt most groups and their leaders,
while the same was not true in Bolivia.

In sum, the capacity of postrevolutionary governments to centralize power and contain conflict depends

in part on the institutions that they develop. However, it also depends on the politicization of domestic classes, the interests and resources of powerful international governments and organizations, and state resources both to coopt and to repress.

NOTES

1. Milton Eisenhower, The Wine is Bitter (Doubleday, Garden City, N.Y., 1963).

2. James Wilkie, Statistical Abstract of Latin America (Latin American Center, University of California at Los Angeles, 1978), pp. 238, 239, 248.

3. Pablo González Casanova, Democracy in Mexico (Oxford University Press, New York, 1970), pp. 24-30, 201.

4. James Wilkie, The Mexican Revolution: Federal Expenditures and Social Change Since 1910 (University of California Press, Berkeley, 1967), pp. 102-103; and World Military Expenditures and Arms Transfers, 1969-1978 (U.S. Arms Control and Disarmament Agency (US-ACDA), 1980), p. 59. Since one of the three main divisions of the military, the division of rural defense, is not a paid force, the actual budget allocated by the federal government to the military does not fully reflect either the size of the military or the political role the military currently assumes. On the division of rural defense, see Jorge Lozoya, El Ejército Mexicano (1911-1965) (El Colegio de México, México, 1970).

5. World Military Expenditures and Arms Transfers, 1969-1978, (U.S. Arms Control and Disarmament Agency (USACDA), 1980), pp. 83-96.

6. One-third of the army was mobilized in the state of Guerrero in 1974 to destroy the guerrilla movement there headed by Lucio Cabañas. His guerrillas kidnapped the prominent Senator Rubén Figueroa, New York Times, 7 July 1974, p. 3.

7. David Ronfeldt, The Mexican Army and Political Order Since 1940 (The Rand Corporation, Santa Monica, 1973).

8. Dominant parties in authoritarian regimes are characteristically weak and without an independent power base. See Juan Linz, 'An Authoritarian Regime: Spain', in E. Allardt and Y. Littunen, editors, Cleavages, Ideologies and Party Systems: Contributions to Comparative Political Sociology (Transactions of the Westermarck Society, Helsinki, 1964).

9. See Patricia Richmond, Mexico: A Case Study of One-Party Politics (University of California, Berkeley, 1965), unpublished Ph.D. dissertation; Roger Hansen, The Politics of Mexican Development (The Johns Hopkins Press, Baltimore, 1971); and L. Vincent Padgett, The Mexican Political System (Houghton Mifflin, Boston, 1966).

10. Robert Scott, Mexican Government in Transition (University of Illinois Press, Urbana, Illinois, 1964); and Bo Anderson and James Cockcroft, 'Control and Co-optation in Mexican Politics', in Irving L. Horwitz, Josué de Castro and John Gerassi, editors, Latin American Radicalism (Vintage Books, New York, 1969), pp. 366-89.

11. González Casanova, pp. 17-18, 201. Initially after the revolution, however, the executive used strong repressive measures to assure its political hegemony over Congress.

12. Elena Montes de Oca, 'The State and the Peasants', in José Luis Reyna and Richard Weinert, editors, Authoritarianism in Mexico (Institute for the Study of Human Issues, Philadelphia, 1977).

13. Robert Shafer, Mexican Business Organizations: History and Analysis (Syracuse University Press, Syracuse, 1973); and Frank Brandenburg, The Making of Modern Mexico (Prentice-Hall, Englewood Cliffs, N.J., 1964).

14. Peter Smith, 'Does Mexico Have a Power Elite?', in Reyna & Weinert, p, 139.

15. Cole Blasier, 'The United States and the Revolution', in James Malloy and Richard Thorn, editors, Beyond the Revolution: Bolivia Since 1952 (University of Pittsburgh Press, Pittsburgh, 1971), pp. 53-110.

16. José Nun, Latin America: The Hegemonic Crisis and the Military Coup (Institute of International Studies, University of California, Berkeley, 1969), p. 11.

17. Jorge Domínguez and Christopher Mitchell, The Roads Not Taken: Institutionalization and Political Parties in Cuba and Bolivia, paper presented at the annual meeting of the American Political Science Association, 1972.

18. James Malloy, Bolivia: The Uncompleted Revolution (University of Pittsburgh Press, Pittsburgh, 1970) p. 239; and Robert Alexander, Bolivian National Revolution (Rutgers University Press, New Brunswick, 1958), pp. 355-65.

12
Equity and Freedom
in U.S.–Latin American Relations

Michael A. Morris

Interaction between theory and praxis complicates
compromise in U.S.-Latin American relations. As for
theory, basic values and policy objectives of the United
States and Latin American states frequently diverge in
important ways, and contribute to aggravation of specific policy differences. As for practice, specific U.S.-
Latin American policy differences often express underlying divergencies in values openly and abrasively,
which may remain latent if confined to an abstract,
philosophical level. If U.S.-Latin American policy differences on key issues are to be reconciled, it is therefore necessary for conflict resolution measures to address interlocking divergencies of both values and policy implementation in tandem.

Consensus-building can contribute to the control of
U.S.-Latin American disputes on both levels, that is,
values and policy implementation. As for theory, shared
values will be identified and possibilities for reconciliation or containment of remaining value differences
will be explored. As for practice, shared interests in
specific policy issues will be identified and compared
with differences. On this basis, strategies for expanding the sphere of common interests and isolating or minimizing differences will be derived.

This paper applies consensus-building as an approach
to conflict resolution to two prominent issues in U.S.-
Latin American relations. The exclusive economic zone

Research for this article was completed during a 1982
National Endowment for the Humanities Summer Seminar
for College Teachers on "Human Rights Issues in the
Third World." The author wishes to thank the Co-
Directors of the seminar, Professors Ved Nanda and George
Shepherd of the University of Denver, for their helpful
comments on an earlier draft of the article.

(EEZ) and human rights illustrate how consensus-
building can assist reconciliation of basic values and
specific policies between the United States and Latin
America. In each case, prospects for consensus-
building will be surveyed in the following logically
progressive order from the general to the specific:
clarification of values; major disputes; consensual and
conflictual trends; and consensus-building. Values underlying policy will be examined first in each case,
with attention given to similarities as well as to the
more prominent differences. Next, for each issue, specific disputes will be surveyed, including their limits
as well as their extent. Emphasis on similarities as
well as dissimilarities in U.S.-Latin American values
and interests in these introductory sections permits
subsequent synthesis of consensual and conflictual
trends for each selected issue. On this basis, a final
section on consensus-building will be derived.

Countries included in the analysis of each issue
will likewise proceed from the general to the particular.
All sections give a fairly accurate picture of U.S.
values and policies, since only one state is involved.
However, Latin America includes over thirty states, so
that an ideal-typical model is used to portray consensual and conflictual aspects of Latin American values
and policies. The final section on consensus-building
is illustrated in greater detail by applying the approach developed in previous sections to a particular
case of bilateral relations (U.S.-Brazil).

CLARIFICATION OF VALUES

For both Latin American states and the United
States, the two selected issues, the EEZ and human
rights, involve equity and freedom as central or core
values. However, both values mean quite different
things for each major group of actors and the relative
priority of the values differs as well.

With respect to the EEZ, the United States has interpreted freedom to mean freedom of the seas, rather
than freedom of coastal states to extend national control offshore at their discretion. For the United
States, freedom of the seas in turn has been regarded as
the basis for the most equitable state of affairs. Were
all states to have equal access to offshore areas with
minimal constraints by coastal states, efficiency would
result. The most competitive states would dominate production because of comparative advantage, and the free
market mechanism would assure that resources would be
distributed at an equitable price. In contrast, unrestrained control offshore by coastal states would undermine common freedoms and limit economic efficiency.

Since equity is regarded as a function of freedom, it is essential for the United States that traditional freedoms be guaranteed through respect for the law. While the new law relating to offshore resources assigns coastal states new EEZ rights, the EEZ also incorporates established foreign-state rights, particularly navigational and military activities or "freedoms," from the old law. The United States and most developed states accordingly regard foreign-state rights in EEZs as anchored in the binding nature of the law, which all states have a duty to respect. Conversely, they insist on a restrictive interpretation of new coastal state EEZ rights, which might otherwise encroach on legitimate foreign-state freedoms.

(In the rest of this paper, "EEZ guidelines" will refer to the internationally-agreed balance between new EEZ rights of coastal states, which mostly relate to economic exploration and exploitation prerogatives, and continuing foreign-state rights in the EEZ, particularly navigational and military freedoms.)

While there is broad agreement on EEZ guidelines, Latin American states generally regard new offshore rights from a distinctive ethical perspective. The traditional freedom-of-the-seas doctrine has been regarded as inequitable, since technologically-advanced developed states have been able to benefit from unhindered offshore access to dominate ocean uses and dictate unfair terms for others. National enclosure through EEZs has been regarded by Latin American states and more broadly by Third World states as a preferable alternative emphasizing meaningful equity by expanding national offshore control and limiting foreign state access therein. (In technical terms, "national enclosure" refers to the tendency in the law of the sea for state jurisdiction to expand offshore from a traditional 3- or 6-mile territorial sea and beyond this out 188 additional miles to include an EEZ.)

To Third World states, including those from Latin America, the EEZ represents belated recognition of the legitimacy of longstanding claims to the national offshore patrimony in the face of foreign exploitation. Third World EEZs allegedly would protect developing states from developed states' predatory deep-water fishing fleets, from rapacious offshore shelf exploitation by transnational oil and hard minerals companies, and perhaps eventually would help insulate them from pressures of the great powers' blue-water navies. The general welfare would therefore be enhanced, including fundamental economic and social human rights.

Inequities in the old law justify more equitable new law, including legal rules sufficiently humane and flexible to accommodate pressing developmental needs of poorer states as they arise. New coastal state EEZ rights

are accordingly viewed expansively by Latin American
states and more generally by Third World states.
Foreign-state rights in the EEZ, it follows, are expected to accommodate to more pressing developmental needs
of Third World states in their EEZs. In essence, foreign-
state EEZ freedoms should defer to equity for Third
World coastal states.

As for human rights, the United States has emphasized political and civil rights more than economic
rights. This does not imply that economic rights are
necessarily subordinate to political rights, but rather
that the former have been regarded as a function of the
latter. In particular, economic equity has been regarded as resulting from respect for individual freedoms.
Democratic institutions would support equality of opportunity through respect for individual freedoms, and
thereby would allow enterprising individuals to receive
their fair share of resources. Political and civil
rights are therefore fundamental, since they assure dig-
nity of the individual as well as provide the foundation
for an equitable polity.

Latin America, in sharing important elements of the
Western tradition, has endorsed U.S. human rights views
in part, but some values have been expressed distinc-
tively. In particular, equity has been regarded much
more in economic terms, and civil and political liberties have been regarded as flowing from this. Poor
countries, it is often argued, must rely heavily on the
state to generate economic progress and provide for
basic human needs, in order to establish economic preconditions for meaningful exercise of individual democratic freedoms. Unfortunately, measures promoting economic equity may need to be postponed until a considerably higher level of development can be achieved; and,
in an economically adverse situation, the exercise of
civil and political liberties likewise must not be allowed to undermine economic progress undertaken for the
common good. Public sector elites, especially the military, also emphasize that pressing security demands
faced by developing states may further require the state
to regulate and even suspend individual rights temporarily in the common interest.

It follows that the role of the state in implementing the values of equity and freedom tends to be regarded differently in Latin America and the United States.
The United States has generally favored a laissez-faire
approach to both values. The proper role of the state
would involve provision of a stable democratic environment, without undue interference in the market place or
in personal affairs, for the pursuit of equity through
competition and the exercise of individual rights. Just
as human rights on land would allegedly prosper with
limited state involvement, so too would economic

efficiency and human welfare be promoted at sea through free competition. Now that EEZs have been accorded widespread legitimacy, the first choice, laissez-faire preference of the United States has been qualified as a second-choice preference for as much foreign access to national ocean zones as possible.

In contrast, Latin American views generally favor extensive involvement of the state. The state would help provide an amenable environment for human rights through promotion of economic progress, and would protect the offshore patrimony through national enclosure. Vigorous state action is often shaped by the traditions of authoritarianism and corporatism, and in some South American cases has become so far-reaching and oppressive as to be characterized as "national security states."

Diverging views on equity and freedom regarding the role of the state lead to contrasting preferences about the relationship of these values to foreign policy. For the United States, state interference in matters involving individual human rights is generally regarded as improper, and justifies international concern. As for the EEZ, coastal state involvement exceedingly carefully defined international guidelines is regarded as "creeping jurisdiction," and similarly justifies international concern. In both cases, the United States has been inclined to oppose Latin American actions which allegedly violate generally recognized norms. The actual degree of U.S. interference in both issues has varied according to a variety of factors, including the U.S. administration, the extent to which U.S. interests have been involved, and other contingencies.

For Latin American states, core international norms instead impose a negative obligation of noninterference on all states and a positive obligation on the United States and other developed states to provide economic assistance and modify global economic structures for the benefit of developing states. Respect for these norms would promote the general welfare of developing states and provide a more amenable environment for individual human rights. Similarly, the nature and extent of foreign involvement in EEZs would largely be a matter of national discretion, and foreign interference would be unacceptable.

MAJOR DISPUTES

The divergence of U.S. and Latin American values in each issue-area has contributed to recurring disputes. As for the EEZ, two periods of inter-American disputes may be discerned.

First, the United States repeatedly objected to EEZ antecedents, from the first expressions of extended offshore jurisdiction by west coast South American states

in the late 1940s until the early 1970s, when a global
consensus about general guidelines for an EEZ began to
emerge. Since this first period involved stark divergence in legal principle and political values, conciliation of U.S. and Latin American differences was extremely difficult and numerous disputes occurred. These disputes included recurring seizures of U.S. fishing vessels and led to U.S. countermeasures, such as restrictions on military and economic aid for Latin American
states violating generally recognized freedoms of the
seas. At times, these inter-American maritime disputes
became linked to other issues and were sufficiently serious to cloud bilateral relations.

The Latin American tendency toward expansive offshore jurisdiction was regarded with particular concern
by the United States, since the precedent was considered as a global challenge to freedom of the seas and
not just a regional one. Once Latin American support
for extended offshore jurisdiction became widespread by
the early 1970s, it indeed added considerable impetus to
longstanding offshore demands by west coast South
American states.[1] Moreover, the Latin American patrimonial sea proposal gained momentum and gradually
merged with the proposal for an EEZ, a related version
of extended offshore resource jurisdiction.[2]

In a second period from the mid-1970s, there has
been inter-American and global agreement on general international guidelines for the EEZ, but new kinds of
problems have been emerging. A brief review of the negotiation process leading to international community acceptance of the EEZ will indicate ways in which there is
discord on matters of detail amidst general consensus
regarding EEZ guidelines.

The Third United Nations Conference on the Law of
the Sea (UNCLOS) involved negotiations to reach multilateral agreement on a global law-of-the-sea treaty from
its formal inception in late 1973 until late 1982, when
the treaty was signed. Nearly all Third World states
signed the treaty, while the United States and a number
of other mostly developed states did not sign the pact.
Even though the United States will remain outside the
treaty regime, protracted UNCLOS negotiations have already made a significant impact on state practice, including that of the United States. In particular, by
the mid-1970s a conference consensus was reached about
a 12-mile territorial sea and a 188-mile EEZ, which reinforced the legitimacy of parallel state practice in
both areas.

U.S. policymakers accordingly have expected to benefit from treaty provisions they accept, such as the EEZ,
which allegedly would apply as customary international
law even to nonsignatories such as the United States.
At the same time, U.S. policy makers have expected that

unacceptable treaty provisions, particularly those on
the deep seabed,could be rejected on a unilateral basis.
This opportunistic U.S. stance toward the UNCLOS treaty
has been widely challenged, among others by a former
U.S. negotiator who claimed that U.S. access to foreign
EEZs would tend to be restricted if it continued to remain outside the treaty regime.[3]

The UNCLOS treaty does broadly reconcile diverging
interests and values of states by establishing a rather
abstract framework for ocean order, but it must be implemented in specific situations where broad legal guidelines offer little clear direction. Different U.S.-
Latin American political and ethical orientations toward the law consequently may be expected to result in
specific differences of implementation in spite of the
treaty consensus regarding EEZ guidelines. On the one
hand, the general Third World preference for expansive
EEZ rights has been expressed particularly vigorously in
South America, where there is a tendency toward territorialization of EEZs. (EEZ territorialization refers
to the contentious tendency to expand generally recognized coastal state rights in the EEZ toward exclusive
control of the EEZ by the coastal state.) On the other
hand, the United States opposes creeping jurisdiction by
continuing to define coastal state rights in the EEZ
restrictively. U.S. insistence that coastal state
rights set forth in the UNCLOS treaty be observed restrictively, even though it does not belong to the
treaty regime, will likely aggravate the clash of U.S.-
Latin American EEZ interests further. U.S. insistence
on freedom of navigation in the EEZ for military, as
well as commercial, purposes is another conflict-prone
source of inter-American disagreement.

Human rights issues have become particularly divisive in U.S.-Latin American relations in recent years.
Agreement there is on both sides that respect for human
rights is desirable, but perspectives differ regarding
acceptable ways of implementing this basic humanitarian
objective. Disagreements between the United States and
Latin American states include the role human rights
ought to have in domestic and foreign policy, as well
as more specific matters of implementation. In essence,
certain communalities of history have led both the
United States and Latin America to endorse respect for
human rights and certain other fundamental values of the
Western tradition, although this consensus does not extend to specific human rights issues.

The hemispheric human rights consensus has remained
rather limited because of distinctive national traditions and interests, and recent efforts to overcome longstanding obstacles have not bridged the gap in human
rights preferences and practices. For example, with
uneven results, the Carter administration actively

pressured repressive Latin American regimes to respect
human rights. At that time, disputes arising from U.S.
pressure on repressive Latin American regimes in favor
of human rights involved U.S. cutoffs of economic and
military aid, Latin American retaliatory measures such
as termination of such aid programs, and consequent
chilling of diplomatic relations. The Reagan Administration has maintained a lower profile regarding Latin
American human rights abuses, but without being able to
produce either international consensus with Latin
American states or domestic consensus within the United
States.
        Current close U.S. relations with authoritarian
Latin American governments with frequently repressive
human rights practices promise to keep the human rights
issue in center stage. The debate continues over whether the United States should oppose, disengage from, or
ally itself with repressive Latin American regimes. Yet
other dimensions to the problem of reconciling U.S. and
Latin American approaches to human rights result from
increasing militarization and instability in the Caribbean basin accompanied by heightened repression and an
apparent trend toward more representative governments in
some South American states. A related debate involves
the question of whether the United States should favor
democratic and democratizing states in Latin America,
including support for improvements in human rights
practices.
        Human rights consensus-building accordingly consti-
tutes an important challenge for U.S.-Latin American relations. International consensus-building between the
United States and Latin American states on human rights
issues poses the most immediate challenge for inter-
state relations, but domestic consensus-building is increasingly important for foreign policy. For example,
part of the Latin American Catholic Church has emerged as
a potent critic of regional human rights abuses and has
significant allies within the U.S. religious community.
At the same time, there is no domestic U.S. consensus on
how best to respond to repressive Latin American governments, and even Latin American human rights activists do
not concur on how U.S. private groups and public policy
could best support their goals.

CONSENSUAL AND CONFLICTUAL TRENDS

        Consensual and conflictual trends are portrayed
systematically for each issue-area in Tables 12.1 and
12.2 by origin (domestic and foreign policy) as well
as by country (U.S. and Latin America). By and large,
national restraints, whether on Latin American human
rights abuses or on expansive EEZ implementation by
Latin American states, offer the potential for

constructive inter-American consensus-building. On the
other hand, trends characterized primarily by national
discretion in both areas often contribute to inter-
American disputes.

However, just as theory and practice are closely related, so are consensual and conflictual trends. Trends
involving national restraints interact with those involving national discretion, usually at the expense of the
former. Policymakers generally prefer to rely on national discretion in the pursuit of objectives rather
than be restrained, whether this involves restraint
through law, morality, or the balance of power. Realistic consensus-building accordingly does not involve a
simplistic strategy for undermining trends characterized
by national discretion and replacing them with restraints,
since the pull of national discretion on policymakers is
pervasive. Instead, restraints must be identified and
encouraged which are compatible with national values
and objectives as much as possible, while containing the
impact of national discretion. A consensus-building
strategy is therefore called for which is at once specific and pragmatic in nature.

Tables 12.1 and 12.2 provide a basis for specific,
pragmatic consensus-building. First, the sixteen cells
of the two tables systematically organize consensual and
conflictual trends for both issues, and thereby facilitate identification and encouragement of consensus-
building opportunities in specific terms. Second, the
double-pronged arrows connecting all sixteen cells into
eight groups emphasize the pragmatic nature of consensus-
building. The arrows suggest that pairs of related consensual and conflictual trends evolve through dynamic
or dialectical tension, so that consensus-building in
each case must be concerned with identification and encouragement of a viable synthesis. In particular, each
of the eight odd-numbered cells ("national restraints")
interact in dialectical fashion with one of the eight
counterpart even-numbered cells ("national discretion"),
with consensus-building involving identification and encouragement of a viable synthesis in each case.

For each issue, consensus-building, while pragmatic,
is nevertheless guided by a fundamental norm. In the
case of human rights, a viable synthesis is regarded as
one which can help reduce abuses of the human person in
Latin America as much as possible without causing undue
stress on inter-American relations. The UNCLOS treaty
is the point of reference for a viable EEZ synthesis,
which would curb expansive EEZ implementation by Latin
American states without causing undue stress on inter-
American relations. This would occur were Latin American states to observe EEZ duties and remain within the
confines of EEZ rights as spelled out in the law-of-the-
sea treaty.

TABLE 12.1.   Consensual and conflictual trends: Human rights practices of Latin American governments and U.S. responses

	United States	
	National Restraints	National Discretion
Domestic (containing cells 1-2 and 5-6)	(1) Liberal, global-order, and other related private sector groups in U.S. criticize Latin American human rights abuses and lobby U.S. government to not support repressive Latin American governments. Similar pressure exerted by some Latin American immigrant communities in U.S. toward related goals (i.e., Cuban-Americans, Chilean-Americans). <⟷>	(2) Human rights emphasis has tended to be a function of the political orientation of the particular U.S. administration. In particular, the views of human rights groups happened to coincide with Carter's active U.S. human rights policy and were hence fairly influential at the time, but have diverged from that of the conservative Reagan administration and hence have been fairly circumscribed since.
	Broad commitment of most U.S. politically-aware groups, including both political parties and successive administrations, to democracy and respect for human rights in Latin America. <⟷>	Tendency of all U.S. administrations to transfer U.S. domestic concept of human rights to Latin America (i.e., U.S. emphasis on individual political rights but not on social and economic rights), with resulting adverse reaction of Latin American states. Tendency of conservatives, U.S. transnational corporations and the governmental security community to emphasize Latin American stability and anti-communism more than Latin American human rights abuses.
	There is considerable support for Latin American liberation theology and its implicit human rights activism among U.S. human rights groups, including numerous members of the U.S. clergy based both in the U.S. and Latin America. <⟵⟶>	Latin American liberation theology is regarded as radical and/or subversive by many established groups and interests in the U.S., including influential currents in the clergy.
National foreign policy (containing cells 3-4 and 7-8)	(3) Official endorsement has been given by all U.S. administrations of democratic governments and human rights in Latin America. Some recent U.S. legislation requires an active foreign policy commitment for human rights (i.e., annual human rights reports and linkage of aid to respect for human rights). <⟵⟶>	(4) U.S. commitment to support Latin American democracy and human rights has varied according to administration and context. --Carter's active U.S. human rights policy toward Latin America was ill-defined and subject to changing U.S. political currents, and was hence precarious. --Congress remains fairly committed, but the executive branch is much less committed under Reagan than Carter with the exception of active criticism of human rights practices of radical Latin American governments (i.e., Cuba).

Table 12.1(cont.)

Latin America

	National Restraints		National Discretion

Domestic (containing cells 1-2 and 5-6)

(5) Latin America shares Western concepts of individual liberty and innate rights of man.[5]

Latin America also has some distinctive kinds of domestic restraints on human rights abuses.[6]
--corporatism
--All human rights (economic, social, cultural, political, civil) should progress in tandem.

<-- -->

(6) Western human rights concepts are not as en-trenched in Latin America as in the U.S.[7]

Restraints such as corporatism are also compatible with authoritarian rule and hence may constitute weak barriers to human rights abuses.
There is a tendency for economic development to gain priority over civil and political human rights.

Latin American liberation theology likewise advocates respect for all human rights. Basic Christian Communities are an expression of this activist approach to respect for human rights.

<-- -->

Latin American liberation theology is regarded as radical and/or subversive by many established groups and interests, often including the military.

Latin American democratic governments tend to respect human rights more than military ones. The legitimacy of democracy as a regional norm is producing sustained pressure for redemocratization, at least in South America.

<-- -->

Latin American military governments generally pay lip service to a return to democracy and to respect for human rights, but often do not have a firm commitment to either goal. National security doctrines, especially in the Southern Cone states, tend to place national security above respect for human rights. Restrictions on civil and political liberties in these states have often been accompanied by growing disparities in the enjoyment of social, economic and cultural rights.

National foreign policy (containing cells 3-4 and 7-8)

(7) Latin American foreign policies emphasize the principle of non-intervention/non-interference by all states in the internal affairs of others. Historically, this principle was intended to limit the impact of U.S. power on Latin American states, and has expanded to bar interference by any American state, including human rights abuses one Latin American state might perpetrate on another.

<-- -->

(8) The non-intervention principle has justified nearly all Latin American governments, whether civilian or military, to oppose U.S. or other international pressure to enforce respect for human rights. Even Latin American human rights activists often oppose U.S. pressure to enforce respect for human rights. Latin American inter-state conflicts and resulting abuses of human rights also continue.

The Organization of American States plays an international role in promoting hemispheric respect for human rights, particularly through the Inter-American Commission on Human Rights (IACHR).

<-- -->

Many Latin American governments favor a limited OAS human rights role. The IACHR is itself primarily limited to the protection of civil and political rights.

TABLE 12.2. Consensual and conflictual trends: EEZ implementation by Latin American governments and U.S. responses

United States

	National Restraints		National Discretion
Domestic (containing cells 9-10 and 13-14)	(9) U.S. deep-water fishing interests have favored restrictive EEZ interpretation by Latin American states.	<--->	(10) U.S. oil interests have long favored exclusive continental shelf control, which was codified in law in the 1960 Geneva Convention on the Continental Shelf. U.S. coastal fishing interests have favored strong coastal state powers in the EEZ.
	The U.S. Navy has insisted on freedom of navigation, commercial and military, in foreign EEZs.	<--->	Influence of the U.S. Navy in U.S. law-of-the-sea policy has tended to decline as influence of coastal state interests has mounted, but remains strong.
National foreign policy (containing cells 11-12 and 15-16)	(11) The United States has supported global freedom of the seas and existing law-of-the-sea rules, including a restrictive interpretation of internationally recognized EEZ coastal state rights.	<--->	(12) Developments in EEZ implementation by several dozen Latin American states in vast areas are hard to monitor. Internationally recognized EEZ guidelines are themselves ambiguous and difficult to monitor. Concerned U.S. interest groups are only attentive to adverse developments for commercial and military interests in strategically-located Latin American offshore areas.
	U.S. cooperation is needed to develop Latin American EEZs, and the United States lobbies strongly for terms favorable to its interests (i.e., U.S. deep-water fishing fleets; U.S. transnational oil and hard minerals companies; naval cooperation, including naval assistance and arms transfers). Resulting dependency of Latin American EEZs tends to reinforce restrictive EEZ interpretations preferred by U.S. and other developed states.	<--->	U.S. focus is on immediately favorable terms for military and commercial interests, without monitoring overall evolution of Latin American EEZs.

Table 12.2.   (cont.)

Latin America

	National Restraints	National Discretion
Domestic (containing cells 9-10 and 13-14)	(13) Restraints on expansive offshore jurisdiction are very weak in terms of domestic ideology or interest groups. Domestic restraints largely involve abstract respect of the Latin American legal tradition for the existing law.	(14) Nationalism and national security doctrines have supported expansive offshore jurisdiction because of their emphasis on the right to economic resources of offshore zones and the right to self-defense therein.

	National Restraints	National Discretion
National foreign policy (containing cells 11-12 and 15-16)	(15) Latin American legalistic tradition emphasizes importance of adhering to duties of international conventions, including the law-of-the-sea treaty.	(16) Ambiguous, internationally-recognized coastal state EEZ rights are interpreted expansively.

The need to cooperate with the U.S. to develop Latin American EEZs imposes restraints, as follows:

--Restraints through naval cooperation with the U.S.: Latin American states have valued benefits of participation in the inter-American Military System, including the Rio Treaty, joint naval exercises with the United States such as UNITAS, and U.S. naval assistance and arms transfers.

Military dependency has tended to decline for a variety of reasons, including general weakening of the inter-American Military System, the Latin American policy of diversification of arms imports away from the U.S. and toward other developed states, and the rise of national armaments industries, including naval warship production by indigenous design and on European license, especially in Argentina and Brazil.

--Restraints through EEZ commercial cooperation with U.S.

Economic dependency has tended to decline as Latin American states have increasingly diversified their foreign policies away from the U.S. and toward other developed states, including EEZ commercial development.

CONSENSUS-BUILDING IN U.S.-LATIN AMERICAN RELATIONS

Three complementary approaches to consensus-building may be derived from Tables 12.1 and 12.2 and involve twelve comparisons between the sixteen cells as follows:

(1) Internal reorganization and/or modification of domestic and foreign policies and approaches (for each of the two issue-areas separately)

    (a) Comparison of cells 1-2 and 3-4 (U.S. domestic and foreign policy approaches to human rights practices of Latin American governments)

    (b) Comparison of cells 5-6 and 7-8 (Latin American domestic and foreign policy approaches to human rights practices)

    (c) Comparison of cells 9-10 and 11-12 (U.S. domestic and foreign policy approaches to EEZ implementation by Latin American governments)

    (d) Comparison of cells 13-14 and 15-16 (Latin American domestic and foreign policy approaches to EEZ implementation)

(2) Reorganization and/or modification of inter-American relations (in each of the two issue-areas separately)

    (a) Comparison of cells 1-2 and 5-6 (U.S. and Latin American domestic approaches and policies toward human rights practices)

    (b) Comparison of cells 3-4 and 7-8 (U.S. and Latin American foreign policies toward human rights practices)

    (c) Comparison of cells 9-10 and 13-14 (U.S. and Latin American domestic approaches and policies toward EEZ implementation by Latin American governments)

    (d) Comparison of cells 11-12 and 15-16 (U.S. and Latin American foreign policies toward EEZ implementation by Latin American governments)

(3) Regional order-building (for both issue-areas)

    (a) Comparison of cells 5-6 and 13-14 (Latin American domestic policies and approaches to the EEZ and human rights)

    (b) Comparison of cells 1-2 and 9-10 (U.S. domestic approaches and policies to Latin American EEZ and human rights practices)

    (c) Comparison of cells 3-4 and 11-12 (U.S. foreign policy toward Latin American EEZ and human rights practices)

    (d) Comparison of cells 7-8 and 15-16 (Latin American foreign policies toward EEZ and human rights practices)

Some general guidelines may be formulated for each
of the three complementary approaches to consensus-
building. (The twelve sub-divisions or comparisons of
the three approaches will be elaborated in the next
section.)

(1) Tables 12.1 and 12.2 demonstrated that restraints
affecting the United States and Latin American
states are not reciprocal in either issue-area,
since many restraints of U.S. origin apply to
Latin American human rights and EEZ practices
but very few regional restraints apply to
counterpart U.S. practices. Latin American restraints or pressure on U.S. human rights practices on U.S. territory and on U.S. EEZ practices in U.S. offshore waters have been minimal,
while Latin American states have had to take
account of U.S. policies and pressures in shaping their counterpart practices. To a considerable extent, this lack of reciprocity is a
function of the central position of the United
States as a superpower and the subordinate position of Latin American states. There are naturally other domestic and global restraints on
U.S. policies, but few restraints are specifically of Latin American origin.

The lack of reciprocity in both issue-areas,
with the United States often being willing and
able to restrain Latin American states but not
vice versa, indicates an important area where
modification of past practices and attitudes
can help build consensus. This is not to propose symmetry in inter-American relations as a
realistic proposition, but rather to indicate
that the uneven or dependent nature of inter-
American relations itself tends to generate
friction, so that the United States should not
abuse its traditionally dominant position in the
hemisphere.

The U.S. tendency is instead to regard asymmetry as requiring action by the dominant power.
According to this view, U.S. human rights practices at home need no restraint and the U.S.
similarly respects existing law-of-the-sea norms
and rules in its home waters as elsewhere, while
restraints frequently need to be imposed on
counterpart Latin American practices in order to
curb abuses. Such an approach distorts Latin
American practice, which is characterized by
some important restraints of national origin,
as well as U.S. practice, which is often characterized by national discretion. Moreover, this
approach, which is condescending and inclined
toward interference, does not promote inter-

American consensus. More positively, in a context of dependency the United States must assume
a particularly heavy responsibility for consensus-
building. Greater U.S. moderation in imposing
its own views need not entail greater tolerance
for Latin American discretion, but rather greater concern with building mutually acceptable
restraints.

(2) It follows that general consensus-building guidelines for U.S. foreign policy, stated negatively,
are avoidance of paternalism and hegemonial
policies, or stated positively, empathy for widely shared Latin American views and concern with
building mutually acceptable restraints. Reconciliation of diverging U.S. and Latin American
views on equity and freedom will play a key role
in this consensus-building process.

This is not to counsel relativism of norms,
but rather to indicate that prudent reconciliation of U.S. and Latin American interests and
views can help strengthen mutually acceptable
restraints. Some irreconcilable differences
will remain and may even include some retrograde governments, but the initial survey of
consensual and conflictual trends has suggested
that considerable scope exists for consensus-
building. It is feasible to strengthen consensus through respect for mutually acceptable restraints among a fair number of hemispheric
governments and among a significant number of
private citizens, interest groups and organizations from both parts of the Americas.

(3) Such a strategy of consensus-building applies
most particularly to the two selected issue-
areas involving equity and freedom in inter-
American relations, but findings of this approach appear to have wider applicability.
First, lessons from consensus-building in the
two selected issue-areas would appear to have
applicability as well to other issues in inter-
American relations, since equity and freedom
are core values for many issues. Second, lessons from consensus-building in the two selected issue-areas would appear to have applicability outside the hemisphere as well. Inter-
American consensus-building for the EEZ and human rights issues is in part distinctive, but
also reflects concern with a larger divergence
between Third World states and developed states
in EEZ and human rights views and practice.
Inter-American consensus-building therefore appears relevant for North-South consensus-
building.

CONSENSUS-BUILDING IN U.S.-BRAZILIAN RELATIONS

The general guidelines for each of the three complementary approaches to consensus-building may be specified by examining a case of bilateral relations, U.S.-
Brazilian relations. Bilateral relations in this case
are important and distinctive, since Brazil has emerged
as the premier Latin American power over the past
decade.

Concomitant with Brazil's rise in status and power,
Brazilian dependency has tended to decline. At the
same time, Brazil still depends on the United States in
some important ways for its development and security, so
that U.S. influence remains disproportionate in the bilateral relationship. Current U.S.-Brazilian relations
are accordingly characterized by a complex web of dependencies and interdependencies.[8]

Through reference to the twelve sub-divisions or
comparisons of the three consensus-building approaches,
the bilateral relationship illustrates distinctive problems and opportunities of consensus-building posed by a
rising power. For this purpose, Tables 12.3 and 12.4
set forth an analytical chronology of key events characterizing U.S.-Brazilian relations in each of the selected issue-areas, human rights and the EEZ. These
data for the bilateral relationship supplement Tables
12.1 and 12.2, in which more general trends were presented. In essence, findings from Tables 12.1-12.4 will
be brought to bear on each of the twelve comparisons in
order to suggest an overall outline of a viable U.S.-
Brazilian consensus for the two issue-areas.

(1a) Overt U.S. governmental pressure on Brazil in
human rights and other issues during the Carter
administration was counterproductive. As an
emerging regional power, Brazil has been increasingly well positioned to resist overt U.S.
governmental pressure. Brazilian governmental
resistance to U.S. pressure was also reinforced
by nationalism, even though the regime was not
popular.

It does not follow that international criticism of human rights abuses is either counterproductive or futile, but rather that heavy-
handed, government-to-government pressure, as
in the case of U.S. Brazilian relations, tends
to be counterproductive. In fact, more discreet, if erratic, U.S. governmental support in
favor of democracy during the same years appears
to have contributed to the Brazilian political
opening. Moreover, the Brazilian regime has
been sensitive and defensive about international
criticism of domestic human rights abuses from
any quarter, including private groups (i.e.,

TABLE 12.3
Analytical chronology of human rights in U.S.-Brazilian relations.

April 1964 to Present:
    Since a 1964 military coup, Brazil has been governed by five
successive military presidents. Suppression of political/civil
human rights was particularly pronounced during the late 1960s-
early 1970s, while there have been some significant improvements
since then.
    Some recent improvements in political/civil human rights have
not been paralleled by similar advances in economic/social human
rights ("basic human needs"). Skewed income distribution and regional disparities, while always a problem in Brazil, in fact have
tended to worsen during the years of military government, at least
until the past few years. The degree of governmental and foreign
responsibility for continuing social and economic inequities, especially including U.S.-Brazilian relations, is a matter of debate.
This is the case since the dominant Brazilian development model,
in which the United States has played a significant role, has emphasized exports and foreign investment as an engine for domestic
growth.
    U.S. relations with Brazil have been important throughout
the period of military government, with political ties being clos-
est during the Castello Branco administration (April 1964-March
1967) immediately following the 1964 coup, which itself received
U.S. support. U.S. economic relations (trade and investment) with
Brazil increased quite steadily in absolute terms over the entire
period, except for aid. The U.S. proportion of Brazil's overall
foreign ties (economic, military, political) nevertheless experienced a relative decline, especially because of Brazil's diversification policy.
1970s to Present:
    Voluntary Brazilian associations committed to democracy and
respect for human rights proliferated and gained strength. Particularly noteworthy is the shift in the Brazilian Catholic Church
toward social activism and the growth of Basic Christian
Communities. During this same period, proliferation and strengthening of U.S. human rights NGOs concerned with Latin America also
occurred.[9]
Costa e Silva (March 1967 - August 1969) and Medici (October 1969 -
March 1974) Administrations:
    These were the peak years of repression against guerrillas
and dissidents. U.S. criticism of Brazilian governmental repression increased, and the Brazilian Catholic Church defended human
rights more actively and itself became a target of repression.
September 1969: U.S. Ambassador C. Burke Elbrick was kidnapped by
Brazilian guerrillas and subsequently released when, under pressure, the Brazilian government acceded to the guerrilla demand for
release of 15 political prisioners.
1970-73: Numerous petitions were received by the IACHR about human rights abuses in Brazil. Brazil denied all allegations and refused to permit any IACHR visit to investigate charges. The IACHR

(Table 12.3 Continued)

nevertheless found the Brazilian government responsible for human
rights abuses.

Geisel Administration in Brazil (March 1974 - March 1979):

Qualified political liberalization ("abertura") began, with
some steps taken toward dismantling of some of the more repressive
elements of the regime.

March 1977: Brazil expressed displeasure with a U.S. State Department report criticizing its human rights situation by cancelling a
longstanding program of U.S. military assistance and rejecting projected U.S. military aid credits. Brazilian opposition groups generally supported the Brazilian government in opposing U.S. pressure
in favor of human rights.

March 1978: U.S.-Brazilian differences, especially human rights
and nuclear proliferation, were prominent when President Carter
visited Brazil. The Brazilian government gave Carter a correct but
chilly welcome and reiterated its resentment of U.S. criticism of
the Brazilian human rights record. Carter emphasized the importance of strong bilateral ties, but caused further irritation by
meeting with some prominent Brazilian civilians who had publicly
opposed the government on human rights and other issues.

June 8, 1978: Prior censorship restrictions were terminated and
led to considerable media freedom, although restrictions continued
in a variety of other ways, including potential invocation of the
National Security Law. Considerable media freedom, as well as
mounting central governmental concern about torture, contributed to
a continuing decline in incidents of torture.

January 1, 1979: Various political reforms were made, including
abandonment of exceptional powers such as Institutional Act No. 5.

Figueiredo Administration in Brazil (March 1979 - Present):

Gradual political liberalization continues, but with opposition from some elements in the armed forces and others. Governmental curbs on trade union activity and political dissent also remain and various measures assure continuing influence of the military in politics. Some measures have been taken to promote more
equitable distribution of income, but income distribution remains
highly skewed and regional disparities continue to be pronounced.

Fall 1979: Various amnesty measures were approved and implemented.

Reagan Administration in U.S. (January 1981 - Present):

New U.S. "quiet diplomacy" approach to human rights issues in
Latin America, including Brazil, is well received by regional military governments, but is criticized by activist groups in both parts
of the hemisphere. In the new context, civil-political human rights
issues decline in prominence in U.S.-Brazilian relations.

Other areas of friction in the bilateral relationship relating
to economic and social human rights persist. In particular, critics
blame the bilateral relationship to varying degrees for Brazilian
dependency, skewed income distribution, regional disparities, and
perpetuation of the military dictatorship.

TABLE 12.4
Analytical chronology of the exclusive economic zone in U.S.-
Brazilian relations.

The 1960s:
November 18, 1966: Brazil enlarged the territorial sea from 3 to 6
miles with an additional six-mile contiguous zone.
April 25, 1969: Brazil extended the territorial sea from 6 to 12
miles.
       Brazil hued to a moderate law-of-the-sea policy during the
1960s, while gradually moving toward more extended national ocean
boundaries. Decrees of 1966 and 1969 moderately extended national
offshore areas in ways regarded at the time as legitimate, and
therefore did not evoke protests by the United States or other
maritime powers.
The 1970s:
March 25, 1970: A Brazilian decree declared a 200-mile territorial
sea. While Brazil asserted national sovereignty out to 200 miles,
the United States and other maritime powers protested this as an
illegitimate territorialist claim and insisted on freedom of the
seas therein. Brazil subsequently compromised somewhat at UNCLOS
by recognizing the value of the EEZ in reconciling diverse interests, but has itself continued to adhere to the essence of its
territorialist position up to the present.
May 9, 1972:
       A U.S.-Brazilian Shrimp Conservation Agreement helped recon-
cile the stark divergence of U.S.-Brazilian legal positions regarding offshore zones, which had threatened to lead to confrontation
following the 1970 Brazilian 200-mile decree. The 1972 bilateral
fishing agreement provided that U.S. fishing vessels would be li-
censed by Brazil and that both countries would cooperate in the development of the national fishing industry. The agreement nevertheless merely suspended basic differences rather than resolved
them, since both sides only agreed to reserve their diverging
legal positions on the territorial sea while cooperating in an interim fishing regime.
June 20 - August 29, 1974:
       Most participants at the Caracas session of UNCLOS, includ-
ing Brazil and the United States, endorsed general guidelines for
the EEZ, although the United States adhered to a restrictive interpretation of coastal state rights and Brazil stressed an expansive
interpretation.
October 9, 1975:
       President Geisel approved risk contracts for foreign oil
companies to explore on-shore and offshore.
September 1977:
       Brazil cancelled the longstanding U.S. Naval Mission in re-
sponse to a March 1977 State Department report criticizing
Brazilian human rights practices. Less intense bilateral naval
cooperation has continued, including the UNITAS series of naval
exercises.

(Table 12.4. Continued)

Late 1970s to Present:
    The interim Brazilian fisheries regime involving periodic re-
newal of bilateral agreements, such as that between the U.S. and
Brazil, evolves toward a permanent, comprehensive offshore fisheries
regime in which foreign access would occur through joint ventures.
April 30, 1982:
    Brazil, like nearly all Third World states, voted to adopt
the UNCLOS treaty, while the United States voted against its
adoption. Brazil adhered to an expansive interpretation of coastal
state EEZ rights within the treaty regime, while the United States,
remaining outside the treaty regime, stressed a restrictive version
of these rights. Similarly reflecting a North-South split, Brazil
signed the UNCLOS treaty in December while the United States did
not.
April - June 1982 Falkland Islands War between Argentina and Great
Britain and aftermath:
    Brazil supported Argentina's claim to the Falklands but not
its precipitate invasion of them, while the United States supported
Great Britain. Because of differences over the Falklands conflict,
Brazil and some other South American states cancelled their participation in the 1982 UNITAS naval exercises with the United States.
    Also in response to the conflict, Brazil has seriously con-
sidered substantial increases in naval spending. This would involve acceleration and expansion of the current naval program for
44 new warships during the 1980s.
The 1980s:
    Past Brazilian advances in ocean and naval affairs point to-
ward increasingly effective national consolidation and control of
the EEZ. With respect to naval power, Brazil has the premier rank
1 navy in Latin America (See Chapter 8 of this volume), and therefore enjoys the greatest regional potential for EEZ enforcement.
The current, ambitious naval expansion program includes foreign purchases, national warship production on foreign license up to frig-
ate size, and indigenous design and production of naval vessels.
Some EEZ-related exports have already occurred, such as fast coastal patrol boats and EMB-111 maritime reconnaissance aircraft.
Brazilian emphasis on naval self-sufficiency and diversification of
naval suppliers has transformed the bilateral relationship with
the United States, with the latter having been Brazil's predominant
naval supplier but now only a minor supplier and a potentially competitive exporter.
    With respect to development of ocean resources, the First
Sectoral Plan for Ocean Resources, 1982-1985, builds on previous
Brazilian efforts and emphasizes greater reliance on national
capabilities. Brazil does continue to rely on the United States
for fisheries and offshore oil expertise in the EEZ and some bilateral naval ties also continue, but the Brazilian policies of
diversification of foreign ties and self-reliance have markedly
decreased dependence on the United States.
    Increasingly effective Brazilian capabilities for EEZ enforce-
ment and exploitation reinforce the Brazilian proclivity toward expansive ocean interests and territorialization of the EEZ.

IACHR, Amnesty International, church groups).
Such private sector criticism seriously em-
barrassed the Brazilian regime and helped gal-
vanize Brazilian human rights activists, and
had the added advantage of not disrupting bilateral relations. A more viable U.S. strategy
for support of political and civil human rights
would therefore involve firm governmental commitment to Brazilian democracy in principle,
in order to complement private sector efforts
to call attention to specific human rights
abuses.
Clear U.S. support for Brazilian political
liberalization and human rights advances, expressed appropriately by the public and private
sectors, would also reinforce progressive tendencies with the Brazilian government. Evidence indicates that those Brazilian military
officers previously involved in torturing have
been isolated by their colleagues and that the
government is trying to demote them or bypass
them in promotions. In contrast, the Argentine
and Chilean militaries have not been critical
of torturers in their midst, and have even appointed some of them subsequently to important
positions within the government, including diplomatic posts abroad.[10]
Instead, U.S. support for progressive tendencies within Brazilian government and society
has been weak, especially during the Reagan administration. Moreover, the Reagan administration has cultivated close relations with both
Argentina and Chile, in spite of their continuing human rights abuses and lack of progress
toward redemocratization. This Reagan approach
has characterized bilateral relations with
Chile up to the present and bilateral relations
with Argentina until the Falklands war and then
again in the aftermath of the war.
The potential U.S. contribution to political
and civil human rights in Brazil has been weakened as well by U.S. reluctance to support
Brazilian economic and social rights. U.S. reluctance to support Brazilian economic and social rights may contribute to a short-term, ex-
pedient government-to-government consensus, but
at the expense of a broader, long-term bilateral
consensus. This is because the sizable U.S.
economic involvement with Brazil, while not
as easily translated into political influence
as previously, still continues to reflect U.S.
complicity with an inequitable social order to
many people in Brazil. At a minimum, the

United States should clearly express support
for tentative Brazilian measures for promoting
social and economic equality which have accompanied political liberalization.

The United States likewise has been slow to
respond to Brazilian governmental demands for
more equitable international economic relations.
To a considerable extent, this is part of a
larger North-South problem posed for U.S. foreign policy, and hence requires integrated bilateral and global responses. Greater U.S.
responsiveness to at least some of the more
moderate Third World demands for a New International Economic Order would have a beneficial
impact on North-South relations in general and
on bilateral relations in particular. Bilateral
political relations would be promoted and U.S.
concern for political and civil human rights
would gain plausibility in Brazilian eyes as
part of a strategy for encouraging all human
rights in the Third World.

(1b) Just as the U.S. approach tends to overemphasize
political and civil human rights at the expense
of economic and social ones, the Latin American
approach tends to place excessive emphasis on
the latter economically-oriented rights at the
expense of the former politically-oriented ones.
This gap, while great in theory, is less marked
in practice and provides ground for reconciliation of differences. In the case of U.S.-
Brazilian relations, divergent approaches to
political and civil human rights did lead to
confrontation in the 1970s, yet in the past few
years Brazilian restraints on governmental
abuse of the person have been reasserted forcefully. This has been expressed through the
governmental policy of qualified political
liberalization, through opposition to torture
within the military (see 1a above), and through
mounting private sector criticism. While the
scope for reconciliation of U.S.-Brazilian approaches to human rights may have been narrow
during the period of Brazilian repression from
the late 1960s through the early 1970s, possibilities for reconciliation are now increasing.

In fact, Brazil is probably the best situated
Latin American state to promote an inter-
American consensus on political and civil human
rights. First, Brazil's internal political
evolution is leading slowly toward redemocrati-
zation and hence greater compatibility with
U.S. concepts of political and civil rights.
Second, Brazil was never as nationalistic or

anti-American in foreign policy as many Latin
American states, so that a tradition of foreign
policy moderation and close relations with the
United States resulted. Accordingly, in spite
of repeated policy differences with the United
States in recent years, the Brazilian foreign
policy tradition of compromise has remained
influential.

Brazil's emergence as a major power likewise
positions it well to promote compromise-factors
three and four. Third, an inter-American consensus must now include Brazil. Increased national self-confidence and capabilities require
that inter-American consensus-building, to be
viable, must respect vital Brazilian interests.
As Brazil has become increasingly less dependent on the United States, it has been able to
assert national interests more forcefully and
effectively, yet has not done so belligerently.
Fourth, Brazilian practice has had an increasing
impact on other Latin American states as the
leading regional state. Domestic advances in
political liberalization and human rights may
accordingly have a beneficial impact on other
Southern Cone governments which have been slow-
er to limit human rights abuses and
redemocratize.

Brazil also appears to be particularly well
situated among Latin American states to promote consensus regarding economic and social
human rights. Brazil's record on political and
civil rights has improved markedly in recent
years, so that at least in this case the U.S.
inter-American human rights approach (emphasis
on political and civil rights at the expense
of economic and social rights) is less
convincing than before. In fact, Brazil's
emergence as a regional power has enabled it to
shift attention increasingly in bilateral relations toward development of more equitable economic relations. The Brazilian policies of
foreign policy diversification and domestic
self-sufficiency add to Brazilian bargaining
power on economic issues in the bilateral relationship. Moreover, Brazil's claim that other
regional states can benefit from Brazilian efforts to reshape economic relations with the
United States and the other great powers is
plausible.

(1c) The United States has essentially been able to
avoid confrontation with Brazil over EEZ implementation because of the willingness of both
sides to temporize about fundamental differences

in legal principle. The basic difference nevertheless remains, with the United States committed to freedom of the seas in foreign EEZs and
Brazil no less committed to expansive ocean interests and consolidation of national control of
its EEZ. But the context of the early 1980s is
different from that of the early 1970s when the
dispute first arose in bilateral relations.

In the early 1970s, Brazil first asserted a
territorialist claim, but was not able to enforce it. While subsequently temporizing about
fundamental differences in legal principle,
Brazil continued to adhere to the essence of its
territorialist claim and gradually began to assert national control over the EEZ more effectively. Brazil's emergence over the last decade
as a regional power with the leading regional navy (see Table 8.1 of this volume) now has positioned it better than any other regional state
to assert territorialist powers in its EEZ. This
threatens to lead to an eventual bilateral confrontation involving EEZ use and control.

This divergence primarily involves the extent of permissible coastal state discretion regarding military uses of the EEZ and other matters. There is already a viable bilateral consensus on economic uses of the EEZ as well as
a larger global consensus on these matters
through UNCLOS.

At the same time, the United States has become less well situated to promote a comprehensive compromise with Brazil reconciling
coastal state and foreign state rights and duties in the EEZ. In essence, over the last
decade bilateral differences in ocean law and
declining bilateral naval cooperation together
weakened previous, interlocking bilateral legal
and strategic consensuses. Possibilities for a
comprehensive bilateral compromise regarding
EEZ use and control decreased accordingly.

There is still a bilateral legacy of strategic consensus in naval affairs which, while
weakened, can help avoid a potential confrontation over the EEZ. Strengthening of the longstanding bilateral strategic consensus would
help forge a comprehensive bilateral EEZ consensus that includes controversial military
uses of the EEZ. Mutually profitable U.S.-
Brazilian EEZ commercial relationships contribute to this end as well.
(1d) While pragmatism and compromise have been hall-
marks of Brazilian foreign policy, Brazilian
EEZ practice involving expansive offshore

interests has threatened to surpass limitations
imposed by internationally-recognized EEZ guidelines. The Brazilian territorialist tendency
is particularly disturbing to the United States
in the security sphere, so that strengthening
of the longstanding bilateral strategic consensus
is essential if confrontation is to be avoided.
A comprehensive bilateral EEZ compromise does
appear feasible. Bilateral cooperation for economic exploitation of the Brazilian EEZ already
exists, so that remaining disagreements, including military uses of the EEZ and creeping jurisdiction, may be contained through consensus-
building.

(2a) U.S. and Brazilian private sector groups active
in the support of human rights pursue compatible
goals, yet strategies for cross-national collaboration have not been shaped. These private
sector groups already have made a constructive
impact in promoting respect and support for
human rights, and greater cross-national collaboration could increase this impact. Cross-
national private sector collaboration also
could help reconcile the narrow U.S. definition
of human rights in vogue in governmental circles
with the broad Latin American definition, since
human rights activist groups throughout the
hemisphere usually have expressed concern with
all human rights.

Government-to-government collaboration likewise has been facilitated as political liberalization has proceeded in Brazil. Domestic
consensus-building, whether involving private
and/or public sectors, therefore tends to complement international consensus-building, at
least in the case of U.S. Brazilian relations.

(2b) Brazil's growing importance during the period
of internal repression from the late 1960s
through the early 1970s posed a difficult dilemma for U.S. foreign policy in terms of the degree to which the United States should associate with and support this key, yet repressive,
Latin American state. In the new context of the
early 1980s, Brazil's position of regional leadership is even more evident than before and domestic human rights practices are much improved
over those of the last decade. Conditions are
therefore much more propitious for international
consensus-building, with the United States now
being able to support both human rights and a
rising regional power and Brazil being able to
consolidate its new status without confrontation
with the former hegemonial power.

(2c) Domestic EEZ interests in Brazil and the United
      States are extremely difficult to reconcile in
      theory because of the divergence in legal prin-
      ciple, but prospects are better for reconcilia-
      tion in practice. First, important U.S. private
      sector interests are already assisting in com-
      mercial exploitation of the Brazilian EEZ.
      Second, UNCLOS establishes an international EEZ
      consensus to which domestic groups must adapt.
      Even though the United States has not signed
      the UNCLOS treaty, the U.S. government has ex-
      pressed its intention to respect the UNCLOS con-
      sensus regarding the EEZ. The Brazilian govern-
      ment has signed the treaty and has expressed
      its intention to abide by it, in spite of
      national territorialist tendencies.

(2d) Ambiguous aspects of the UNCLOS consensus in-
      clude military uses of the EEZ and permit creep-
      ing jurisdiction, and strain international ties.
      Strengthening of longstanding U.S.-Brazilian
      naval ties would help contain remaining bi-
      lateral differences about EEZ uses, just as
      they helped prevent a confrontation in the
      early 1970s over Brazil's 200-mile territorial
      sea declaration.

          Rigid law-of-the-sea policies, embodying
      contrasting concepts of freedom and equity,
      further complicate international consensus.
      The legacy of pragmatism in bilateral relations
      can continue to help resolve such differences
      in principle when both sides are disposed to
      enter into meaningful negotiations. Pragmatism
      has in fact permitted substantial bilateral
      EEZ cooperation, while deferring resolution of
      remaining EEZ differences.

(3a) As Brazil becomes a more autonomous actor
      domestically with mounting impact international-
      ly, prospects for regional order will be af-
      fected increasingly by Brazilian practice and
      initiatives. A case in point is domestic EEZ
      and human rights practices, which affect other
      regional states through example as well as
      through foreign policy.

          While trends affecting the two selected
      issue-areas are ambivalent, the domestic set-
      ting in each case is much more propitious at
      this time than previously for Brazilian prac-
      tice to constitute a constructive example for
      other regional states. Domestic respect for
      political and civil human rights, if not eco-
      nomic and social ones, has been considerably
      enhanced. Similarly, Brazil's conflict-prone
      territorialist stance in the early 1970s has

been moderated through acceptance of the UNCLOS consensus on the EEZ. It is therefore all the more important that the United States respond constructively to this relatively favorable Brazilian situation.

(3b) As traditional U.S. dominance in the hemisphere recedes and the influence of regional powers rises, especially that of Brazil, it is particularly important for the United States to recognize that consensus will increasingly occur through dialogue, not through fiat as often occurred in the past. In this changing situation, it is incumbent on the United States to cooperate with regional states in mutually acceptable consensus-building and restrain its own national approaches which are not compatible with a constructive inter-American consensus. For the EEZ, U.S. domestic responsiveness to international change could be reflected through greater willingness to consider, as potential components of a comprehensive EEZ consensus, Latin American security concerns in the EEZ which do not obstruct foreign navigation. Greater U.S. willingness to acknowledge the importance of social and economic human rights could also express constructive adaptation to change.

(3c) U.S. pressure on Brazil in favor of human rights and for a more restrictive EEZ definition proved counterproductive, while an evolving dialogue between equals has held forth the promise of a mutually compatible consensus. Traditionally close bilateral ties, as well as the current relatively favorable Brazilian situation with respect to both issue-areas, also can facilitate development of such a consensus. Consensus-building, at least in the context of U.S.-Brazilian relations, therefore provides a way for the United States to promote important concerns and interests without unnecessarily antagonizing the leading regional power.

(3d) Strengthening of the U.S.-Brazilian consensus appears feasible and would have a significant, constructive impact on regional order-building. Obstacles to international consensus-building still should not be underestimated. The depth of new-found Brazilian respect for political and civil human rights is uncertain, and Brazilian practice continues to give little weight to generally recognized economic and social rights. Brazil also continues to endorse a territorialist position, and is better able to enforce it. In each case, U.S.

and Brazilian theory and practice continue to diverge.

The consensus-building challenge for Brazil is to accommodate national growth and regional leadership to internationally-recognized norms, whether internationally-recognized human rights or the UNCLOS consensus on the EEZ. The consensus-building challenge for the United States is to encourage Brazil's emergence as a compatible major power. This involves both accommodating itself to Brazil's rising influence as its own influence in the region declines and encouraging Brazilian regional leadership compatible with internationally-recognized norms.

NOTES

1. For historical background and evolution of Latin American law-of-the-sea claims, including the territorialist claim of the leading regional state, Brazil, see Chapters 3 and 4 of Michael A. Morris, International Politics and the Sea: The Case of Brazil (Boulder, Colorado: Westview Press, 1979).

2. Among other issues discussed, a special theme issue of Ocean Development and International Law Journal on "Influence and Innovation in the Law of the Sea: Latin America and Africa," Vol. 7, Nos. 1-2 (1979), edited by Michael A. Morris, analyzed the impact of Latin American law-of-the-sea claims on other regions and on the development of the EEZ.

3. Leigh S. Ratiner, "The Law of the Sea: A Crossroads for American Foreign Policy," Foreign Affairs 60 (Summer 1982): 1018-1019.

4. Philip L. Ray, Jr., and J. Sherrod Taylor, "The Role of Nongovernmental Organizations in Implementing Human Rights in Latin America," Georgia Journal of International and Comparative Law (1977): 478-479. Ray and Taylor analyze the activities of "the most active and most effective" nongovernmental organizations (NGOs) located in the United States and Europe for promoting internationally recognized human rights in Latin America. Three of these NGOs are internationally-based and nonsectarian (International League for Human Rights, International Commission of Jurists, and Amnesty International) and three are U.S.-based and church-related (United States Catholic Conference, National Council of Churches and the Washington Office on Latin America).

5. H. Gros Espiell, "The Evolving Concept of Human Rights: Western, Socialist and Third World Approaches," in Human Rights: Thirty Years after the Universal Declaration, ed. G. B. Ramcharan (The Hague: Martinus Nijhoff, 1979), pp. 49, 60.

6. Howard J. Wiarda, "Democracy and Human Rights in Latin America: Toward a New Conceptualization," in Human Rights and U.S. Human Rights Policy, ed. Howard J. Wiarda (Washington, D.C.: American Enterprise Institute for Public Policy Research, 1982), pp. 30-52.

7. Ibid.

8. Robert Wesson argues that the ability of the United States to influence a large and relatively advanced state such as Brazil is restricted to areas of parallel or complementary interest. The United States and Brazil: Limits of Influence (New York: Praeger Publishers, 1981). Michael Morris, in International Politics and the Sea: The Case of Brazil, analyzes the relationship of Brazil's emergence as an ocean power to its larger emergence as a major power, and concludes that this rise in status was not primarily directed against the United States and did not usually involve U.S.-Brazilian confrontations.

9. Ray and Taylor, pp. 478-479.

10. For Brazil, see "Brazil: Torture revelations spark angry response from army," Latin America Weekly Report WR-81-08 (February 20, 1981): 7. For Chile, see "Torturer in Washington," UPDATE Latin America 7 (July/August, 1982): 10. For Argentina, see "Latin Letter," Latin America Weekly Report WR-82-18 (May 7, 1982): 3.

Selected Bibliography: Latin American Conflicts and Conflict Control

Michael A. Morris and Victor Millán

INTRODUCTION

There is a close relationship between Latin American conflicts and control of these conflicts, so that enhanced understanding of the former is crucial for generating more appropriate regional approaches to conflict control (Chapter 1). Bibliographical materials accordingly are included here which relate to both regional conflicts and control of these conflicts. The bibliography has been divided into two sections, covering books and articles.

The literature on Latin American conflicts and conflict control tends to be clustered around certain topics, while other topics, even though of considerable importance, have received very little attention. While understanding of selected areas of focus has been advanced, the literature as a whole is of very uneven quality.

On the one hand, considerable attention has been given to identification of general characteristics of Latin American conflicts, yet this has often been impressionistic rather than rigorous. Some specific conflicts have been analyzed in some depth as well, but all too often in a polemical context. As for conflict control, the Treaty of Tlatelolco has been the object of considerable popular and scholarly attention.

On the other hand, there are many gaps in the literature outside the most prominent clusters. For example, the impact of simultaneous, multi-tier change (national, sub-regional, regional, inter-American, global) on Latin American conflicts and conflict control has not been given careful, sustained attention Chapter 1). There is also a lack of literature presenting a thorough account of many currently unresolved conflicts between Latin American states (Figure 1.1). Likewise, there has been very little analysis of appropriate regional measures for conventional arms control and their relationship to nuclear arms control (Chapter 7). Finally, apart from this book, there has been no attempt to thoroughly and systematically generate approaches for regional conflict control (Chapter 1 and <u>passim</u>).

246

While these conclusions emerge from study of the entire literature, the bibliography which follows is selective rather than comprehensive. The objective was to be
sufficiently thorough to indicate the structure of the
literature without overwhelming the reader with many ci-
tations of secondary importance. The enclosed list of
bibliographical entries does aspire to include the most
important contemporary sources for Latin American conflicts and conflict control.

Books

Arbaiza, Norman D., Mars moves South: the future wars of South
    America (Exposition Press, Jericho, N.Y., 1974).

Atkins, Pope G., Latin America in the International Political
    System (The Free Press, Riverside, N.J., 1977).

Azar, Edward E., Probe for Peace: Small State Hostilities (Burguess
    Publishing Co., Missouri,1973).

Barber, Willard F., and Ronning, C. Neale, Internal Security and
    Military Power: Counterinsurgency and Civic Action in Latin
    America (Ohio State University Press, Columbus, 1966).

Benavides Correa, A., ¿Habrá una guerra próximamente en el Cono Sur?
    (Siglo XXI Editores, Mexico, 1974).

Bologna, A.B., Conflicto Honduras-El Salvador, Colección Progreso
    14 (Tierra Nueva, Buenos Aires, 1977).

Boulding, E., Passmore, Robert J., Gassler, Scott, R., Bibliography
    on World Conflict and Peace, second edition, (Westview Press,
    Boulder, Colorado, 1979).

Butterworth, Robert L. & Scranton, Margaret E., Managing Interstate
    Conflict, 1945-74: Data with Synopses (University Center of
    International Studies, Pittsburgh University, Pennsylvania, 1976).

Calvert, Peter, Latin America: Internal Conflict and International
    Peace (St. Martin's Press, 1969).

Castor, Suzy, La Ocupación Norteamericana de Haiti y sus conse-
    cuencias (1915-1934), (Siglo XXI, Mexico, 1971).

Castro Martínez, P.F., Fronteras Abiertas: Expansionismo y Geo-
    politica en el Brasil Contemporáneo (Siglo XXI, Mexico, 1980).

Child, J., Unequal Alliance: The Inter-American Military System,
    1938-1972 (Westview Press, Boulder, Colorado, 1980).

Day, Alan J. (ed.), Border and Territorial Disputes (Gale Research
    Co., Detroit, 1982).

Díaz, Albónico R. (ed.), Antecendentes, Balance y Perspectivas del Sistema Interamericano (Editorial Universitaria, Universidad de Chile, 1977).

Domínguez, Jorge I. (ed.), Economic Issues and Political Conflict: US-Latin American Relations (Butterworths, London, 1982).

Donelan, M.D. & Grieve, M.J., International Disputes: Case Histories 1945-1970 (Europa Publications, London, 1973).

Duff, Ernest A., and McCamant, John F., Violence and Repression in Latin America: A Quantitative and Historical Analysis (Free Press, New York, 1976).
Encinas del Pando, J.A., Gastos militares y desarrollo en América del Sur (Univ. de Lima, Lima, 1980).

García Robles, A., El Tratado de Tlatelolco (El Colegio de Mexico, Mexico, 1967).

García Velasco, Rafael, El Territorio del Ecuador en el Siglo XX (Publitécnica, Quito, 1981).

Gregg, David, The Influence of Border Troubles on Relations between the United States and Mexico (Johns Hopkins Press, Baltimore, 1958).

Gregg, Robert W. (ed.), International Organization in the Western Hemisphere (Syracuse University Press, Syracuse, New York, 1968).

Guglialmelli, Juan E. (ed.), El Conflicto del Beagle (El Cid Editor, Buenos Aires, 1980).

Haavelsrud, Magnus (ed.), Approaching Disarmament Education (Woburn, Ma., Butterworth Publishers, 1981).

Herrera, Amílcar O. et al, Catastrophe or New Society? A Latin American World Model (International Development Research Centre, Ottawa, Canada, 1976).

Inter-American Treaty of Reciprocal Assistance: Applications, Vol. I-1948-1959, Vol. II-1960-1972, Vol. III-1973-1976 (General Secretariat, Organization of American States, Washington, D.C., 1977).

Ireland, Gordon, Boundaries, Possessions and Conflicts in Central and North America and the Caribbean (Harvard University Press, Cambridge, Mass., 1941).

Ireland, Gordon, Boundaries, Possessions and Conflicts in South America (Harvard University Press, Cambridge, Mass., 1938).

José, James R. An Inter-American Peace Force within the Framework of the Organization of American States (Scarecrow, Mutuchen, New Jersey, 1970).

Kane, William Everett, Civil Strife in Latin America: A Legal History of United States Involvement (Johns Hopkins University Press, Baltimore, 1972).

Lagos, Gustavo, International Stratification and Underdeveloped Countries (Univ. of North Carolina Press, Chapel Hill, North Carolina, 1963).

Lagos, Gustavo and Godoy, Horacio, H., Revolution of Being: A Latin American View of the Future (New York, The Free Press, 1977).

Luard, Evan, Conflict and Peace in the Modern International System (Little, Brown & Co., Boston, Mass., 1968).

Luard, Evan (ed.), The International Regulation of Frontier Disputes (Thames and Hudson, London, 1970).

Machicote, Eduardo, Brasil: La Expansión Brasilera (Editorial Ciencia Nueva, Buenos Aires, 1973).

Marchant, Alexander, Boundaries of the Latin-American Republics 1493-1943: An Annotated List of Documents (Department of State, Office of the Geographer, Washington, D.C., 1944).

Meira Mattos, C., A Geopolítica e as Projeções do Poder (Livraria José Olympio, Rio de Janeiro, 1977).

Meira Mattos, C., Brasil: Geopolítica e Destino (Livraria José Olympio Editora, Rio de Janeiro, 1979).

Meira, Mattos, C., Uma Geopolítica Pan-Amazónica (Livraria Jose Olympio Editora, Rio de Janeiro, 1980).

Morris, Michael A. International Politics and the Sea: The Case of Brazil (Boulder, Colorado: Westview Press, 1979).

Nordlinger, Eric N., Conflict Regulation in Divided Societies (Occasional papers in International Affairs No. 29, Harvard University, January 1972).

Nye, Joseph, Peace in Parts: Integration and Conflict in Regional Organization (Boston, Little, Brown, and Co., 1971).

Paarlberg, Robert L. (ed.), Diplomatic Dispute: US Conflict with Iran, Japan and Mexico (Harvard Studies in International Affairs, No. 39, Harvard University, 1978).

Parkinson, F., Latin America, The Cold War, and the World Powers: 1945-1973 (SAGE, Beverly Hill, California, 1974).

Payne, James L., Patterns of Conflict in Colombia (Yale University Press, New Haven, Conn., 1968).

Rodley, N.S., and Ronning, C. Neale, (eds.), International Law in the Western Hemisphere (Nijhoff, The Hague, 1974).

Rojas, I.F., Ofensiva Geopolítica Brasileña en la Cuenca del Plata: La Defensa y el Rechazo Argentinos (Marymar, Buenos Aires, 1982).

Rojas, I.F., & Medrano, Arturo L., Argentina en el Atlantico; Chile en el Pacífico (Marymar, Buenos Aires, 1982).

Ronning, C. Neale, Law and Politics in Inter-American Diplomacy (John Wiley and Sons, New York, 1963).

Rout, Leslie B., Politics of the Chaco Peace Conference, 1935-39 (University of Texas Press, Austin, 1970).

Salguero, Ramón, Todo Sobre el Beagle (El Cid Editor, Buenos Aires, 1979).

Silvert, Kalman H., The Conflict Society: Reaction and Revolution in Latin America, rev. ed. (American Universities Field Staff, New York, 1966).

Taylor, Philip B., Law and Politics in Inter-American Diplomacy (John Wiley and Sons, New York, 1963).

Thomas, Ann Van Wynen, and Thomas, A.J., Non-Intervention: The Law and Its Import in the Americas (Southern Methodist University Press, Dallas, Texas, 1956).

Walbek, Norman V., and Weintraub, Sidney, Conflict, Order, and Peace in the Americas, Parts I and II (The University of Texas, Austin, 1978).

Wood, Bryce, The United States and Latin American Wars, 1932-1942 (Columbia University Press, New York, 1966).

Wöhlcke, Manfred, Die Karibik im Konflikt entwicklungspolitischer und hegemonialer Interessen: Sozio-ökonomische Struktur, politischer Wander und Stabilitätsprobleme (Nomos, Verlagsgesellschaft, Baden-Baden, 1982).

Zook, David H., The Conduct of the Chaco War (Bookman Associates, New York, 1964).

Zook, David H., Zarmilla-Marañon: The Ecuador-Peru Dispute (Bookman Associates, New York, 1964).

Articles and Monographs

Aftalion, Marcelo E., "Poder Negociador Latinoamericano," Foro Internacional, April-June 1975.

Agor, Weston H., "Latin American Inter-State Politics: Patterns of Cooperation and Conflict," Inter-American Economic Affairs, vol. 26, Autumn 1972, pp. 19-33.

Aguayo, Sergio, "Consenso y Desacuerdo en la Política Exterior Norte-Americana de la Postguerra," Foro Internacional, October-December 1980

Alcántara Sáez, M., 'Diez años de conflicto armado entre El Salvador y Honduras,' Revista de Estudios Internacionales, Madrid, July-September 1980.

Aleixo, Juan Carlos Brandi, "El Conflicto El Salvador-Honduras y la Integración Centroamericana," Geosur, February 1981.

Alonso, Enrique, "Notas Acerca de la Coexistencia Pacifica," Estrategia, May-August 1980.

Azicri, Max, "Cuba and the U.S.: On the Possibilities of Rapprochement," Caribbean Review, vol. 9, 1980, pp. 26-29, 50-52.

Baron, Donna, "The Dominican Republic Crisis of 1965: A Case-Study of the Regional vs. the Global Approach to International Peace and Security," in Cordier, A., (ed.), Columbia Essays in International Affairs, vol. III (Columbia University Press, New York, 1968).

Bibliografía de artículos sobre las relaciones internacionales de América Latina y el Caribe: 1975-1981 (Organización de los Estados Americanos, Secretaría General, SG/Ser. L./I.2., 16 September 1981).

Bloomfield, Lincoln P., Leiss, Amelia C. et al, The Control of Local Conflict: A Design Study on Arms Control and Limited War in the Developing Areas, prepared for the US Arms Control and Disarmament Agency (Washington, D.C., US Government Printing Office, 1967).

Bloomfield, L.P., Leiss, A.C., Controlling Small Wars: A Strategy for the 1970s (The Penguin Press, London, 1970).

Bologna, Alfredo Bruno, "Consequencias del Conflicto entre Honduras y El Salvador," Revista de Ciéncia Política, October-December 1979.

Bonilla, H., 'La dimensión internacional de la Guerra del Pacífico,' Revista de Desarrollo Económico, Vol. 19, No. 73, 1979 (Bogota) pp. 79-93.

Brauch, H.G., "Confidence Building Measures, Regional Security, Arms Control and Disarmament - Three Examples: Europe, Latin America, Indian Ocean," in Proceedings of the Twenty-Ninth Pugwash Conference, 18-23 July 1979, Mexico City, pp. 153-162.

Cabrera Báez, M.M. 'Acción y reacción en política internacional. El Conflicto de Leticia," Mundo Nuevo - Revista de Estudios Latinoamericanos, Vol. II, No. 4, April-June 1979 (Caracas), p. 7-42.

Caetano, Alcides C., 'Planeamiento territorial: instrumento para la geopolítica,' Geosur, Abril 1981 (Montevideo).

Castellanos, Diego Luis, "Estrategia de Grupos en las Negociaciones Internacionales," Comercio Exterior, October 1980.

Cavalla Rojas, A., '¿Guerra en el Cono Sur? Hipótesis de guerra y balance de fuerzas,' Cuadernos Semestrales: Estados Unidos, Perspectiva Latinoamericana, No. 4, 1978, pp. 227-254.

Child, J., Conflicts in Latin America: Present and Potential (American University, Washington, D.C., September 1980).

Child, J., 'Military aspects of the Panama Canal issue,' U.S. Naval Institute Proceedings, January 1980, pp. 46-51.

Clissold, Stephan & Hennessy, Alistair, 'Territorial Disputes,' in Veliz, Claudio, (ed.), Latin America and the Caribbean (London, 1967), pp. 403-13.

Conference on Energy and Nuclear Security in Latin America (The Stanley Foundation, Vantage Conference Report, 1979).

Conference on the Inter-American System and World Order (The Stanley Foundation, Vantage Conference Report, 1974).

Cortés Rencoret, Gerardo, "Los tratados de armamentos en America," Seguridad Nacional, January-March 1978.

Dallanegra Pedraza, Luis and Anglarill, Nilda Beatriz, "Aptitud de los Estados Latinoamericanos para Adoptar Decisiones Conjuntas," Revista Argentina de Relaciones Internacionales, January-April 1976.

Dario Lopez, Rubén Z., "El Mar Territorial, la Plataforma Continental y el diferendo Colombo-Venezolano," Estudios de Derecho, March-September 1976.

The Denuclearization of Latin America: Implications for Arms Control, a study prepared for the U.S. Arms Control and Disarmament Agency (Security Studies Project, University of California, Los Angeles, June 30, 1968).

Diaz, Jaime, "Disarmament Education: a Latin American Perspective," Bulletin of Peace Proposals, no. 3 (1980), pp. 273-279.

Díaz Albónico, Rodrigo, "El sistema de seguridad interamericana y sus neuvos desarrollos a través del Tratado de Tlatelolco," Estudios Internacionales, Vol, 13, no. 51, July-September 1980, pp. 345-381.

Documentos Básicos sobre el Protocolo de Rio de Janeior de 1942 y Su Ejecución (Ministerio de Relaciones Exteriores del Peru, Lima, 3a. edición, 1981).

Domínguez, Jorge I., "Consensus and Divergence: The State of the Literature on Inter-American Relations in the 1970's," Latin American Research Review, Vol. 13, 1978.

Domínguez, Jorge I., Ghosts from the Past: Territorial and Boundary Disputes in Mainland Central and South America since 1960. (Department of Government, Harvard University, 1979, unpublished).

Dreier, John C., "The Western Hemisphere," in The role of alliances and other interstate alignments in a disarming and disarmed world (Washington Center of Foreign Policy Research, School of Advanced International Studies, Johns Hopkins University, Washington, D.C., July 1965).

Eckhart, W. & Azar, E., 'Major world conflicts and interventions: 1945-1975,' International Interactions, Vol. V, No. 1, 1978, pp. 75-110.

Einaudi, Luigi, et al., Arms Transfers to Latin America: Toward a Policy of Mutual Respect (R-1173-DOS, Rand Corporation, Santa Monica, Calif., June 1973).

El Incidente Fronterizo Peruano-Ecuatoriano de la Cordillera del Condor (Ministerio de Relaciones Exteriores del Perú, Lima, 1981).

El Problema Territorial Ecuatoriano-Peruano (Ministerio de Relaciones Exteriores del Ecuador, Quito, 1981).

En torno al Tratado de Tlatelolco: Algunas Consideraciones sobre aspectos específicos (OPANAL, Mexico, 1978).

Farer, Tom J., 'Limiting intraregional violence: the cost of regional peacekeeping,' in Farer, Tom J. (ed.), The Future of the Inter-American System (Praeger Publishers, New York, 1979), pp. 195-203.

Fernández Cendoya, A., '¿Una nueva guerra del Pacifico?,' Estrategia, No. 27, March-April 1974.

Ferris, Elizabeth G., "The Andean Pact and the Amazon Treaty: Reflections of Changing Latin American Relations," Journal of Inter-American Studies and World Affairs, May 1981.

Flores Pinel, Fernando, "Entre la Guerra y la Paz: El Conflicto Honduro-Salvadoreño 1969-1979," Eca, July-August 1979.

Galindo Pohl, Reynaldo, Solución de Controversias Relacionadas con el Derecho del Mar, (Ministerio de Ralaciones Exteriores, San Salvador, El Salvador, 1977).

Galtung, Johan, Mora y Araujo, Manuel, and Schwartzman, Simon, "The Latin American System of Nations: A Structural Analysis," in Hoglund, Bengt and Ulrich, Jorgen Wilian (eds.), Conflict Control and Conflict Resolution (Munksgaard, Copenhagen, Denmark, 1972).

García Robles, Alfonso, The Latin American Nuclear-Weapon-Free Zone (The Stanley Foundation, Occasional Paper 19, May 1979).

García Robles, Alfonso, The Denuclearization of Latin America (Carnegie Endowment for International Peace, New York, 1967).

Geiser, Hans-J., Conflicts and conflict resolution in the context of Caribbean integration. Paper presented at the International Conference on Development and Cooperation in the Caribbean, 20-25 August 1979 (Mexico), pp. 20-25.

Gerstein, J.A., 'El conflicto entre Honduras y El Salvador. Análisis de sus causas,' Foro Internacional, Vol. 11, No. 4, April 1971 (Mexico), pp. 552-568.

Glick, E.B., "The Feasibility of Arms Control and Disarmament in Latin America," Orbis, vol. 9, no. 3 (1965).

Goldblat, Jozef, and Millán, Victor, "Militarization and arms control in Latin America," World Armaments and Disarmament, SIPRI Yearbook, 1982 (Taylor and Francis Ltd., London, 1982), pp. 391-425.

González Aguayo, L., 'Las relaciones entre paises vecinos: el estado o la situación de conflicto,' Cuadernos Americanos, 2, March-April 1979 (Mexico), pp. 18-39.

González Aguayo, L., 'Panorama general de los conflictos entre paises vecinos,' Revista de Relaciones Internacionales, Vol. VII, No. 26-27, July-December 1979 (Mexico), pp. 39-50.

González, Aguayo, L., 'Los vecinos de las grandes potencias,' Cuadernos Americanos, No. 4, July-August 1979 (Mexico), pp. 82-96.

Gorman, S.M., 'Present threats to peace in South America: the territorial dimension of conflict,' Inter-American Economic Affairs, Vol.33. No. 1, Summer 1979, pp. 51-71.

Gorman, S.M., "The high stakes of geopolitics in Tierra del Fuego," Parameters, Vol. 8, January 1980, pp. 45-56.

Gottemoeller, Rose E. The Potential for Conflict between Soviet and Cuban Policies in the Third World (Rand Project 6668, August 1981).

Grabendorff, Wolf,"Inter-state conflict behavior and regional potential for conflict in Latin America," Journal of Interamerican Studies and World Affairs, vol. 24, August 1982, pp. 267-294.

Grabendorff, Wolf, 'Tipología de los conflictos en América Latina,' Nueva Sociedad, No. 59, March-April 1982 (Caracas), pp. 39-46.

Greño Velasco, José Enrique, "Implicancias del Pacto Amazónico," Revista Argentina de Relaciones Internacionales, January-April 1978.

Gros Espiell, El Tratado de Tlatelolco: Diez Años de Aplicación (OPANAL, Mexico, 1978).

Gros Espiell, "The Non-Proliferation of Nuclear Weapons in Latin America," International Atomic Agency Bulletin, August 1980.

Husbands, Jo L., "Nuclear Proliferation and the Inter-American System," in Farer, Tom J., (ed.), The Future of the Inter-American System (Praeger, New York, 1979), pp. 204-231.

Ince, Basil A., Boundary disputes as an obstacle to integration in the Commonwealth Caribbean (The University of the West Indies, St. Augustine, August 1979).

International Organization in the Western Hemisphere, 3rd ed. (Maxwell Institute on the United Nations, Racine, Wisconsin, 1966).

Jaguaribe, H., 'Brasil-Argentina: Breve análisis de las relaciones de conflicto y cooperación,' Estudios Internacionales, Vol. XV, No. 57, January-March 1982 (Santiago), pp. 9-27.

Kemp, Geoffrey, "The Prospects for Arms Control in Latin America: The Strategic Dimensions," in Schmitter, Philippe C. (ed.), Military Rule in Latin America: Function, Consequences and Perspectives (SAGE, Beverly Hills, California, 1973), 189-243.

Klock, Roberto D., "Gulf of Venezuela: A Proposed Delimitation," Lawyer of the Americas, Winter 1980.

Lafer, Celso, "Una Redefinición del Order Mundial y la Alianza Latinoamericana: Perspectivas y Posibilidades," Estudios Internacionales, July- September 1975.

Lagos Escobar, Ricardo, "Latin America and the Creation of a New International Order," Economic Bulletin for Latin America, 1975.

Leonard, M.T., U.S. Policy and Arms Limitation in Central America: The Washington Conference of 1923 (Calif.St.Univ., Los Angeles,1982)

Lewis, Vaughan A., 'Focus on major tasks facing CARICOM in the 80's, Caribbean Contact, January 1980.

Lewis, Vaughan A., 'Problemas y posibilidades de la Comunidad del Caribe,' Nueva Sociedad, No. 28, January 1977 (Caracas), pp. 52-66.

Maier, G., 'The boundary dispute between Ecuador and Peru,' American Journal of International Law, Vol. 63, No. 1, January 1969, pp. 28-46.

Marcella, Gabriel, "Cuba and the Regional Balance of Power," Parameters: Journal of the U.S. Army War College, no. 2, 1977.

Marcella, Gabriel, "Las Relaciones Militares entre los Estados Unidos y America Latina: Crisis e Interrogantes Futuros," Estudios Internacionales, July-September 1980.

Marin Bosch, Miguel, "Mexico y el Desarme," Foro Internacional, July-September 1977.

Martz, M.J.R., "Conflict Resolution and Peaceful Settlement of Disputes," in Governance in the Western Hemisphere (Aspen Institute for Humanistic Studies, New York, June 1982), pp. 151-178.

Martz, M.J.R., "OAS Reforms and the Future of Pacific Settlement," Latin American Research Review, vol. 12, 1977.

Mayorga Quirós, Román, "Una solución política negociada para el Salvador: Una propuesta," Foro Internacional, vol. 21, no. 4, April-June 1981, pp. 363-387.

Maza, E., 'Belize en la geopolítica Antillana,' Revista de Política Internacional, No. 154, November 1977, pp. 101-112.

Melo, Artemio Luis, "La Mediacion de la Santa Sede en el Conflicto Argentino-Chileno en la Zona Austral," Revista de Derecho Internacional y Ciencias Diplomáticas, nos. 48-49, 1981.

Menon, P.K., 'The Anglo-Guatemalan territorial dispute over Belize,' Carribbean Yearbook of International Relations, 1977 (St. Augustine, Trinidad & Tobago), pp. 115-145.

Mesa Lago, Carmelo, Blasier, Cole and Moreno, José, "Mesa Redonda sobre el Restablecimiento de Relaciones entre Cuba y los Estados Unidos," Arieto, September-December 1975.

Milenky, Edward S., "Latin America's Multilateral Diplomacy: Integration, Disintegration and Interdependence," International Affairs, January 1977.

Moneta, Juan Carlos, "América Latina y el Sistema Internacional en la Decada del Ochenta: ¿ Hacia un Nuevo Orden Antártico?," Estudios Internacionales, October-December 1980.

Moneta, Juan Carlos, "Conos Sur de Africa y América: Aspectos Conflictivos de sus Relaciones," Geosur, May 1980.

Moreno, Antonio Federico, "Desarme. Análisis del Documento Final Aprobado en el Décimo Periodo Extraordinario de Sesiones de la Asamblea General de Naciones Unidas," Estrategia, March-April 1980.

Morris, Michael A., Expansion of Latin American Navies (Stockholm, Sweden, Institute of Latin American Studies of the University of Stockholm, 1980). Research Paper Series, Paper No. 25.

Morris, Michael A., "Latin America and the Third United Nations Law of the Sea Conference," (an annotated bibliography) Ocean Development and International Law: The Journal of Marine Affairs, vol. 9 (1981), 101-175.

Morris, Michael A., and Millán, Victor, "Arms Control in Latin America," in Hopkins, Jack W. (ed.), Latin America and Caribbean Contemporary Record, Vol. I: 1981-82 (Holmes and Meier Publishers, Inc., 1983).

Moss, Robert, The Stability of the Caribbean (Institute for the Study of Conflict, 1973, London).

Myers, David J., Frontier settlement in the Amazon: International Provocation or National Development (Pennsylvania State University, 1978). Unpublished.

Narayanan, R., "Brazil's Policy towards Nuclear Disarmament," The Institute for Defence Studies and Analyses Journal, vol. 3, no. 2, October 1970, pp. 178-191.

O'Brien, Brighid, 'Conflict resolution: a selected annotated bibliography,' Peace and Change: A Journal of Peace Research, Vol. VIII, No. 2-3, Summer 1982, pp. 139-148.

Orrego Vicuña, Francisco, "Análisis de la práctica latinoamericana en materia de solución de controversias," Derecho de la Integracion, vol. 4, 1974.

Padilla, David J., "The Judicial Resolution of Legal Disputes in the Integration Movements of the Hemisphere," Lawyer of the Americas, vol. 11, pp. 75-95.

Parker, Franklin D., "The Futbol Conflict and Central American Unity," Annals of the Southeastern Conference on Latin American Studies, vol. 3, March 1972, pp. 44-59.

Pearson, S.F., 'Foreign military interventions and domestic disputes,' International Studies Quarterly, Vol. 18, No. 3, September 1974, pp. 259-290.

Pollard, Duke, 'The Guyana-Surinam boundary dispute in International Law,' The Caribbean Yearbook of International Relations (Trinidad & Tobago, 1976).

Prats, Raymond, "Le conflit Honduras-El Salvador," Notes et Etudes Documentaires, vol. 21, October 1971, pp. 8-36.

Puig, Juan Carlos, "El Principio de No Intervención en el Derecho Internacional Público Interamericano. Influencia de las Nuevas Relaciones Internacionales," Anuario Jurídico Interamericano, 1979.

Redick, John R., "Nuclear Proliferation in Latin America," in Fontaine, Roger, and Theberge, James, (eds.), Latin America's New Internationalism: The End of Hemispheric Isolation (Praeger, New York, 1976), pp. 267-309.

Redick, John R., "Nuclear Trends in Latin America," in Governance in the Western Hemisphere (Aspen Institute for Humanistic Studies, New York, June 1982), pp. 213-265.

Redick, John R., "Prospects for Arms Control in Latin America," in Kincade, William H., and Porro, Jeffrey D. (eds.), Negotiating Security: An Arms Control Reader (The Carnegie Endowment for International Peace, Washington, D.C., 1979), pp. 211-217.

Redick, John R., "Regional nuclear arms control in Latin America," International Organization, Vol. 29, no. 2, Spring 1975, pp. 415-445.

Redick, John R., "Regional Restraint: US Nuclear Policy and Latin America," Orbis, Vol. 22, Spring 1978, pp. 161-200.

Redick, John R., "The Tlatelolco Regime and Non-Proliferation in Latin America," International Organization, Vol. 35, Winter 1981, pp. 103-134.

Robinson, Davis R., "The Treaty of Tlatelolco and the United States," American Journal of International Law, vol. 64, April 1970, pp. 282-309.

Ronfeldt, David F. & Einaudi, L.R., 'Conflict and cooperation among Latin American States,' in Einaudi, L. (ed.), Beyond Cuba: Latin America takes charge of its future (New York, 1980), pp. 185-200.

Ronfeldt, David F., and Einaudi, Luigi R., "Prospects for Violence," in Einaudi, Luigi R. (ed.), Beyond Cuba: Latin America Takes Charge of Its Future (Crane, Russak and Company, New York, 1974), pp. 35-43.

Ronfeldt, D. & Sereseres, C., U.S. Arms Transfers, Diplomacy and Security in Latin America and Beyond (Rand Corporation, P-6005, Santa Monica, California, 1967).

Rout, Leslie B., Which Way Out? A Study of the Guyana-Venezuela Boundary Dispute (Michigan State University Press, East Lansing, 1971).

Salgado, Germánico, "Integración, Conciliación de Políticas y Diferencias de Estructura Económica," Estudios Internacionales, April-June 1977.

Stinson, Hugh and Cochrane, James, "The Movement for Regional Arms Control in Latin America," Journal of Inter-American Studies and World Affairs, vol. 13, January 1971, pp. 1-17.

Tambs, Lewis, 'The changing geopolitical balance of Latin America,' Journal of Social and Political Studies, Spring 1979, pp. 17-35.

Tomassini, Luciano, "Intereses Mutuos: Las Verdaderas Bases del Diálogo Norte-Sur," Estudios Internacionales, January-March 1978.

Tomassini, Luciano, "Tendencias Favorables o Adversas a la Formación de un Sistema Regional Latinoamericano," Estudios Internacionales, January-March 1975.

Tossi, Jorge Luis, "Salto Grande, Integración Geopolítica, Geopolítica, July-December 1976.

U.S. Nuclear Policy and Latin America (The Stanley Foundation, Vantage Conference Report, 1977).

Valdés, Nelson P., "Cuba's Involvement in the Horn of Africa: The Ethiopian-Somali War and the Eritrean Conflict," Cuban Studies, January 1980.

Valenta, Jiri, The U.S.S.R., Cuba and the Crisis in Central America, The Latin American Program, Woodrow Wilson International Center for Scholars, Smithsonian Institution, Washington, D.C., April 1981.

Valois Arce, Daniel, Reseña histórica sobre los limites de Colombia y Venezuela (Editorial Bedout, Medellin, 1970).

Varas, A. and Portales, C., 'El problema militar: carrera armamentista y conflicto local en América del Sur,' Chile-America, No. 41-42 (Roma, 1978), pp. 67-87.

Vargas Carreño, Edmundo, "La Solución a las Controversias en el Derecho del Mar," in Vargas, Jorge A., and Vargas, Edmundo, (eds.), Derecho del Mar: una visión latinoamericana (Editorial JUS, Mexico, 1976), pp. 311-328.

Velasquez, Rolando et al, El Salvador y su diferendo con Honduras (Imprenta Nacional, San Salvador, 1970).

Ware, David, "The Amazon Treaty: A Turning Point in Latin American Cooperation?," Texas International Law Journal, Winter 1980.

Wilson, Larman C., "International Law and the United States Cuban Quarantine of 1962," Journal of Inter-American Studies, vol. 7, October 1965, pp. 485-492.

Wilson, Larman C., "Multilateral Policy and the Organization of American States: Latin American-U.S. Convergence and Divergence," in Davis, Harold Eugene and Wilson, Larman C., (eds.), Latin American Foreign Policies: An Analysis (The Johns Hopkins University Press, Baltimore, 1975), pp. 47-84.

Wilson, Larman C., "The Settlement of Boundary Disputes: Mexico, The United States, and the International Boundary Commission," The International and Comparative Law Journal, vol. 29, Jan.,'80, pp. 38-53.

Wilson, Larman C., "The Settlement of Conflicts within the Framework of Relations between Regional Organizations and the United Nations: The Case of Cuba, 1962-1964," in Netherlands International Law Review, vol. 22, pp. 282-318.

Wood, Bryce, Aggression and History: The Case of Ecuador and Peru, (Ann Arbor, University Microfilms International, 1978).

Wood, Bryce, "How Wars End in Latin America," Annals of the American Academy of Political and Social Science, No. 392, November 1970, pp. 40-50.

Wyman, D., 'Dependence and conflict: U.S. relations with Mexico 1920-1975,' in Paarberb, L.P., (ed.), Diplomatic Dispute, Harvard Studies in International Affairs No. 39, 1978 (Cambridge, Mass.), pp. 83-141.

Zelaya Coronado, Jorge, "La Coordinación entre los Sistemas Universal y Regional de Seguridad Colectiva y de Solución de Controversias, in Primeras Jornadas Latinoamericanas de Derecho Internacional (Caracas, 1979), pp. 237-242.

Index